BUSINESS INFORMATION TECHNOLOGY SERIES

INFRASTRUCTURE

BUILDING A FRAMEWORK FOR
CORPORATE INFORMATION HANDLING

Tony Gunton

Prentice Hall

NEW YORK   LONDON   TORONTO   SYDNEY   TOKYO

First published 1989 by
Prentice Hall International (UK) Ltd,
66 Wood Lane End, Hemel Hempstead,
Hertfordshire, HP2 4RG
A division of
Simon & Schuster International Group

Printed and bound in Great Britain by
A. Wheaton & Co. Ltd, Exeter.

British Library Cataloguing in Publication Data

Gunton, Tony, 1943–
  Infrastructure. – (Business information
  technology series)
  1. Business firms. Information systems.
  Management
  I. Title II. Series
  658.4'038

  ISBN 0-13-465535-4
  ISBN 0-13-465543-5   Pbk

---

1 2 3 4 5 93 92 91 90 89

ISBN 0-13-465535-4
ISBN 0-13-465543-5 PBK

BUSINESS INFORMATION TECHNOLOGY SERIES

INFRASTRUCTURE

BUILDING A FRAMEWORK FOR
CORPORATE INFORMATION HANDLING

CONTENTS

LIST OF FIGURES

PREFACE

Up to a couple of years ago, I earned my living by doing consultancy assignments for the top companies in Europe, sometimes bespoke assignments for individual clients, sometimes market research projects funded jointly by a number of clients. It is a rewarding career, certainly financially and, if you take to it, also personally. You get a privileged inside view of the workings of a diversity of major companies, and the satisfaction of applying your own experience to solve other people's problems. Furthermore, as cynical managers constantly remind you, consultancy differs from normal managerial work in one important way – when one assignment is over, there is usually no long, hard slog putting plans into action, but it's off again to the next assignment and the next problem. Consultancy does not quite give you power without responsibility, the privilege of the harlot, because major companies do not often let you get away with mistakes or sloppy work, but it gives you something uncomfortably close to it.

After more than a decade of consultancy work, I had begun to feel uncomfortably like an intellectual harlot, and I had also recognized another drawback of that type of work. If, as I do, you get your kicks from solving complex management problems, especially those where advanced technology is involved, then it is great to be able to move on from one problem to the next, without a lengthy intervening period. Those left behind have to persuade their colleagues to back them, then painfully overcome the huge inertia built into all large companies, before they can actually make anything happen. As a problem-solver rather than a do-er, I did not particularly miss that, but I did realize that the consultant butterfly, flitting from problem to problem at the cutting edge of management experience, was perhaps finding the sweetest nectar, but not (to mix a metaphor) gathering much moss.

So, being blessed with a career wife and some money in the bank, I gave up (well, almost) consultancy, and sat down to look back over all the material and knowledge I had gathered in the past ten years plus of consultancy and research, determined to work out what it all added up to. That, I can tell you, is not easy. Thinking is hard work at the best of times, and it is even harder when you are trying to reverse-engineer thought processes of years ago that have created today's assumptions. Only by challenging these, sometimes rebuilding them and sometimes throwing them away, do you come to understand what you really know. This book is one of the results, and I hope not the last, of that process.

I have explained all this not just because it might be interesting on its own account, but more because I feel there is a lesson in it for anyone reading this book, and particularly for managers or information technology specialists who have already built up a valuable fund of knowledge and experience. This book presents a blueprint for an infrastructure to support information systems in business organizations. In so doing, it looks forward to the 1990s, but the blueprint has been assembled by standing back and studying the lessons of the recent past. The clues as to where we should be heading, and the hard evidence to bear out those clues, are all there for those who look for them.

Information technology, though, is a restless and fascinating technology, and most people making a career in information technology find it very difficult to escape the pressures it generates – pressures to keep up with its breakneck advance; to learn about the latest and the best; as well as to meet project deadlines and cope with chronic skill shortages. These technology pressures do not make it easy to think through the implications of what is going on. The technology is very important, but we must not let fascination with its power mesmerize us. We need to watch very carefully what people, end-users as well as specialists, are doing with the technology. And then we need to stop the headless chicken act long enough to work out what it all means, then have the confidence to draw the appropriate conclusions. This book is the result of my own attempt to do just that.

It is also the result of countless discussions and arguments with people struggling, like me, to understand how best to apply and how best to manage one of the key technologies of our time. Many people have helped to shape the thinking presented in this book, and I would like to acknowledge their contribution and thank them all.

Upminster, Essex
August 1988

Tony Gunton

INTRODUCTION

Evidence of the astonishing advance of information technology is all about us in the form of new consumer products, ever more powerful business machines, and new publishing and media ventures. And yet, if we look at the application of information technology within many business organizations today, we find that the same rapid technological advance which has driven these other developments does not seem to be reflected in the performance of business information systems.

Why should this be so? Many senior managers, for their part, put at least some of the blame on their information systems departments. A recent survey of 70 senior managers from Europe's largest companies summed up its findings as follows:

> Less than a third of the senior managers in our survey were fully satisfied with the performance of their systems departments. Well over half were satisfied in some respects only, and nearly one in ten was not satisfied at all.
> The most common complaint is that of late delivery of information, and responsiveness to user needs comes a close second.[1]

The skins of information systems managers have been thickened by years of criticism and resentment, both justified and not. From where they stand, it often looks as if senior managers do not appreciate the problems caused by high rates of technological change and by skill shortages, and that they have naïve expectations fed by uncritical readings in *Business Week*.

Dissatisfaction with the performance of information systems started to grow well before the personal computer boom of the early 1980s. When personal computers arrived on the business scene, they were seen by some as a solution to the problem of unresponsive information systems departments but, in the event, they have served to throw that problem into greater relief. Personal computers have not reduced the 'applications backlog' – the queue of applications waiting for the attentions of the information systems department. Instead, they have revealed the existence of a *hidden* backlog – a whole range of information handling problems, faced mainly by managers and professional staff, either too small or too transient or too 'soft' to be worth even putting up for consideration as development projects.

At first, most personal computers were installed as stand-alone machines, and were used for tasks such as budgeting or managing personal data files. Subsequently many were linked to central computers for access to operating data. While this added to the value their users gained from them, it also showed up the limitations of central data file structures. These files had often not been designed for the purposes to which they were now being put. For example, files were segmented by topic, whereas management users generally needed data organized by department. Such users also found it extremely difficult to 'navigate' data files designed, first, for operating purposes, and second, by and for systems specialists rather than 'naïve' end-users.

Finding that they had a number of stand-alone personal computers installed, some departments decided to link them together so that users could exchange and share information, perhaps using inexpensive local area network technology. This exercise revealed that data sharing is an order of magnitude more difficult than stand-alone personal computing, and sometimes uncovered a whole new range of difficulties, major and minor, when attempts were made to link into corporate systems.

Information technology started moving out of the air-conditioned machine room and into the department with the minicomputer, and the personal computer extends the move right on to the end-user's desk. This may have suggested that now, at last, information systems could be organized to fit the business problems, rather than vice versa, and that office work could be organized according to its own logic, rather than reshaped to suit the technology. Sadly, this is not yet possible, or at least not without an inordinate amount of pain and effort. Certainly we are moving closer to this desirable goal, but the problems of managing a complex technology, not to speak of the problems of managing its human impact, keep that goal tantalizingly out of reach.

While information systems departments and business managers struggle with the practical problems of managing information technology, the pressures to make a success of the task grow more intense. Markets worldwide are becoming more volatile and more demanding. Legislation – on data protection, on health and safety, on environmental protection – provides more and more information handling hurdles for administrators, designers, marketing staff and planners to clear. In some respects, by establishing Information Centres to support end-users and by adopting advanced development tools, systems departments have improved their ability to respond to users' needs. But most continue to struggle with a heavy maintenance workload, and, while new tools make minor changes easier to implement, many existing systems can only be improved through major surgery and through projects measured in years rather than months.

One explanation sometimes offered for the gap between senior management expectation and the performance of the information systems department is poor communication. Information systems managers are urged to develop a new awareness of internal politics, rather than spend all the time nursing their expensive machinery. If possible, they should join the Chief Executive's golf club and murmur propaganda in his (or her – do female Chief Executives play golf?) ear on the way to the seventeenth tee. This may indeed smooth the department's path to higher budgets, but it is no substitute for making a real contribution to business success. The evidence suggests that in many companies it is the latter which is in doubt.

The search for ways to improve the contribution of the information systems department has been on for some years now and is going in a number of different directions. In a number of well-publicized instances information technology has been used as a potent competitive weapon,[2] and search strategies have been devised to help to identify such 'competitive edge' applications.[3] The methods used to design and develop applications systems are under scrutiny, and new tools and techniques are being introduced. Human resource management is receiving less attention, but surely is equally important in view of the chronic shortage of skilled staff.[4]

These are three important topics that deserve attention, but this book concentrates on a fourth key area – the deployment of the technology itself. It is now becoming widely recognized that success depends on deploying the technology resources in a radically different way. In the past, information systems specialists thought of that task principally in terms of specific projects for which equipment had to be provided. In addition, scale economies were achieved by sharing expensive resources such as large-scale computers and telecommunications networks. Yet in many organizations today far too much is going on, and the opportunities are far too diverse and widespread for such an approach to work. Instead, we must think of information technology as an enabling mechanism, and build an *infrastructure* to support all of the information systems activity taking place right across the organization. This infrastructure will serve the information users within the business in much the same way that the road and rail networks, plus a whole range of supporting services, serve transport users. Speaking of organizations that have gone through the initial stages of growth in data processing, Richard Nolan explains why an infrastructure is needed:

> we have discovered that companies in the advanced stages stagnate when they spend less than 35 per cent of their total computer budget on infrastructure computer resources. Initially, short-term gains and enthusiasm from user computing are realized, but then the more sophisticated uses resulting from the integration of CAD and CAM, downloading institutional systems databases such as financial information to personal computer-based spreadsheet models, and document transfer through electronic mail systems, are stopped dead in their tracks because of the lack of an integrated architecture. If the technological discontinuity is not resolved, each technology develops its individual infrastructure, leading to excessive duplication of investment and functional incompatibility.[5]

Why, at this stage in the development of information systems, is it so important to provide an infrastructure? There are three main reasons, all hinted at by Nolan. The first reason is to unify a fast-growing new domain within information systems, which I term *end-user systems*, with the established operational systems – the data and transaction processing systems that support the production, logistical and control processes of the organization. Only thus can you protect the huge investment in operational systems whilst safely releasing individual initiative by means of end-user systems. The personal computer is the most visible representative of this domain at present but, as Figure 1 illustrates, end-user systems draw not only on personal computer technology, but also on distributed data processing (sometimes called departmental computing) and on office automation technologies. End-user systems provide information handling power at the point of use, and for skilled knowledge workers rather than for the low-level staff most heavily affected by operational systems.

Second, a considered architectural approach, embodied in an infrastructure, is the surest way to build in the kind of flexibility that yesterday's systems conspicuously lack. This will enable information systems to keep pace with users' needs as both business strategies and their own ability to exploit information evolve. It will also make it easier to take rapid advantage of new technologies, where these offer important opportunities for the organization.

Third and by no means least, the information systems department must recognize the change in its internal market and in its own role in providing service and support. If it is to succeed in servicing an emerging mass market with the limited resources at its disposal, then it must think more in terms of providing infrastructure and utility services, less in terms of projects to develop specific business applications.

The idea of an architectural approach to information systems has been around for some time. As usual, IBM got in the first telling punch, by announcing Systems Network Architecture (SNA) in 1974. SNA and

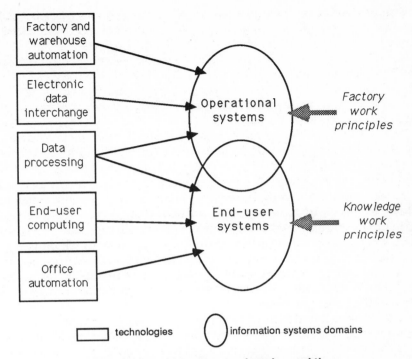

Figure 1 Information systems domains and the technologies that contribute

other suppliers' architectures have made a contribution, but they have by no means answered all the questions that must be addressed. They have helped to address some of the technical questions but not the business questions. Defining an architecture, and beyond that building an infrastructure, involves a great deal more than deciding how to interconnect the equipment, which is where suppliers' architectures help most. Judgement must also be brought to bear, for example, to trade off the merits of control and discipline conferred by centralization, against those of local accountability and innovation conferred by decentralization.

The task, in summary, is to design an infrastructure for information systems that combines these desirable properties:

- It is sufficiently practical and cost-effective to be implemented today, with the resources, human and financial, likely to be available.
- It is flexible and robust enough to absorb inevitable change as it arises, without excessive cost or delay.
- It is comprehensive, capable of covering the full range of corporate needs as they exist today and as they can be foreseen in the near future.
- It is appropriate, in a strategic sense, for the business it must serve.

Impossible? Certainly not. This book is based on what business organizations, staffed by highly competent but otherwise quite normal managers, have actually achieved. Only two ingredients have been added to their practical experience. First, the analysis necessary to recognise how they made their choices and why they went wrong (which, of course, they sometimes did), and, second, the synthesis needed to draw general lessons from their experience and to present those lessons in a structured way.

What *is* impossible, perhaps, is to lay down a cut-and-dried method for justifying expenditure on infrastructure, or for deciding how much you should invest in it, and this I do not attempt to do. Money spent on motorways is not justifiable in terms of specific benefits gained by having them. We build motorways, it seems to me, because our political masters believe we have to have them in order for our economy to remain competitive, and also because a lot of voters drive motor cars and dislike traffic jams. And, at any particular time, we spend as much on them as our political masters believe we can reasonably afford. Information technology infrastructure, I believe, must be seen in similar terms. You should build the best infrastructure your organization can possibly afford, at the lowest possible cost.

The book is divided into two parts. Part One examines the forces shaping the infrastructure, in order to define what requirements it should set out to meet and what principles should be applied to its design. In Part Two of the book I go on to show how these requirements and principles can be turned into a workable infrastructure, appropriate for a particular organization with particular needs.

Notes and references

1   *Information technology: value for money* (Butler Cox & Partners Ltd, 1987).
2   See, for example, 'Ten ways to get ahead with information technology', *Business Week,* Oct 14 1985, pp. 108-116.
3   For a review of several such methods, see Malcolm C. Munro and Sid L. Huff, 'Information technology and corporate strategy', *Business Quarterly,* Summer 1985, pp. 18-24.
4   For a comprehensive and up-to-date treatment of this important topic, see a forthcoming book in this Business Information Technology series by John Westerman and Pauline Donoghue: *Managing the human resources.*
5   R. L. Nolan *et al,* 'Creating an information utility', *Stage by Stage,* 6, 2, pp. 1-9.

PART
ONE

REQUIREMENTS AND PRINCIPLES FOR THE INFRASTRUCTURE

To design a building to meet a specified purpose, an architect draws on a long-established body of knowledge. Information systems have had a relatively short and turbulent history, and during that short time a considerable body of knowledge has been assembled, but one that is highly fragmented. What is more, much of it has become obsolete almost as soon as it took shape, because of the unprecedented rate of change of information technology.

So, before we can begin the task of defining an information technology infrastructure, we must first, starting from the requirements, derive a set of architectural principles that can be applied to derive a workable result. The requirements reflect the purpose that the infrastructure must serve – in short, to facilitate the handling of business information – and they also reflect the environment within which the infrastructure must function. For information systems, just as for buildings, the environment comprises the needs, social as well as technical, of those people who will make use of them; the strengths, weaknesses and economics of the technologies available; and the stresses to which they can expect to be subjected during their useful life.

Thus, to recognize what the requirements are, we need to look at the infrastructure from three points of view:

- From a marketing viewpoint – What are the customers' needs? How should we aim to satisfy them?
- From an engineering viewpoint – What structural qualities should the infrastructure have? What topology? How should we fit the component parts together?
- From a procurement viewpoint – What are the characteristics of the components we will use to build the infrastructure? Hence, what guidelines or restrictions should we apply to purchasing?

The marketing viewpoint, in fact, is not a single viewpoint, but two. In the first place, there are the various corporate customers – departmental heads, senior managers, professional staff, support staff, and so on. Of course, the infrastructure is shaped by their individual and shared needs for better means of handling information. But it is also shaped by the needs of the organization as a whole, and particularly by the methods chosen to co-ordinate the activities of all those working on its behalf.

Thus we have four viewpoints – the applications of customers, both as individuals and as members of work groups; the demands of the organization as a whole; an engineering viewpoint; and a procurement viewpoint. In this first part of the book I explain, under each of those four headings, what the forces are that shape the infrastructure, and what design requirements and architectural principles they imply.

CHAPTER 1

APPLICATIONS AND CUSTOMER NEEDS

Looking at infrastructure requirements from a marketing viewpoint, it is logical to begin by identifying the growth areas in the application of information technology, and also the general trends reflected in priorities for the information systems effort. But, as information technology spreads out into the business and is used by an ever wider range of staff – by managers, professionals, salesmen, and their support staff, as well as by clerks – it is important also to recognize the needs of these staff as individuals and as members of work groups. Many of these new users of information technology are more senior than the clerks who were the users (and sometimes the victims) of the data processing systems of the past, which means that they are better able to resist unwelcome change. What is more, most of them are knowledge workers who can exercise a high degree of discretion to decide when, and sometimes whether, they will use information technology tools, rather than established ways of completing their tasks.

Drawing on the lessons of experience to date, I begin by identifying the application growth areas and the requirements of different types of user. Since much of the growth is carrying information systems deeper into the domain of knowledge work, I continue by summarizing the information systems requirements of knowledge workers. Finally, I draw out the key implications for the infrastructure.

Growth areas in information systems

In all the diversity of information technology activities in business organizations, both in the private and public sectors, certain key growth areas can be recognized. To illustrate where these are, I have drawn up a simple model of those business information flows and information handling processes on which information systems have made an impact, shown in Figure 1.1. The figure is divided into three 'layers':

- At the top, the *production systems* which control the production and logistical resources of the enterprise – manufacturing plant, distribution networks, manpower and so on.
- At the bottom, the *environment* within which the business operates, consisting of customers, agents, suppliers, competitors, regulatory bodies, government.
- In between these two layers, the *information systems*, consisting of both information technology and older technologies, and operated mainly by white-collar staff. The information systems react to the demands of the business environment as these arise and, through planning, they also attempt to anticipate those demands. They buffer the production

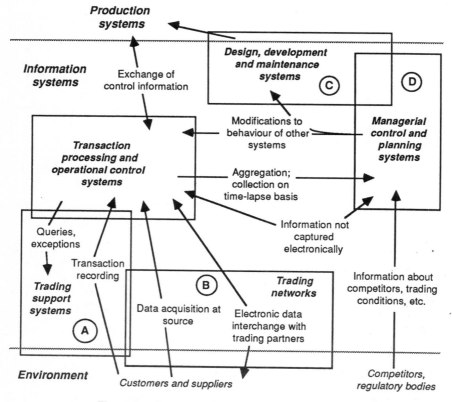

Figure 1.1 Growth areas in information systems

systems from much of the volatility of the environment, enabling these to operate in a stable manner which minimizes and controls costs. They also coordinate the human resources outside the production area – the knowledge workers – and control the financial resources of the business.

Information flows up and down across the layers, and also along the layers. In the information systems layer, the flow is mainly from left to right. Beginning as a record of business transactions, information is used first to drive and control the production and clerical operations which service those transactions, then to feed the management control and planning systems, which in turn feed back instructions, guidance and modifications. Information technology is, of course, only one of the technologies in use within the information systems layer, but it is of considerable and growing importance. For this reason, and for lack of an alternative term, I use the term 'information systems' throughout the remainder of this book in the narrower sense, to mean computer-based information systems.

We can identify a number of applications growth points within information systems, in terms of this model, and also two general trends, and I outline these briefly below.

Applications growth points

I have identified the growth points on the figure, in no particular order, by the letters A to D. In brief, they are as follows.

A: SUPPORT FOR CUSTOMER SERVICE

Throughout the 1980s, information technology has been applied to the link between the organization and its customers. Online terminals have been introduced into branch offices and sales departments. At first, effort was concentrated on capturing transaction data and on back office activities, but this has given way to a broader approach aimed at improving customer service in general, and involving front office staff and staff such as dealers and brokers, who conduct transactions directly with customers. Benefits, previously measured in reduced administrative costs, are now measured in terms of increased sales effectiveness.

To give just one example among many available, Thomson Holidays' computerized reservation system has saved its travel agents about £1.5 million in telephone charges over three years. It has also doubled the sales productivity of Thomson's own reservation staff and enables the company to capture sales very quickly – 105,000 holidays were booked in one day at the start of the 1986 summer holiday booking season. Other applications include the use by travelling sales staff of hand-held terminals to do on-the-spot checks on product availability; dealing systems in financial services companies; laser scanners at supermarket checkouts, providing itemized bills.

What underlies developments in this area is a recognition that front-line staff often need support with other aspects of their work apart from transaction recording, such as in assembling quotations rapidly or in collating information from a number of different sources. Often, this implies an intelligent system installed locally, rather than just a 'dumb' online terminal.

B: TRADING NETWORKS

In the latter half of the decade, telecommunications networks have been used to capture data at source, such as via 'hole-in-the-wall' banking terminals and transaction telephones at point of sale, and to exchange data directly with trading partners. The objectives may be to externalize labour or eliminate errors, thus reducing costs; to accelerate data flows, perhaps bringing down inventory levels or improving the utilization of capital assets; or to gain a marketing advantage by reducing the bargaining power of customers or trading partners.

C: SUPPORT FOR PROFESSIONAL WORK GROUPS

Work groups consisting mainly of highly skilled technical or professional staff usually manipulate information intensively, and often in *ad hoc* ways. They sometimes include a number of sub-specialities, and members of the group work together closely to bring their combined skills to bear on their common tasks. Until recently, these characteristics made them difficult to support with information technology. Now, though, what I call *work-group systems* – systems combining applications to manipulate information in specific ways with general-purpose utilities to present and disseminate the results – are being applied successfully, sometimes with dramatic gains in performance. In the next section I give examples of the types of work group that have been helped in this way.

D: SUPPORT FOR MANAGERIAL CONTROL AND PLANNING

Operational systems, used to record business transactions and to control operational processes, have always included some features for reporting and analysis, intended to help management monitor current activities and plan ahead. Recently, organizations have started to develop systems to support managerial control and planning, separated from the operational systems. This has been done for a combination of reasons, but one powerful reason is to enable reporting and analysis routines to be changed more frequently and more rapidly than is possible when they are embedded in the operational systems. Additionally, all the base data required may not be available from those operational systems, or cannot easily be put together in the right form.

Two general integration trends

To these four specific areas of growth can be added two general application trends, each of which is a particular manifestation of integration, by which I mean combining disparate parts of a system into a coherent whole.

The first of these is the desire to lower the barriers to interchange of information across functional boundaries or 'information frontiers'. Information frontiers have been created by the introduction into different parts of a business of information systems between which information cannot easily be exchanged, and also by the introduction of information systems into manual systems, thereby creating a new barrier between the information held on the new system and the information still handled manually. In some organizations, integration of this kind is seen as a business necessity, as a means of introducing product changes more quickly or responding more effectively to volatile trading conditions. Many more look at the problem from the negative side, and see today's incoherent or fragmented information systems as a severe handicap for the business, constraining their room for manoeuvre or their marketing options.

The search for better integration of information systems with one another is under way in many industries, but it is most visible in manufacturing, where it has attracted the label *computer-integrated manufacturing*. Definitions of the concept, and also attempts to realize it, vary considerably, but it can be summarized as bringing product design, manufacturing and business information together in such a way that different parts of the business can all draw on it as they need. Manufacturing companies see improved response to the market and/or improved internal communications as the main benefits, sometimes plus reduced lead times, reduced inventory or reduced manufacturing costs.

In general, the driving force behind integration efforts is to improve response to customers and to markets that are becoming increasingly volatile and increasingly demanding. In their book *In search of excellence*, Peters and Waterman give the example of a company which needed 223 formal linkages between organizational units before launching a new product. Taken by itself, they say, each linkage made perfectly good sense, but the outcome did not: 'Needless to say, the company is hardly first to the marketplace with any new product.' Ironically, information systems have sometimes made the problem of co-ordinating corporate response on major decisions more rather than less difficult, because, as mentioned earlier, they have created new information frontiers that are not easy to bridge.

The second trend is toward the incorporation into information systems of forms of information previously outside their scope entirely. At the present time, it is image information that is starting to come within their scope – images of paper documents, plant diagrams, signatures, maps, in fact any visual information that cannot be captured or keyed in text format. The technological driving forces here are high-resolution scanning, display and printing technologies, combined with the low-cost processing power and memory that is needed to manipulate and store images, which are at least an order of magnitude more demanding of these resources than coded data or text. A number of utilities, for example, are installing mapping information systems which permit them to superimpose diagrams of their outside plant and equipment on to street maps. These are linked to the existing data processing systems, and pick up the plant attributes and other information from the computerized records already held there. In a very real sense, these systems add an extra dimension – the visual or spatial dimension – to information systems.

Systems such as these are highly specialized, but they are the forerunners of document image processing systems that will have a much wider impact. By document image processing I mean the capture and storage of information as images rather than as coded data or text. In addition, key information is associated with the stored images, so that they can be retrieved in a flexible manner for examination. These systems do not permit the detailed manipulation of images associated with computer-aided design applications, but they normally allow users to make changes which do not involve manipulation of the images, such as by annotating them or by 'stapling' several of them together electronically. They also assist with comparison and analysis, by enabling users to cut-and-paste portions of images on to different parts of the display screen. Applications of this technology include existing paper archives which have to be retained for lengthy periods for legal or other reasons, and for which manual re-keying would take far too much time and be much too expensive, and current documents, generated internally or received from outside, which contain signatures, drawings or pictures, and which cannot be keyed in at all.

Until recently, information of this kind, estimated to comprise nearly two-thirds of the paperwork used in business, was partially or completely outside the reach of digital information systems. In the 1988 Computer Weekly/BCS lecture, Robb Wilmot, formerly chief executive with Texas Instruments and ICL, expressed the magnitude of the new opportunity in these terms:

> optical storage will be less than 50 cents a megabyte in five years, will be erasable, removable and have similar performance to magnetic DASD storage.
>
> Using these parameters for a minute to assess the forces for change, a full four drawer file cabinet holds 30 Mbytes of ASCII text, requiring $20 of optical storage with annualised costs of probably $5 or so. The equivalent four drawer file occupies 10 square feet including access, and at today's London space rates is £500 a year.[1]

The range of end-user needs

If we move the camera in closer, to look at the needs of individuals, we find a variegated picture. In the early days of what was then called *office automation*, suppliers tried to persuade us that a limited number of utilities, such as word processing, messaging, diary management, and so on, would solve the 'office productivity problem'. What has since become clear is that this was a simplistic view of what goes on in offices. Although the utilities offered as a basis for automating the office can and do contribute, behind and beyond them office work has thrown up a huge variety of applications. What is more, the attitudes and level of confidence of individual end-users vary dramatically.

To define an infrastructure, though, it is essential to latch on to certain key characteristics of end-users' needs which can be used to shape the overall approach. My purpose here is to bring out those key characteristics, rather than to take on the impossible task of cataloguing the whole range of needs in detail. For that purpose, end-users can usefully be characterized in two different ways – in terms of their job function and as members of work groups.

Office workers by job function – some patterns

Before the personal computer boom, several different types of office worker were already established users of computer devices. Many clerks, of course, had online terminals for transaction entry; some secretaries had word processors; scientific and technical staff used timesharing terminals, now rapidly being displaced by personal computers; some salesmen had videotex or portable data capture terminals. The personal computer has displaced a number of these devices and has also substantially extended the use of computer devices into the ranks of professional and managerial staff. Few, however, are used by higher-ranking managers.

Based on accumulated experience to date, some valid generalizations can be made about how different types of office worker use computer devices, and hence what their needs are. I describe these briefly below.

SENIOR MANAGERS
The computing activity of those few senior managers who do use computer devices is distinct from that of more junior managers and staff professionals, notably because executives require highly refined information, with a strong emphasis on external information. A system developed for senior executives at British Petroleum is a good example. They have been equipped with colour terminals which give them access both to external oil price information and to various internal business indicators.

COMMERCIAL MANAGERS

Commercial managers, by contrast, tend to be heavy users of operating data, retrieved from centralized data processing systems. To monitor business operations, they wish to select from this data and present it in various ways, sometimes *ad hoc*. They may also use messaging services to keep in touch with their staff and other members of their management team, especially where these are geographically distributed or highly mobile.

PROFESSIONALS

By *professionals* I mean all those staff who carry out tasks depending on professional knowledge, excluding *sharp-end staff*, covered below. This category covers a wide range of specializations such as research chemists, design engineers, computer programmers, financial accountants, architects, and so on.

Some of them use highly specialized computer-based tools and applications, but many carry out modelling and analysis using personal computer applications packages like Lotus Corporation's *1-2-3* and Ashton-Tate's *Dbase III*. Word processing, desktop publishing and business graphics packages are used for presentation of results. Some professionals are heavy consumers of information, drawing on a variety of sources both inside and outside their business; others key in limited quantities of data themselves.

Typically, professionals are organized in teams, either to bring a range of specialized knowledge to bear on a complex task, or to economize on scarce skills or expensive equipment. As I explain further below, this makes many teams of professionals candidates for workgroup systems, although they also gain high levels of benefit from stand-alone personal computers.

ADMINISTRATIVE SUPPORT STAFF

As one would expect, administrative support staff such as secretaries do use what was originally termed 'office automation' – utilities such as word processing and electronic mail. These are used as improved substitutes for typewriter, telex and internal mail. But they also tend to be drawn into what I call *local data processing*.

What happens is that once-off applications are implemented locally, usually on the initiative of managers or professionals, occasionally by support staff themselves. Sometimes these meet a short term need then fade away, but on other occasions they are extended or generalized and become assimilated into office procedures. When this happens, responsibility for operating them is handed down to the most junior member of the team capable of coping, such as marketing assistants or senior secretaries. These applications are usually written in high-level languages like

BASIC or APL, or are generated by means of (relatively) easy-to-use file management packages such as *DBase III*.

SHARP-END STAFF
By *sharp-end staff* I mean people with professional skills who take trading decisions, usually under pressure – dealers, sales staff, buyers. Their information systems activity is usually what I term *enhanced transaction processing* – in other words, it provides a means for them to obtain information about customers and to record business transactions, but enhanced in particular ways which help them to operate more effectively. Citibank, for example, has installed personal computers to support its foreign exchange dealers. These devices are linked via a local network to a shared system handling transaction documentation and accounting.

CLERICAL STAFF
The needs of clerical staff are comparatively well known, since they have been the main target of data processing systems in the past. However, this does not mean that those needs are necessarily well met. Data processing systems have often created new problems, as well as solving old ones, because of their inflexibility or because of their narrow scope. This has created opportunities for local systems, perhaps replicated across a number of similar work groups, which help to support or unify fragmented work patterns or handle problems outside the scope of the main system.

A health insurance company, for example, had installed centralized systems to record insurance contracts. Staff at the branch offices found that these systems were not responsive enough to enable them to calculate price quotations in the course of a phone call. In addition, the company wanted to give the branch office managers the flexibility to strike special deals reflecting local needs. The solution was to develop a pricing program to run on personal computers installed in the branches. Head office distributed a standard version of the program whenever policy changed, and branch office managers could add in local pricing rules when they wished.

Four categories of work group

Personal computers, and before them personal computing via time-sharing terminals, have led the growth of end-user systems, but it is misleading to think of requirements principally in terms of the personal needs of different types of office worker. No office worker in business is an island, since all contribute jointly to the corporate goals. Most form part of one or more teams or work groups, and have close working relationships with the other members of their own work group and with work groups elsewhere in the business.

The work group or department generally delivers defined business results that can be measured objectively. For this reason it is the correct focus for the justification and design of information systems, and thus is a key building block for the infrastructure also. The range of work groups, line and staff, is naturally greater and more diverse than the range of office workers. Looking, however, at the systems which have been installed to support the work of particular groups, it is possible to recognize four distinct categories. Although different equipment solutions may be used for any one of these and a range of different applications may be implemented, the nature of the benefits tends to be common within each category. The types of work group and the characteristic benefits gained from information technology are outlined below.

THE COMMERCIAL TEAM

The first category I refer to as the *commercial team*. It consists of a vertical slice of the staff handling the line activities of a business. Depending on how the business is organized, the slice may relate to a particular product or group of products, or perhaps to a particular category of customer or trading partner.

The best way to identify the boundaries of such a work group is to study who communicates and shares data with whom in day-to-day work. One such study was conducted within a chemical company which was divided up into business groups dealing with different types of product, and functional groups handling such activities as distribution, manufacturing and accounts for all the business groups. The study was centred on a business team in one of the business groups. The team consisted of commercial product managers and technical services managers plus supporting staff, and had marketing responsibility for a particular group of products. The study focused on data sharing patterns rather than on communication alone. It revealed that, in addition to the business team itself, the work group included other people within the business group, such as the technical planner, and some in the functional groups, such as the plant managers and plant engineers dealing with the team's products. Consequently, the initial installation was extended to include these people.

Although work-group systems can certainly be expected to improve administrative efficiency for commercial teams, the main payoff is usually intangible. They enable the team to respond faster to market needs; to better coordinate product changes; to manage crises more effectively.

THE CRITICAL PROFESSIONAL TEAM

My second category I describe as the *critical professional team*. As the name implies, these contribute to business performance principally by applying professional knowledge rather than by means of managerial skills. Many such groups need well-validated data from a number of sources, including data processing systems. For the team itself, the advantage of work-group systems is that they can access, manipulate and distribute information easier and faster. They can also monitor and regulate their own activities better. This is a great advantage for them because the quality of their work is often a key factor, but difficult to monitor and control precisely.

A further characteristic of these work groups is that they are on the critical path of the business, which means that time savings or quality gains translate directly into business benefits. For example, one successful system is used by a team of chemists preparing submissions to statutory bodies responsible for approving new drugs. Time savings in the approval process mean that drugs are introduced to market sooner, a key competitive advantage. Another is used by a team of engineers preparing proposals for major capital projects. In this case, the more carefully their proposals are worked out, the more likely that the subsequent capital project will run to cost.

However, there is a problem with targeting work-group systems at teams such as these. When the pressure on the team is at its greatest, the disruption of introducing a new system can be least afforded. Conversely, when the pressure is off, the business need is much weaker. Also, because they are on the business critical path, the cost and visibility of failure are high. For this reason, I have heard opportunities like these referred to as 'the bleeding edge of technology'. By the same token, though, the benefits of success are considerable.

Systems for professional teams also tend to be more challenging technically than those for commercial teams. As indicated earlier, professionals usually operate as integrators of a varied body of information, applying their background knowledge and professional judgement to validate and select from this information, then to hammer it into the particular form that is needed. Hence, systems to support this kind of work may have to span a variety of specialized information and processing needs, whereas commercial teams usually have much more of their support and information requirements in common.

THE PROFESSIONAL SKILLS COMPOSITE
Head Office departments are typical of the third category of work group. Examples are a group charged with a range of corporate accounting tasks; a secretarial and legal department, which carries out all the tasks requiring legal skills. I describe this type of work group as a *composite* rather than a team, because they usually do not have a central business mission to which all contribute, as do both the *commercial team* and the

critical professional team. What unites them as a work group is the fact that they share a particular professional skill which is applied to a range of corporate tasks.

Such groups typically find it virtually impossible to increase their headcount even while they face a growing workload, so their prime objective for work-group systems, naturally enough, is to improve productivity. Work-group systems directly improve the productivity of individuals or teams within the group, but, more importantly, they also make it possible to assign tasks more flexibly and thus to handle peaks or crises more easily. Hence a greater payoff is gained where workloads are very variable. For example, the accounting group mentioned above used to run into huge peaks of work every month when they produced monthly management reports. Their system eliminated most of the overtime, and also sliced several days off the lead time from receiving data from business units to delivering the reports to top management. With financial markets as volatile as they are today, that was a valuable benefit.

Alternatively, the main benefits may be gained where a great deal hangs on the ability of a team to operate effectively in a crisis, such as a secretarial team engaged in a takeover battle.

THE SENIOR MANAGEMENT TEAM

Work-group systems for senior management teams are often referred to as executive support systems. These have been much discussed for some years,[2] but success, defined as a real impact on the way executives work, remains elusive. Systems have been installed with widely varying motives, some to demonstrate the Chief Executive's commitment to exploiting information technology, others to solve urgent business problems. Success is more common in the latter case than in the former. The Centre for Information Systems Research at the Massachusetts Institute of Technology (MIT) looked at five US installations, and the researcher summed up the difference between the successful and unsuccessful ones in this way:

> . . . A distinct difference in development and use exists between . . . [an] executive support system in firms where it is initiated as a problem-solving tool and firms where it is brought in for other reasons.
>
> The problem-solving systems begin small in number of applications and number of users and then grow. They gradually evolve into planning systems. The efficiency systems begin with a larger number of users and then atrophy. At the end of two years, only the problem-initiated systems survived. Distinction between the two types of systems is the relationship of the executive support system to the core of the business.[3]

The situation which seems to supply just the right problem for a work-group system to address is where senior management wants to redirect the mission of the business unit, for example to switch from product orientation to a customer orientation. The trigger tends to be the arrival of a new Chief Executive or Chairman, or a radical change in the external trading environment. The work-group system serves to supply the new information which the senior management team requires. Almost always, this information can only be generated by building new data files, so only a marginal cost is incurred by making the information available directly to senior management via the new system, rather than having them continue to rely solely on middlemen. (Staff with information skills are always needed to feed and water the new data files, though.)

As one would expect, in all cases the senior management team, or its leader, were strongly committed to the idea of using information technology as a catalyst to bring about the necessary changes. The reason for applying the technology to their activities, rather than lower down the hierarchy, was that middle management was more likely to feel threatened, and therefore to resist change or, as often happens, to downgrade objectives to deal with low-level problems. The system serves to reinforce the change in mission, by defining new indicators and reporting formats. Lower level managers have no choice but to conform to these new information requirements if they wish to communicate with senior management. The CISR researcher again:

> The reports and data in the executive support system are the message to the rest of the organization as to what indicators count, and the staff who manage the executive support system become the gatekeepers of information.

Those staff which lead the exploitation of a work-group system will inevitably bend it to their own purposes before they will bend it to those of someone else. An engineering company installed a system consisting of networked workstations, aimed at improving communication between directors and senior managers. To break these senior staff in gradually, the information systems staff installing the system concentrated first of all on equipping and training the managers' secretaries. The final result of the exercise was great popularity for word processing, but not much benefit for senior managers. The qualities of the technology adopted had an influence here – word processing was one of its strengths – but the message is clear. The technology is passive – if senior managers do not seek benefits for themselves, people lower in the hierarchy will find the benefits that suit them.

Work-group systems – three key requirements

When we look at office workers' requirements for information technology support as work groups rather than as individuals, three additional

[margin note: SPECIFIC WK GRP APPLIC⌐S]

requirements come to the fore. The first requirement is for applications which address business problems specific to the work group. A number of leading edge companies have discovered this, among them DuPont.

DuPont were pioneers in the application of office automation tools and subsequently work-group systems. Two major pilot systems were initiated within their US Divisions in 1982. The objectives set for those pilots were to provide tools for professionals and managers to increase productivity and improve effectiveness, and also to implement what DuPont called an *extended value* approach – in their words, 'to identify individual and organizational missions, functions and tasks' and provide applications specifically to support them. Experience with office automation had taught them that the general-purpose tools, although useful, were not enough on their own. The pilots confirmed the validity of their *extended value* approach, showing that individual productivity will pay for the system after the assimilation period, but that major benefits come from specific applications and from personal computing. (As a result of their experience, they also 'changed the focus of the technology from individual to organization' and 'changed the focus of justification from strict cost/benefit to improved organizational effectiveness and competitive advantage'.)

The second requirement is for members of the work group to be able to share information selectively – data, documents, perhaps in the near future images also. Applications solving specific business problems provide the early impetus, but the second ingredient is equally crucial, because it ensures that the system's contribution is sustained long enough for it to become an essential part of people's jobs, rather than just a new form of office furniture. This crucial ingredient is added-value that the members of the work group gain by sharing data or documents with one another. They derive particular value from information-sharing mediated by a computer system if they exchange volatile or time-sensitive information, or if they match information obtained from different sources or obtained by different people. The potential benefit is further increased if communication by normal means is difficult, such as, for example, if people in the work group are widespread geographically, are in different time zones, or are highly mobile.

3ND. Work-group systems also bring a greater range of services to the desktop. As a result, a wider range of staff than gain sufficient value from personal computing alone become users, and this in turn places greater demands on the quality of the human/computer interface. That is the third extra requirement. Today, most end-users have relatively few applications, which they use heavily. Surveys of personal computer users show that most of them divide their computing activity between spreadsheet, retrieving data from mainframe computers, word processing, and managing local databases. As they are offered a richer range of services, some types of staff, and especially managers, begin to use a wider range of applications, and in shorter bursts. As their confidence in their new equipment grows, so also do they use it for more critical tasks, and as a result become more dependent on it and place greater urgency on results.

Knowledge workers' integration needs

If we pause for a moment and look back at the recent history of information systems in business, it is clear that they have often delivered no more than partial solutions to the business problems they addressed. This is neither surprising nor blameworthy, since the technology itself has strict limitations, which it pays to respect, and since people usually find it easier, in the first instance, to assimilate partial solutions. But, in the course of time, the result has been that information frontiers have been created. These have grown up both between these partial solutions and the human systems within which they operate, and also between the solutions installed in different parts of a business. The effort and inconvenience incurred in crossing these information frontiers is now recognized in many organizations as the main barrier to wider or more intensive use of information technology.

The existence of these information frontiers was recognized some time ago in the data processing era, when commentators pointed to the *islands of automation* that had developed in the different functional areas of complex businesses.[4] Subsequent technological developments have sometimes exacerbated rather than eased the problem. We now find, for example, that electronic messaging services are often divorced from obviously related functions such as word processing; that access from personal computers to operational systems, if automated at all, is unreliable and difficult to use; and that personal computers have good processing tools but can only disseminate results to others by means of paper.

If we turn from the technology itself to look at individuals' success in coming to terms with that technology, we find that, despite the runaway success of the personal computer, everything in the garden is not as beautiful as might be supposed. Personal computers seemed to represent a turning point, computing with a human face and on a human scale. But there is a reverse side to the attractive face of personal computing – the so-called *one-application syndrome*. People new to personal computers usually find that they invest far more time and effort than they imagined to learn one application. Naturally, they are reluctant to go through the same process to learn a second application, but stick doggedly to their hard-won, but very narrow skills. As a result, the machines are not used to their full potential and the end-users gain minimal benefits. They teach themselves to drive, but the experience is so intimidating, they hardly dare go out on the roads. When they do, they only use first gear.

It is also a fact, and a disappointment to many information systems people, that personal computers and other tools for knowledge workers have not penetrated very far up the management hierarchy in most businesses. The chemical company, ICI, which has placed a high corporate priority on the adoption of information technology, surveyed a sample of 2,000 personal computer users within the group companies in March 1986. The results showed that most personal computer users were relatively low level staff who had been directed to use them, supplemented by a scattering of self-selected enthusiasts among the ranks of professionals and managers. This is represented in Figure 1.2.

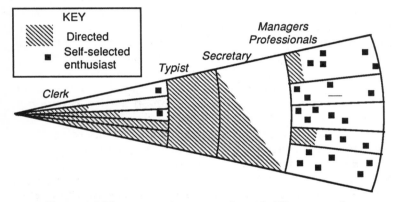

Figure 1.2 The personal computer base in ICI – pressed men and self-selected enthusiasts

Broadly based surveys of US businesses show a similar picture. Arthur D. Little's 1986 Integrated Office Survey was sent to over 300 US 'bell-wether' companies, excluding information technology vendors. The survey showed that a typical business has standalone word processors and personal computers, often with fledgling links to mainframe computers, one or two departmental systems, and numerous on-line terminals to the mainframes. There is little communication among the various camps. 65 per cent of the respondents hoped to build systems that would allow office workers to perform office tasks in a fully integrated manner, and over half had already embarked on the task. Only two per cent claimed to have made significant progress.

If we look more closely at what 'integration' means, we immediately recognize the difficulties. Each individual end-user has a particular combination of needs for information systems, which in turn imply a particular range of processing functions and applications, integrated together in a particular way. Those needs reflect, obviously, the type of job he or she is doing, but they also reflect personal preferences and habits of working. While it is reasonable to expect people to change some of their working practices to fit in with new information systems, it is *not* reasonable to expect them to abandon ingrained thinking and working processes altogether, nor to expect all to adapt in precisely the same way. Variety is the spice of knowledge work, as well as of life.

To serve its purpose as a vehicle for integration, then, the infrastructure must accommodate the combined needs of *all* end-users, or at the very least a large enough subset of those needs for each individual to feel reasonably well served. So, to understand the potential scope of the infrastructure, we must start by recognizing what end-users' overall requirements for integration consist of. To do that, it is helpful to separate those requirements out along three main dimensions. Those three dimensions are illustrated in Figure 1.3, and I now explain for each in turn what current experience shows to be needed.

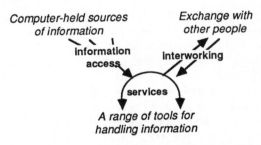

Figure 1.3 There are three dimensions to end-users' integration needs

Access to information – order out of chaos

It is clearly a fundamental requirement that knowledge workers should be able to access the information[5] they need to do their jobs with a minimum of effort. More and more of that information is finding its way on to computer systems, and hence more and more knowledge workers benefit by accessing information by means of a terminal or workstation.[6] The aim of integration along what I term the *information access* dimension is to make it easier for knowledge workers to obtain complete, relevant information from computer-based sources.

To date, attention has focused on linking personal computers directly with the operating and corporate data typically held on centralized mainframe computers. This brings three particular advantages. First, re-entry of computer-generated data, such as from printed reports, is avoided. This is still a widespread practice in large organizations. Not only is it a waste of effort, it is also an opportunity to introduce errors.

Second, integration into the highly structured data processing environment makes it easier to apply central controls on the integrity and security of data processed by end-users on their own local systems, where this is appropriate. Third, it lowers the effort demanded to acquire information and extends end-users' reach, thus enabling them to exploit a wider range of information resources and add more value by doing so.

The expense of providing direct electronic access to data is not trivial when all the costs are taken into account, but cost is a declining barrier. Direct access is near-essential for heavy consumers of data (typically ten per cent of the office workforce). It is also potentially valuable for anyone who needs to manipulate operating or corporate data extensively, because it brings data directly into the easy-to-use tools available on personal computers.

But the problem of access to data is only the tip of an iceberg of problems faced by knowledge workers, especially in larger organizations. The problem is not just getting at the data, but getting at the *right* data. This is a widespread difficulty, especially for managers. To put it another way, managers do not want data, they want information. A study carried out among executives in 45 industrial and financial organizations in California in 1985 illustrates why they find it so difficult to do so.[7] All those managers had access to a computer-based management information system for at least a year. Many of them found that the information available to them via the system lacked one or more of five important properties – accuracy, timeliness, completeness, conciseness and relevance. Completeness, conciseness and timeliness were missed much more often than accuracy or relevance, with miss ratings of 64, 50 and 46 per cent respectively! Not surprisingly, the managers felt that their decision-making was adversely affected, and rarely used a terminal themselves to initiate requests for information.

They also complained that software for building queries was difficult to use. Difficulty arises not only from the inadequacy of enquiry languages themselves, but also because operational files, the original source of much of the management information, are usually badly structured for the new purpose to which they are being applied. Management information, too often, is seen as a by-product of operational systems. As a result, it tends to be organized by topic, whereas managers most often need end-to-end information relating to a business process or to a departmental sphere of action.

But the limitations of operating data for management control and planning purposes are much more fundamental than that. In the first place, organizations have discovered the dangers of management over-reacting to operational data. Tactical and strategic decisions are often based on time-lapsed data, and war-game logic must be applied to decide when and when not to react. For this purpose, managers need refined, relatively noise-free information, whereas operational data contains a great deal of noise. In the second place, operational data tends to provide a one-dimensional picture of a multi-dimensional world. In other words, the same information can assume different values depending on the purpose to which it is applied and the person for whom it is intended. Examples are not hard to find of systems, designed carefully and conscientiously by head office staff to supply information to operating companies or to regional offices, where the output has to be re-hashed almost out of recognition to be of any real use to the intended beneficiaries. Degrees of detail, accuracy and urgency will vary with the purpose. For day-to-day control, for example, speed may be more important than accuracy, whereas for auditing purposes accuracy is a *sine qua non*.

To summarize, managers, and particularly senior managers, need complete and relevant (in their terms!) information, and expect to have exactly, or nearly, what they want delivered to the desk. Frequently, they need a great deal of external information, such as stock or commodity prices. Whether information is delivered by hand or by electronic means is almost immaterial, provided delivery is timely. If delivered electronically, then access has to be at least as easy for the manager as it is when delivered by hand. These complications mean that successful systems to provide managers with information have usually been built as bespoke systems, rather than based on general-purpose data management packages using standard query languages. This in turn means high development and maintenance costs, which to date has limited their application to the senior management of the largest organizations. With the move to develop work-group systems at departmental level, however, applications to meet the information needs of departmental managers are increasingly being built into these systems.

For professional staff, both the problems of obtaining the right data and the benefits of computer support are different. These staff add value to information by applying their professional skills to various tasks of analysis and synthesis. Often, they draw information from a variety of different sources. As well as helping with this logistical problem, a workstation with appropriate software makes it easier for them to associate and manipulate information without calling on middlemen. Swedish Telecom studied the effect of this and found that, by interacting directly with information, professionals improved the quality of their output. A middleman, without the same level of professional knowledge, sometimes filtered out information which the professional otherwise would have picked up and made something of.

Professionals sometimes achieve surprizing gains in productivity as a result of gaining full control of activities previously shared with support specialists – see Figure 1.4. Professionals, in summary, need both

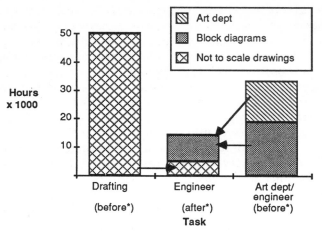

* before/after the introduction of information technology

**Figure 1.4 Integration of professional work
brings surprising gains**

easy access to their major sources of information, and also tools that
enable them to associate and manipulate that information in such a way
that they can apply their knowledge and creativity to best effect.

There is a further aspect of integration which, with data processing
and personal computing dominating information systems budgets, it is
easy to overlook. The fact remains that much of the information used in
offices is still held on paper. This includes existing paper archives which
have to be retained for lengthy periods for legal or other reasons. It also
includes current documents, generated internally or received from outside, which contain signatures, drawings or pictures. As indicated above,
until recently information of this kind, estimated to comprise nearly two-
thirds of the paperwork used in business, was partially or completely
outside the reach of digital information systems.

As is well known, paper filing systems are labour-intensive and
prone to a number of severe shortcomings – they include high risk of
misfiling or loss; lengthy retrieval times; and physical bulk. Information
systems people, I believe, are much less aware of the magnitude of the
paper handling problem than their colleagues who specialise in records
management and than end-users themselves. Hence there is a risk that
they will underestimate the potential contribution of document image
processing systems.

Far from solving the paper handling problem, the recent spread of
technology out into the workplace has served to highlight it. I have come
across a number of managers and professionals who key (or have their
support staff key) selected information about incoming correspondence

into their desktop systems for later analysis or retrieval. I know many more who would dearly like to bridge the gap between their existing data/text handling systems and incoming or stored correspondence, if only they knew of a practical, affordable way to do it. As I elaborate later, the arrival of document image processing affects the position and role of the workstation within the infrastructure and the structure of the corporate network.

Services – matching the pattern of work

Most end-users cut their teeth on simple, stand-alone processing tools on personal computers. Not only are personal computers appearing on more and more desks, they are also getting more and more powerful. Large organizations, able to buy in bulk, already find that the marginal cost of equipping all personal computers with a 20-megabyte hard disk is small enough to disregard. This desktop processing power, combined with a huge range of applications software packages and growing end-user sophistication, is widening the range of applications which end-users find it worthwhile to adopt.

One of the key attractions of the more sophisticated general-purpose office systems, such as DEC's *All-in-1* or Wang's *Office*, is that they integrate into a coherent whole the services which the end-user calls on to manipulate information. Integration of this kind brings ease of use and other convenience benefits for the individual end-user. Among those there are two particularly significant advantages.

First, it means that the user does not need to adjust continually to different application interfaces. The overhead of this 'context-switching' can be very high, and the advantages of integration at the application level are correspondingly great. This form of integration led to the success of the one of the world's best-selling personal computer packages, Lotus *1-2-3*, which integrates data management, spreadsheet and business graphics.

A consistent interface is an advantage for all types of staff, but especially for managers. Their needs are rather different from those of professionals. Their 'work style' is typically event-driven and their tasks are fragmented. To support this kind of work style, workstations must not only provide a consistent interface, but must also be capable of switching rapidly from one application to another, leaving the first application neatly and safely parked, with all its information intact, so that the manager can pick it up again later when it suits.

If applications all have a consistent 'look and feel' about them, it also makes it easier for occasional or sporadic users – such as many senior managers – to pick up the reins again after a lay-off

A second advantage of integration is that it can enable the user to associate information of different types – for example, to include numbers from a company database in a budget spreadsheet, to embed graphics into a proposal or specification, to return spoken comments on a draft report. Integration of a variety of information-handling tools is a characteristic requirement of professional staff charged with research or analysis tasks.

Integration at application level presents a severe dilemma, hinted at above. One key reason for the success of the personal computer is the dynamism of the industry supplying its application software, which, in a relatively short time, has delivered a huge range of packages, many of high quality. Unfortunately, this range of packages is anything but coherent, in the sense that they treat the user interface in all kinds of different ways. (At least, this is true of those aimed at the IBM PC and 'clones' – as I elaborate later, the Apple Macintosh is an honourable exception.) They also use a number of different proprietary formats to represent information. Furthermore, today's popular personal computers are essentially single-user, single-task machines. This means that they cannot easily support the kind of effortless task-switching needed to match the managerial work style. Nor can they easily link with other systems and services as required to support the interworking dimension of end-users' needs, which I come on to next.

The general-purpose office systems mentioned above, by contrast, offer the coherence which personal computer software lacks, but cannot rival the personal computer for range and quality of applications software. To meet end-users' evolving needs, it is necessary to marry the range of choice and the accessibility offered by the personal computer with the coherence built into proprietary packages such as *All-in-1*.

Interworking – breaking down the walls

As more and more end-users have their own desktop workstations, so it becomes increasingly worthwhile for them to link those workstations directly with those of their colleagues, and occasionally those of customers or trading partners, so that they can exchange and share information – in other words, so that they can *interwork*. The motive for linking workstations in this way is not merely speed of transfer. Integration along the interworking dimension helps end-users to exchange information in a secure and orderly manner, and to assimilate what they receive into their information handling activities with a minimum of effort and risk of error.

An effective scheme to support interworking is essential if information systems are to unite rather than divide the workforce as end-user systems spread. But there are also positive gains to be had by improving communication across functional barriers.

Successful work-group systems give us numerous examples of the breakdown of functional barriers which the technology has revealed as meaningless. At Dupont, for example, a system was introduced into a business unit in the synthetic fibres division. In that division, customer complaints had always been handled in the marketing organization. A marketing man broadcast an appeal for help with a particularly difficult complaint via the system, and received some valuable suggestions from the engineers. Subsequently, the process of handling customer complaints changed to include the active participation of the engineers. This produced the dual advantage that complaints were handled more effectively and that the engineers got early warning of possible product problems.

A second example, from the UK, has an ironic twist. A public utility arranged that all the transactions handled by different specialist departments at its regional offices could be accessed from any terminal. This was made known to the staff, quietly, but no organizational changes were made. In the course of time clerical staff began to handle transactions outside their specialist area to save unnecessary work and to help one another out. Ironically, while these functional barriers were breaking down naturally at regional offices, the Chairman was fighting a battle at Head Office to break down the entrenched functional orientation of his Board colleagues, so that he could swing the whole business round to a customer orientation.

As the examples above show, the benefits of interworking are not solely those of speed and immediacy. Information technology can also act as a catalyst for change, by establishing new communications paths through large or complex businesses. As I discuss later on, the extent of that requirement varies.

Since interworking is not only about speed, it follows that effective interworking demands a great deal more than a physical communications path. It also depends on mechanisms that coordinate the exchange of information, and, often, routines to convert information between the different internal formats used by sending and receiving systems.

Implications for the infrastructure

These then, are the general and specific trends in the application of information technology which the infrastructure must take on board. Naturally, applications will have differing priorities in different organizations, and will evolve over differing timescales, but it is possible to recognize some clear implications for the information technology infrastructure.

Trading networks – growth area B – will have a major impact on the structure, procurement and management of corporate networks and on particular data processing applications, but they have little impact outside these areas and do not affect the topology of internal information systems. Leaving them aside for the moment and concentrating on the other growth areas and the general trends, we can recognize three important features.

The first is that information technology is increasingly being used to support knowledge work. This is most obvious in that professionals and managers have been the main beneficiaries of the personal computer boom. But it also manifests itself in a more subtle way, in the sense that information systems are being deployed in a more holistic way than in the past, to embrace knowledge work as well as rote work. In situations where information systems are already in use, then the latest systems in a sense *re*-integrate work patterns that have become fragmented. Thus, for example, front office systems open up new ways of meeting customer demands by combining transactions that previously had to be handled separately, or by drawing in information not held on the data processing system. Similarly, work-group systems are both a rationalization of the piecemeal tools available on personal computers and an escape from the limitations of reporting and analysis features grafted on to operational systems. In other cases, new systems become worthwhile because they are able to accommodate some of the less structured and *ad hoc* aspects of knowledge workers' activities, as well as the structured, predefinable activities which have always been the focus of data processing systems.

The second common feature is a move away from support for individuals carrying out largely independent activities towards support for groups working on pooled activities. This is explicit in support for professional work groups and for management decision-making – growth areas C and D. The trend towards integration of information systems across functional barriers is a higher level manifestation of the same thing – the organization is seen as a team of work groups that must work more closely together.

The third feature is a move to distribute computing power and storage. This reflects changing technology cost ratios, but is also a consequence of the increasing sophistication and the widening scope of systems used to support the activities of knowledge workers. This can only be achieved by providing power at or close to the point of use of information, so that it can be handled according to needs and within the normal pattern of work.

In summary, then, the infrastructure must provide a framework for systems installed to support knowledge work and the groups that perform it. An architecture serving this purpose is shown in Figure 1.5, and is taken up in detail in Part Two. The infrastructure must also, to the

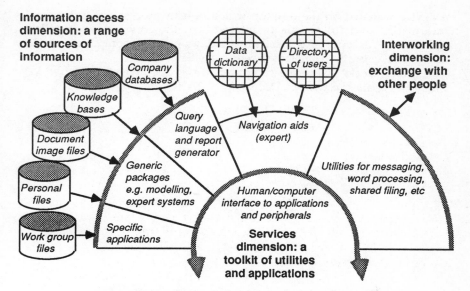

Figure 1.5 An architecture to support knowledge work

extent required in a particular business, serve to unify systems installed in different parts of that business. It must unify them in a way that is consistent with the methods used within the organization to co-ordinate the activities of its various component parts. This topic – how the demands of the organization influence the information technology infrastructure – is the subject of the next chapter.

Notes and references

1 R. Wilmot, Computer Weekly/BCS lecture; transcript in *Computer Weekly*, March 10/17, 1988.
2 The Centre for Information Systems Research at MIT has carried out much of the authoritative research on executive support systems. This is documented in *The Rise of Managerial Computing* (Dow Jones-Irwin, 1986).
3 Eliot Levinson, 'Support Systems for the Executive', *Computerworld*, Nov 26 1984, pp. ID/3-ID/16.
4 The classic paper is by James L. McKenney and F. Warren McFarlan: 'The information archipelago – maps and bridges', *Harvard Business Review*, Sept-Oct 1982 pp. 109-119.
5 In this book, I use the term *information* to mean 'facts to which a meaning can be attached'. Those facts may be in any form – structured data, text, image.
6 Originally, the term *workstation* was associated with very powerful desktop graphics systems used by engineers. I use the term more generally to mean

a device installed on the desktop which (a) can process and store local information and (b) is able to interwork with workstations installed elsewhere. With appropriate software, today's personal computers can do this, even if clumsily. Tomorrow's certainly will.

7   V. Thomas Dock, 'Executive computer use is doomed without five key properties', *Data Management*, Dec 1985, pp. 27-30.

CHAPTER 2

THE DEMANDS
OF THE
ORGANIZATION

If we look on the organization as a likeness of the human body, then information systems are its nervous system. Inevitably, some of those considerations which shape the organization influence the information systems and, in turn, the infrastructure that underpins them. In fact, I would put it more strongly than 'influence'. It is vital to decide a 'strategic direction', to be reflected in the infrastructure, which genuinely reflects the underlying needs of the organization. This essential preliminary step is often neglected on the grounds of being 'too difficult' or out of sheer lack of nerve. Without a clearly formulated strategic direction there is a real and ever-present danger that all the day-to-day pressures come to exert an excessive influence. Indeed, because of the power of these pressures, the chances of arriving by accident even close to where the organization needs to be are extremely slim. As the Chinese proverb has it: 'If you don't know where you're going, any road will take you there'. Information technology offers a wide, and widening, choice of roads.

The day-to-day pressures come both from the past and, as it were, from the future. The pressure from the future is the enormous potential of information technology – the motive power we are aiming to harness. The prime danger is that its contribution is not set in correct proportion with that of the people who, in the end, must exploit its potential to deliver results. It is difficult to overstate the importance of the issues concerning people – skills, attitudes, organization, methods, etc. – but this book only deals with them insofar as they affect the infrastructure.

The past is represented by the enormous inertia of existing information systems. This often becomes evident only with hindsight. It builds up insidiously year by year to the point where it can easily dominate both thinking and action. To appreciate how strong that inertia can become, you only need to look at many of those organizations for which data processing has played a key role in the recent past. One of the UK clearing banks, for example, found that its marketing policy was effectively being determined by the data processing department, which dictated how quickly changes could be made to the operational systems which drove their network of branches and teller machines. Many marketing moves, in turn, depended on these changes. The bank had been attempting to come to grips with this problem for some time, but the deregulation of the UK financial services industry finally forced them into action. With the aim of overcoming the inertia, they launched a study to draw up a picture of the information systems they hoped to have in about five years' time, and then attempted to reverse engineer back from this picture to the present day. This, they believed, would force all concerned – bankers and information systems specialists – to face up to any unpalatable changes which they had to make.

What this example shows is that the road ahead – the strategic direction – is not always apparent from a position in the thick of information systems activity. Indeed, in present circumstances of volatile business conditions and volatile technology, I would again put it more strongly and say that the strategic direction is rarely apparent unless you make a real effort to distance yourself from the confusion. Like the generals of the past, you have to get up on a hill over the battlefield so that you can look down over it.

And how do we get up on to this hypothetical hill over the information systems battlefield? Here we face a problem, because formal methods used for planning information systems are good at generating a design when objectives are clear, weak at translating business requirements into overall objectives. There are historical reasons for this. In the past, the targets for the information systems effort were obvious. The issues at stake were relative priorities (in the face of limited resources) and how best to structure the systems (so that they met fundamental business needs and could better absorb change). Proven and widely used planning methods, such as IBM's Business Systems Planning (BSP) and its derivatives, reflect these concerns. Now, in the arena of data processing at least, most organizations find that all the obvious things have been done or are already in the queue for future development. Meantime, end-user systems have widened the scope of information systems and diffused their objectives across a whole range of business activities.

As the scene has changed, so have the questions which planners must try to answer, as a preparation for defining an infrastructure. Now, the key questions are these:

- How can we express the collective business needs of a range of departmental and individual users as a single coherent theme?
- How can we reconcile these collective needs with the demands of the

business as a whole, reflected both in the operational systems and in the strategic aims of the enterprise?
- Finally, how can we translate these requirements into practical, technological terms?

At this point, it is useful to remind ourselves what strategy is for. The origin of the term is military, and in the military context it refers to the overall plan for a campaign. The strategy sets the ground rules for all involved, and is supplemented by tactical decisions taken on the battlefield in response to prevailing circumstances. Business organizations are involved in a campaign in a competitive sense or in order to meet externally defined objectives, but this is a campaign for excellence rather than for military victory. Thus strategy, whether at the level of the business as a whole or for information technology alone, has both a negative and a positive purpose:

- It defines the limits within which tactical manoeuvre may take place, and thus prevents those implementing the strategy from pursuing inconsistent or mutually incompatible objectives;
- It highlights those particular ways in which the organization seeks to excel, because these are judged to be at the heart of its mission, so that these aims can be given priority.

My purpose in this chapter is to provide some ways of looking at organizational requirements in order to recognize the most appropriate strategy to pursue. My starting point is a description of the strategies being pursued by leading-edge business organizations at the present time. I then go on to provide some 'windows' through which you can look at your particular requirements and judge the relevance of those various strategies.

Four generic strategies

By analysing how a range of different businesses were organizing their information systems effort, I recognized that, in terms of overall approach, there were essentially two dimensions along which their perceptions of what was best for the business diverged. Without over-simplifying, it is possible to divide businesses into two categories along each of these two dimensions, giving four categories altogether.

Before I describe and illustrate these categories, it is important to point out that I am dealing here only with individual businesses, or with groups of closely related and homogeneous businesses. The generic strategies reflect fundamental features of the way particular businesses work, and this means that conglomerates of diverse businesses will not easily be able to apply one strategy across all the group members – some are bound to be square pegs that will not fit into the round hole designed for them by group staff. I comment on the implications of this later on.

How much autonomy for end-users?

First, organizations differ on the measure of autonomy which it is desirable to give to end-users. This difference is apparent if we compare two large US companies, both very progressive and sophisticated users of information technology, each of which has reported its strategy to recent meetings of the Office Technology Research Group.[1] At the time, Bank of America had 20,000 timesharing users, 8,000 office workstations, and a worldwide electronic mail community of 8,000 people. Both the latter were growing fast. The second company, Hughes Aircraft, had an installed base of 7,000 personal computers. Both companies place strong emphasis on supporting work-group and departmental computing, but arrive at very different conclusions as to the best way to do this. Bank of America is keen to 'blend' operating systems and end-user systems, and also places heavy emphasis on security of data and on data management. Arguing that distributed data means distributed risk, they are phasing out departmental processors and plan to interconnect powerful desktop workstations directly to centralized mainframe computers.

At Hughes they were concerned about security as well. In fact, personal computers producing thousands of floppy disks, stored locally, had created security and other problems which had caused them to look round for a better solution. But, by contrast with Bank of America, security was not Hughes' prime concern, but was secondary to another – to avoid interfering with the independence and the emphasis on local initiative then prevalent throughout the company. As a result, they opted for departmental computers linked both to communities of personal computers and to the mainframe computers. These departmental computers provide an intermediate level of computing power and enable more sophisticated applications to be developed locally than can be handled by personal computers alone. Bank of America, on the other hand, although it *does* want end-users to develop *ad hoc* decision-enabling systems locally, specifically wishes to discourage them from developing day-to-day operating systems.

A common feature of both these companies' strategies is that they are developing corporate telecommunications networks which link together equipment at all levels – local, corporate and, in the case of Hughes, departmental – so that data and other forms of information can be exchanged rapidly and easily. To make such networks a practical proposition, both organizations place heavy emphasis on data administration, and on standardization of equipment and telecommunications interfaces. The difference between them lies in the importance they place on giving end-users the autonomy to develop the applications which manipulate information to support day-to-day decisions and operations. For Hughes, end-user autonomy to develop local applications overrides other considerations; for Bank of America, security and consistency of operational data are paramount.

Tightly or loosely coupled?

I said that both these organizations were developing a high-performance integrated network and emphasized data administration. What underlies this common emphasis is the fact that both these organizations are what I term *tightly-coupled*. In other words, it is important from a business point of view that the activities of different functions within business units, and sometimes across them, should be closely coordinated. This arises, for example, because products or services have a short life or because there are high costs associated with product inventory or distribution. But there are many (*loosely-coupled*) companies where these conditions do not exist, or not to the same degree. *Coupling* defines the second dimension along which business needs diverge.

Let me give a couple of examples to illustrate how loosely-coupled companies tend to look at infrastructure. The first of these is the Swedish National Roads Administration, which is responsible for the engineering and maintenance of the road network throughout Sweden. Because of the nature of its activities and also as a consequence of a policy of decentralization of Government offices, it is a highly dispersed organization, with large numbers of small administrative and engineering sites spread right across Sweden. They have used centralized mainframe computers in the past and expect to continue to make some use of them, but their future strategy is built around the use of advanced system building tools by end-users. The idea is to put the geographically dispersed sites in a position to solve their own problems in their own way, using whatever equipment – personal computer, engineering workstation or departmental system – is appropriate for the task. The system building tools and preferred equipment have been chosen so that, as far as is possible (at the beginning, for example, engineering workstations were temporarily excluded from the scheme because no suitable tools were available), applications can be transported between different types of equipment and different sites. Arrangements are also being made for electronic exchange of data, messages and applications, but mainly via public data networks rather than via a sophisticated corporate network.

This organization is a counterpart of Hughes in terms of attitudes to end-user autonomy, but differs in giving data administration and networking a much lower priority. This reflects the fact that rapid access to shared operating data by individual end-users is not a pressing business requirement.

Bank of America, an organization which attributes a low value to end-user autonomy, also has loosely-coupled counterparts. For examples we can take a number of large professional service companies or partnerships, such as lawyers, accountants or consultants, operating out of offices distributed across many city- and town-centre sites. Firms such as these typically have centralized administrative systems, and additionally both professionals and support staff may be equipped with workstations used for word processing, analysis and messaging. Unlike Swedish Roads, most staff use only the standard utilities available through their workstations, and very few bespoke applications need to be developed. Unlike Bank of America, the centralized systems are seen as background utilities rather than foreground sources of operating or management information, essential for everyday work. Again, data administration and networking take a relatively low priority.

Four generic strategies for information systems

As illustrated by the four examples given above, the technical strategies adopted by a wide range of business organizations can be differentiated in terms of two variables. These are:

Autonomy: How important it is that end-users should be free to work out new ways of processing information rather than handling it largely in a predefined manner.

Coupling: How important it is that end-users should have immediate access to data on corporate files, rather than working, for example, with aggregated summaries produced weekly.

By using these variables as the axes of a two-by-two matrix, we arrive at the four categories shown in Figure 2.1. The names given to each of the categories express the nature of the associated technology strategy.

The *corporate information engine*, Bank of America's category, favours a hierarchical structure, with end-user systems closely linked via a high-performance communications network to centralized databases.

Distributed information system also has a high-performance network, as Hughes Aircraft does, but its structure is mesh-like rather than hierarchical. Both processing power and storage are distributed more widely out into the business functions.

The *office utility network* places a low emphasis on network performance and on sharing of data. End-user systems are general-purpose utilities, rather than the means of accessing and processing shared data.

Finally, *end-user computing environment*, for which I used Swedish National Roads as the model, concentrates on enabling end-users to develop their own applications, again with limited emphasis on networking or shared data. Here, sharing of applications is more important than sharing of data.

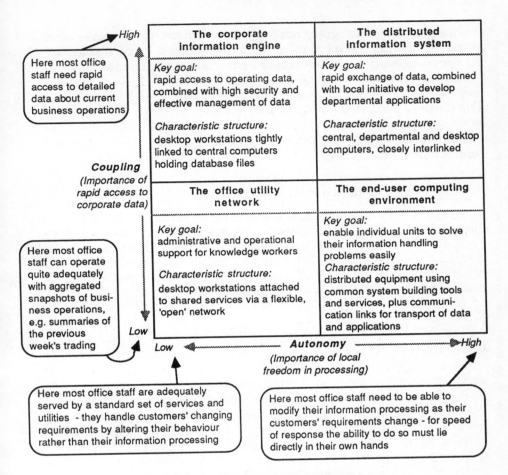

**Figure 2.1 Strategies for information systems
depend on two business variables**

As you look at these categories and try to relate your own business to one of them, there is one important thing you should bear in mind. Whereas each puts greater stress on certain aspects of its end-users' needs than on others, that does not mean that it neglects those other aspects entirely. There is a minimum level of service which end-users in all businesses are entitled to expect, and that level is rising all the time. To emphasize what I said above, strategy, which is what we are talking about here, is a question of deciding those aspects in which you it is vital that you should excel.

Each of the categories defined in Figure 2.1 has a distinct set of success factors, both organizational and technical, and that is why this scheme is such a useful guide not only to infrastructure, but also to other scheme is such a useful guide not only to infrastructure, but also to other aspects of the management of information systems. In particular, as I now go on to explain, each embodies a particular control philosophy.

The control philosophy

The infrastructure reflects the mechanisms adopted for co-ordination and control in two main ways:

- Via the methods used to manage information
- Via the methods used to develop applications

In each case, very different benefits and countervailing disadvantages are obtained by adopting tough or tender control policies, in other words by being restrictive or permissive in setting the limits for individual initiative. First I review those policy options briefly,[2] then I return to the four generic strategies, showing how each of them embodies distinct control policies within a coherent overall architecture.

Information management – security versus flexibility

In deciding information management policy, we are concerned with how end-users exploit the information resource – how they access, manipulate and exchange information. Permissiveness will enable end-users to respond flexibly and rapidly to new or changing information needs. On the other hand, restriction may be needed to protect the security and integrity of information exchanged within and by the organization – to make sure, for example, that department A understands the same by information transmitted to it by department B as the latter intended. This is the conflict to be resolved.

This is not a new conflict. It has had to be faced by data processing departments as end-users have pressed for improved management information to be made available from operational systems. For some time, suppliers have been devoting considerable efforts to developing techniques and tools for the management of data, aimed at meeting this need. But end-user systems have added a new dimension, since the threat to the security and integrity of computer-based information grows in proportion to the range of people using it directly. End-user systems, of course, are increasing that number. As a Bank of America executive put it: 'Distributed data means distributed risk.'

In deciding how to manage that risk, you face a choice which has more to do with management philosophy than with technology. Proponents of information resource management[3] advocate developing new management disciplines with regard to information, much as there are already disciplines with regard to finance. Others place the emphasis on end-users' rights and accountabilities in a new, information-rich environment These two contrasting philosophies are exemplified, respectively, by Gulf Oil's 'business-driven five-year information resources plan' and by the information policy of Sweden's largest employer, Swedish Telecom.

Gulf's study was commissioned by senior management. It required each business function to develop a business plan supported by an information resources plan. To do this, they identified critical success factors; inventoried equipment, applications, personnel and expenses; assessed the effectiveness of current applications; and looked at the impact of new technologies and the activities of competitors. Out of these were developed statements of direction and action plans. The overall statements of direction were:

1. Link information resources planning to business planning.
2. Manage the existing computer applications portfolio as an asset.
3. Develop the technical and management skills of information resources personnel.
4. Manage emerging technologies.
5. Develop information resources for managing skills among users.[4]

In 1975, Swedish Telecom introduced a new organization based on the four principles of decentralization; result orientation; management by objectives (MBO); and co-operation and co-determination. This reorganization revealed the defects of the current information systems, then mainly centralized, and in 1985 an information handling policy was formulated. This included the following key points:

Productivity Achieved by eliminating some steps in document production and decreasing need of clerical staff support.

Flexibility Achieved by geographical independency (offices may be where is convenient) and functional independency (whatever your normal function, systems must support you to temporarily perform other functions).

Motivation of personnel By making all information easily accessible to all, supporting professional development, and letting the individual perform more steps in the office production process.

Well-informed personnel All employees will get all information they need in their current work situation when they need it, selected as they want it, compiled in the way they wish, and excluding all information they do not want.

Security Both data security and personal integrity must be protected.[5]

These two approaches to information policy share similar objectives, but embody quite different management philosophies. Every company must have an information policy to underpin its information systems activities, and must choose the philosophy with which it is most comfortable.

Information policy affects the infrastructure fundamentally, since it determines the extent to which information, and responsibility for it, is decentralized. At a more basic level, it also influences the methods used to give end-users access to operational files held centrally. To do this, the information systems people responsible for operating central systems face practical difficulties. Searching of data files can be very expensive in computer power. End-users are unlikely to be aware of the implications of entering particular queries which happen to be expensive in machine terms. Finding this out when the bill arrives, or when nothing happens for 15 minutes after the query was entered, is, to say the least, bad for relationships. Unrestricted activity of this kind is also unwelcome, since it may interfere with the performance of operational systems. When, as manager responsible for centralized information systems, you have to choose between delaying the issue of invoices and delaying replies to senior managers' urgent requests for information, resignation is probably the only way out.

Because of difficulties such as these, access by end-users to central data files is usually mediated in some way, both to insulate the end-user from the inadequacies of file structures and access languages, and to insulate the central data files from uncontrolled interference. End-users are given access to central data files in three basic ways. These are sometimes applied selectively for different categories of information (for example, operational or not; within the scope of auditing procedures or not), and sometimes for different categories of end-user (for example, according to authorization level). The three ways are:

1. End-users are given powerful tools which enable them to create extracts from the central files, either held on the disks at the central site or down-loaded to local storage. Having done so, they can then search and manipulate this data as they wish.
2. Information systems staff, working in an Information Centre, draw off selective extracts of data from the central files for end-users to access, when requested. Sometimes they may go further and also carry out a search to supply precisely the report that is needed. This enables end-users to satisfy *ad hoc* information requirements.
3. Periodically, as part of normal computer operations, selected data are drawn off from the main files and are then restructured to provide the kind of 'view' of the data which particular groups of end-users need. End-users use terminals or personal computers to access and search these 'user view' files directly.

Each of these solutions has merits in particular circumstances. Solution 1 is attractive because it involves limited up-front effort, and is appropriate where end-users must have current data, and cannot make do with extracts created the previous night or the previous weekend. But it is not a complete solution and can prove very expensive in disk storage space, unless end-users can be persuaded or coerced to get rid of extract files as soon as they have outlived their usefulness. Some organizations have found disk storage requirements at their central sites growing at 50 per cent per year or more, mainly because of extract files generated by end-users.

Solution 2 has the merit that it keeps control in the hands of the information systems professionals, but by the same token is politically risky. It is also expensive in skilled manpower. Some organizations set up Information Centres to meet end-users' demands for a faster response to *ad hoc* requests for information, failed to keep up with the demand, and found that they had merely succeeded in shifting the focus of dissatisfaction from the information systems department to the newly-formed Information Centre.

A growing number of companies are adopting solution 3, because it is the most sustainable in the long term. Its main drawbacks are a high up-front cost, and a sustained support and housekeeping effort imposed on the information systems department.

My purpose here has been to show the conflict that information policy must address and introduce some of the key options. I return to the topic and discuss the options in more detail in Chapter 5.

Applications development – quality versus speed of learning

Policy for applications development is no longer solely a matter of which tools or languages the information systems department should adopt. With the growth of end-user systems, we are also concerned with how end-users decide which applications to attempt and how they develop those applications.

The great advantage of a permissive policy is that it 'lets a thousand flowers bloom', as end-users experiment and learn from their own mistakes and from those of their colleagues. A restrictive policy, by contrast, leaves the key decisions on applications and the responsibility for development with the information systems specialists. This makes sure that yesterday's mistakes are not all repeated, and, by imposing professional standards, guards against the longer term costs of maintaining badly constructed applications.

Policies, then, are very much about roles and responsibilities. They must encourage end-users to focus on the business application of end-user systems, rather than be distracted by technicalities or low-level problems, and they must help to ensure that specialist technical skills, always at a premium, are applied where they will contribute most. The difficulty is to maintain the correct balance between the discipline needed to manage the innovation process, and the freedom which end-users require to develop confidence and, ultimately, a high degree of self-sufficiency.

One particularly contentious issue is whether end-users should be allowed, or even encouraged, to design and program their own applications. About 30 per cent of the organizations I have studied had what I would describe as a permissive attitude to end-user programming. About 20 per cent had a restrictive attitude, not permitting any end-user development (although a few of these admitted that it did go on, regardless). The remainder, about half, were either neutral on the question, or permitted end-user programming only under certain circumstances, for example if there were no audit implications or if programs would only be used infrequently. Those organizations that adopted a permissive attitude generally had a higher penetration of end-user systems.

I see growth in end-user design and programming as an inevitable development, as the tools get better and as end-users become more confident. Where the information systems department is not well regarded, this end-user development activity substitutes for central development, short-cutting the applications backlog. But it is also happening where the information systems department *is* successful, and in this case the activity is often different from and complementary to central development work, focusing on local decision-making. The challenge to information systems management is to channel this activity so that it runs alongside the main stream of data processing, to the mutual benefit of both streams.

To achieve this, many organizations have defined standards and guidelines, which specify whether and how end-users should develop applications. One purpose of these standards and guidelines is to prevent end-users from taking on applications which do not belong in the end-user systems domain, but which, for various reasons, should be handled by the information systems department. Included in this category would be applications which, for example, make heavy demands on centralized files or exceed the processing limits of equipment which can practically be installed under local control.

Another purpose is to ensure that applications can be learnt reasonably easily and can be adopted by people other than the originators. This makes it possible to propagate applications from one part of the organization to another and keeps the learning barriers low for newcomers. By ensuring that applications have a familiar 'look and feel' about them, it also makes it easier for people to settle down with new systems after they change jobs within the organization.

To sum up, restrictive approaches enable the information systems department to maintain the quality of end-user systems, but at the price of slower progress, higher support costs and, often, end-user resentment. Permissive approaches have converse merits and demerits.

The generic strategies revisited

To bring together the elements discussed above and to show how they affect the infrastructure, I return to the four generic strategies. As Figure 2.2 illustrates, each of those embodies a distinct approach in terms of information management and applications development. Furthermore, the experience of organizations that have implemented strategies such as these shows that they are coherent and practical.

	Topology	Information management	Application development
Corporate information engine	All major systems centralized; local systems limited to *ad hoc* decision support; heavy hierarchical flows of information.	Centralized data management using advanced tools; strict control over downloading to local systems.	Central development shop, also supporting approved PC and office packages; certification of local applications.
Distributed information system	Centralized systems for operational and corporate control, linked to powerful departmental systems; heavy flows of information, laterally and hierarchically.	Central group concerned with directional issues; decentralized accountability for data, backed up by data description and data interchange standards.	Central shop for corporate systems; joint projects and end-user computing support for departmental and local applications.
Office utility network	Shared utility services, such as for messaging, with specialized and generic packages used locally; *ad hoc* lateral and local traffic.	Data integrity is local responsibility; low-key, informal management practices, centred round approved packages.	Small central unit looks after shared utilities and corporate systems, and provides technical support for approved packages; little local development.
End-user computing environment	Distributed machines used for operational applications and to support knowledge work; *ad hoc* access to corporate systems and to system building tools.	Data integrity is local responsibility; low-key, informal management practices centred around approved system building tools.	Centre provides technical support and rapid development service; system building tools used for local applications; design standards to promote application sharing.

Figure 2.2 How the generic strategies handle information management and application development

Window 1 – driving forces

I have identified two key aspects of the information systems environment – *coupling* and *autonomy* – which determine the best generic strategy to pursue. For some organizations it may be easy to decide where you stand in terms of these two factors. Those not so certain need some way of translating the characteristics of their organization into the terms I have used to identify the generic strategies. Here is one way of doing so. I begin by identifying the forces which drive the adoption of different forms of information technology. These forces operate on different organizations with different strengths, thus causing them to adopt different strategies. So, by identifying those characteristics of an organization that determine the strength of the driving forces, you can establish a link with the appropriate strategy.

Information systems fall into three domains

My starting point is to consider briefly what territory systems based on information technology occupy within business organizations today. As is obvious, that territory has widened steadily since the early days of data processing.

The contribution of data processing in the past is reflected now in the operational systems supporting the basic administrative and production processes of most of today's businesses. Since the days when many of those systems were first developed, information technology has both improved its cost/performance and widened dramatically in scope. In particular, communications systems have removed geographical barriers, while end-user systems have penetrated into new areas of the business and brought different and more senior staff into direct contact with information systems.

The three branches of information systems I have mentioned – operational systems, end-user systems and communications systems – represent three separate dimensions to the contribution of information systems to business performance. The contribution of each has a different value in different types of business, so they will naturally command varying priorities in organizations' investment plans.

As a preliminary, then, I examine more closely what capabilities information systems, in each of those three branches, do offer to today's business organisations, and what characteristic form the benefits take.

DATA PROCESSING – FAMILIAR TERRITORY

Beginning on the familiar territory carved out by data processing, we know that information technology has been widely applied to the basic administrative and production processes. For the purpose of this analysis, I class these systems under the heading of *operational systems*.

Systems in this category essentially serve to handle business transactions. Most of the benefits they deliver have to do with the reduction of operating costs. This is achieved in a number of different ways:

- By displacing human clerical labour.
- Through economies of scale in the processing and distribution of business transactions.

- Through the coordination and optimization of linked administrative or production processes.
- By embodying the organization's learning in applications software.
- By better utilization of production capacity, via monitoring and control mechanisms.

Initially, the technology was applied principally to internal operations, but more recently we have seen businesses establishing external links direct to the data processing systems of customers, trading partners or suppliers, through the medium of electronic data interchange (EDI) networks. Here again, some of the benefits are to do with operating costs, since the manual effort needed to enter transactions is either eliminated entirely or externalized (for example, banking customers using on-line terminals enter transaction details themselves).

But these trading networks also deliver benefits of a different order, which I call *linkage* gains, because they increase the speed with which trading information can be exchanged or matched. While speed may equate to cost, such as where, for example, it makes it possible to reduce inventory for a given level of service to the customer, it may equally be used to gain a marketing advantage. I return to *linkage* a little later on.

KNOWLEDGE WORK – THE NEW FRONTIER
I call my second major category of information systems *end-user systems*. This category includes those technologies where end-users, or their managers, have a high element of discretion as to whether or when to use the technology, rather than other methods of carrying out their work. With operational systems, by contrast, there is no such discretion – the system *becomes* the process it supports. The category includes 'office automation' (with qualifications), personal computing and work-group systems.

Office automation can be viewed as the beginning of end-user systems, although at first it headed off in much the same direction as operational systems, even if starting in the office rather than in the central computer room. At first, office automation equipment was aimed at assembly-line tasks such as typing. It focused heavily on support staff, whose activity could be analysed and systematized (it was thought) in the same way as the administrative and production processes supported by operational systems. Later, with the realization that three-quarters of office costs were represented by professionals and managers, it moved to eliminate their so-called 'unproductive' activities. Results, however, were disappointing. Levels of support staff were reduced, but neither easily (more often than not, they had to be reorganized into larger support units) nor dramatically. The big productivity gains for professionals and managers rarely materialized and, even when they did, it was not clear that the office was contributing substantially more to business success than it had done in the past.

In several telling cases, however, the really worthwhile gains came from quite unexpected directions. A UK engineering company provides a typical example. They installed 32 advanced workstations to improve communication between directors and senior management and to contain administration costs. In practice, the first objective was only partially achieved and administration savings only covered running costs. The main business benefit was one which had not been anticipated at all. Engineers responsible for making estimates and preparing tenders began using the equipment directly, and cut tendering times by a large margin. Equipment installed to streamline administrative processes had in the event enabled knowledge workers to improve their effectiveness.

Personal computers, by contrast, were seen from the outset primarily as the knowledge worker's personal productivity tool. The typical personal computer user in business today is a manager or a professional (such as an accountant or a marketing specialist) using a spreadsheet package for budgeting or planning, or a communications package for data retrieval.

Since the personal computer boom, companies have started to install work-group systems, which combine office services such as word processing and messaging with support for personal computing and for departmental applications. Often, personal computers installed previously are incorporated into the new system. Sometimes these work-group systems do give a clearcut pay-off in straight cost terms, but more often the benefits are intangible. Lead times to produce documents or respond to service requests are cut, sometimes dramatically; staff morale rises and staff retention is improved; crises are handled much more effectively; and so on. The staff, at all levels, using these systems almost invariably value highly the benefits which accrue to them. Individually, they gain greater control of their work and greater flexibility to organize it in the way which suits them best. As a team, they are able to respond more promptly to requests for information or for service, and to interact more easily and more effectively with colleagues.

To sum up, the key contribution of end-user systems is to support knowledge work. This includes much of the work of professional and managerial staff, and is an important component in the work of many clerical and support staff also. End-user systems support knowledge work in the following ways:

- By recording, manipulating and disseminating less structured (than normally handled by operational systems, that is) information, to support creative activities such as analysis, design and decision-making.
- By permitting more flexible work assignment and organizational structures.
- By achieving greater leverage with specialized and scarce skills.

- By capturing organizational know-how in the form of personal and departmental applications, and (in due course) knowledge in the form of expert systems.

End-user systems may reduce office costs, but the main business benefits are often intangible – higher quality sales proposals; better informed product designs, marketing plans, or whatever; an improved ability to respond to change or to handle crises; more effort devoted to revenue-related activities, rather than to the office routine.

THE GROWING IMPORTANCE OF INTERCOMMUNICATION

However effective work groups are individually, the organization will only benefit from their activities if the work they do meshes with that of other work groups and reflects the overall aims of the enterprise. That means that a co-ordinating mechanism is needed, a means of linking the various activities of the business so that it can act and react as a disciplined corporate body. Co-ordination is achieved by means of organizational structure, by allocation of responsibilities within that structure, and by a range of control and communication mechanisms.

Information technology adds some new ingredients to the co-ordination recipe. It makes it possible for people to share, exchange and manipulate large amounts of information more reliably, more rapidly, or more productively than in the past. By so doing, it brings two particular advantages:

- It enhances the speed and effectiveness of corporate response to events or to changing circumstances.
- It improves co-ordination and optimization of complex decision-making and consultation procedures (for example, an engineering company deciding whether to launch a new product line; a telecommunications carrier deciding what tariffs to set).

To realize these advantages, telecommunications systems will often be used to link people and their workstations with the information they require, but it is a mistake to think that telecommunications systems alone meet the need. For telephony, indeed, all that is needed is a switched link that can be used to establish a connection between two handsets. The conversation that ensues is controlled and guided by the two people involved. For computer-based devices, by contrast, the complex signalling conventions that people use to guide a telephone conversation must be built into the equipment that is communicating, and must be sufficiently well known to the telecommunications system that it can play its part in the exchange. Only where these conditions are met will it be possible for the people and information systems involved to *interwork*, in other words, to share and exchange meaningful information. This implies considerably more than a reliable telecommunications service. Over and above that, it demands integration of the various components into a coherent total system, from information structures downwards – I elaborate later on what that entails.

Each domain has a distinct driving force

These three branches of information technology – operational systems, end-user systems and intercommunication – are three substantial items on an information technology menu which not long ago held only one. Each has a price tag attached, and resources – both money and people – are limited. One way of deciding priorities is to decide the relative importance of the contribution each can make to the success of the business. Ideally, it should be possible to derive this directly from the business strategy, but business strategy is often couched in terms which do not equate directly with information systems requirements.

To help you to make the connection, I have identified a number of drivers. These are observable features of the way a business works, of the products or services which it offers, or of the markets in which it operates. They correlate with the importance different types of business attach to each of the three branches of information systems outlined above. The correlation is reflected both in past spending patterns and in immediate plans for information systems. These are:

- *Structure* drivers, indicating the potential contribution of operational systems.
- Drivers of *information intensity*, indicating the potential contribution of end-user systems.
- *Linkage* drivers, indicating the importance of intercommunication.

STRUCTURE DRIVERS
Data processing systems have been targeted principally at highly structured business activities. These are amenable to economies of scale in processing and to precise control mechanisms. For this reason, structure tends to be associated with high volume, but the real touchstone is predictability. Those businesses, or those areas within businesses, with highly predictable activities (because the variety of products, customers or suppliers is low) or with a predictable sequencing of tasks (because the variety of procedures is low) have attracted the heaviest investment in the past.

A high degree of structure is also found where staff are permitted low discretion, because they are unskilled or have a very narrow specialization – in typing pools, for example. But this form of structure is an artefact of the methods used to organize work, rather than inherent in the activities the business carries out. This means that it is dangerous to take current working methods as a measure of the structure inherent in the business, because those methods are liable to change. For example, by setting out to differentiate its products or services, an organization will probably increase the level of discretion exercised by some of its staff.

It is impossible to provide precise measures of structure, which can be used to decide which business activities are, or are not, candidates for operational systems. This is because the amount of variety which operational systems can cope with has been increasing steadily for some time, as the equipment itself and our understanding of how to exploit it have both improved. Indeed, structure itself is a variable, as markets, trading patterns and competitive strategies change. But the problems most data processing departments are experiencing in maintaining operational systems indicate that we may have already reached or surpassed the practical limits with which the technology can easily cope. If structure is imposed on business activities by means of operational systems, but in inappropriate circumstances, the price is loss of flexibility.

INFORMATION INTENSITY DRIVERS
Information intensity derives from high complexity, a high information content, or high innovation and change. Complexity may reside in the product itself (such as in the aerospace industry), or in functions such as procurement, distribution, or marketing (as, for example, in the pharmaceutical industry). Information content, similarly, may be in the product itself (electronic publishing) or may consist of a high service content (consultancy). Finally, high innovation and change may result because key technologies are evolving rapidly (information technology), because markets are changing (financial services), or because customers are fashion-sensitive (clothing).

As you would expect, the information intensity of a particular business is reflected in the composition of its workforce. Thus you can use the proportion of managerial and professional staff in the white-collar workforce as a broad measure of information intensity. In *professional* I include accountants, chemists, designers, marketing, legal and systems specialists, architects – in other words, people who earn their keep by applying specialist knowledge. This proportion varies from 90 per cent or more in professional service companies, or 70 per cent in knowledge-based manufacturing firms such as pharmaceutical companies, down to about 20 per cent in low-technology manufacturing and in some distribution companies.

LINKAGE DRIVERS
High linkage businesses are those where high variety is present at the same time as factors that place a premium on speed of response. High variety may arise because the products or services themselves are varied (travel agents); because those products or services are delivered in a

variety of forms (specialized machine tools); or because they are customized to meet individual requirements (aircraft simulators).

Two groups of factors place a premium on speed of response. The first is where time itself has a value. This may be because the product or service has a short life (an aircraft seat; perishable goods); because immediate availability is important to the customer (health care); or because demand or supply is irregular (fashion goods). The second is where time equates to high cost – high inventory costs (vehicles); high distribution costs (building materials); or high fixed assets (power station construction).

But it is competition which really heightens the pressure for linkage. Electronic data interchange (EDI), for example, extends linkage outside the business to provide faster access to customers or to distribution channels. The adoption of EDI is driven by, and at the same time intensifies, competitive pressures. Thus linkage forces are much stronger in highly competitive industries, and much weaker in the public sector.

Driving forces vary by industry

As I have explained, differences in product and market characteristics determine the strength of the driving forces acting on an organization. Sometimes these are common to all companies in an industry sector, and sometimes they differentiate companies because of varying business strategies or different positioning within the industry. With that qualification, and the further one that industry characteristics change over time, it is possible to make some valid generalizations about industries, and hence about the priorities companies within that industry are likely to set for information systems. My purpose in doing this is to help readers to position particular organizations, rather than to make definitive statements about the industries themselves.

If, first of all, we examine industries in terms of the structure and information intensity dimensions, we find (top right in Figure 2.3) that industries high on both scales are the high spenders on all forms of information systems. These are highly capital-intensive businesses, with high levels of innovation and competition – motor vehicle manufacturers, airlines, petro-chemical companies, computer systems companies.

High structure businesses with low information intensity, by contrast (lower right in Figure 2.3), tend to be more labour-intensive with lower spending on end-user systems. They also control information systems tightly from the centre. Among service industries, this category includes retailing, retail financial services (clearing banks, building societies and life insurance), travel agents, the distribution arms of public utilities, and public sector administrative (i.e. rather than policy-making) operations. In manufacturing, it includes low-technology process manufacturers

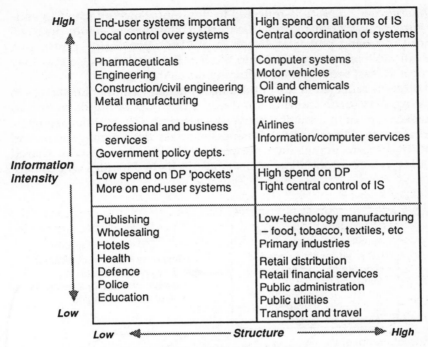

**Figure 2.3 Industry sectors allocated in terms of
structure and information intensity**

(food, tobacco, textiles) and high-volume discrete manufacturers.

Information intensive businesses with low structure, such as construction, high-technology engineering and pharmaceutical companies in manufacturing, or professional services firms (top left), spend relatively little on central data processing. Many of their systems are controlled locally – departmental systems, CAD/CAM, office systems.

Finally, the low structure, low information intensity companies have labour intensive service activities, and mostly low capital intensiveness – publishers, wholesalers, hotels. They spend little on operational systems, relatively more on end-user systems. This category also includes some public sector operations with unusual characteristics which make them difficult to pigeon-hole – some parts of health care, police, education.

As Figure 2.4 illustrates, the strategies being adopted by different types of business today are driven principally by levels of *information intensity* and *linkage*, rather than by levels of *structure*. This clearly reflects the fact that most of the development effort (if not the maintenance and fine tuning) has already been put into the operational systems. End-user systems and measures aimed at improving intercommunication are still in their infancy, and hence are the current focus of attention.

Information intensity is reflected in the importance attached to end-user autonomy. Hence, information intensive businesses favour distribution of processing power and seek to put both processing power and application development tools into the hands of end-users, so that they can meet at least some of their requirements as they arise.

Linkage is reflected in the importance attached to immediate access to operating data (or to information derived from operating data) and to rapid exchange of information between systems in different departments. For that reason, high linkage businesses stress data management and install high-performance data networks to link end-users with shared data files. Where information intensity also is high, data files will usually

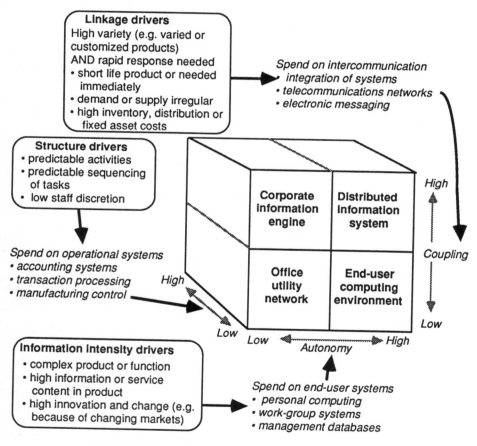

**Figure 2.4 Information intensity and linkage drive
today's information systems strategies**

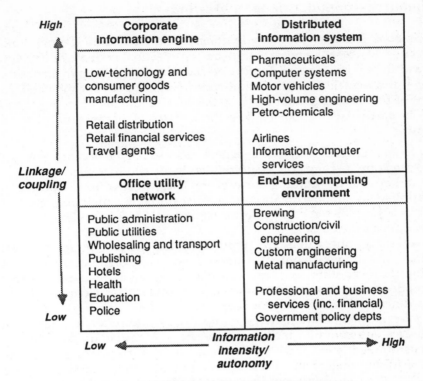

**Figure 2.5 Industry sectors allocated in terms of
information intensity and linkage**

be shared at corporate and at departmental level, whereas businesses
with low information intensity favour simpler structures with tighter
central control.

Low linkage, low information intensity businesses, finally, adopt a
much more low-key approach both to end-user development and to data
management. Operational and end-user systems appear in 'islands' of
high structure or high information intensity, with low central co-
ordination. Sometimes utilities are provided, such as common administrative systems or messaging services, which are accessed on an 'as
needed' basis.

Figure 2.5 shows how industries can be distributed across the four
categories, and hence which generic strategies organizations in them are
most likely to pursue. This is provided for guidance and illustration
rather than as a definitive statement about the industries concerned. To
repeat the qualifications made above – industry sectors are not entirely
homogeneous, and industry characteristics change.

Window 2 – organizational work-flow

In his book *Understanding organizations,*[6] Charles Handy defines three ways of describing the operations of an organization, each of which relies on a different method of control or coordination. The infrastructure serves as a vehicle for control and coordination by favouring standard ways of performing certain tasks, so this way of looking at an organization is particularly apposite. The three types of organization are as follows:

- *Facsimile* operations are those where each part of the organization is a close copy, perhaps on a different scale, of another, such as supermarket chains, building society branches, post offices. Control is applied by standardization – of prices, display methods, clerical procedures, data recording forms, and so on – and is implemented by *rules and procedures*.
- *Sequential* operations are typified by the oil and petro-chemical industries, in which outputs from one part of the organization become inputs to another, but any complex integrated business fits this model, such as an aerospace or vehicle manufacturer. Control and co-ordination is achieved by *planning and scheduling*.
- *Independent* operations have no necessary interrelation except that they share common facilities or services. Manufacturers of highly customized products, professional service companies such as consulting engineers, and hospitals operate predominantly in this manner. Control and coordination is less important and centres on the use of cash or scarce shared facilities. Coordination is achieved mainly via *direct personal interaction* between individuals.

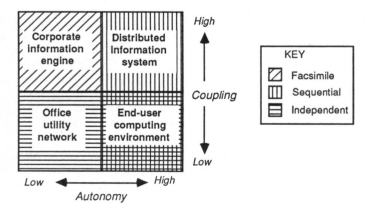

Figure 2.6 Relationship between generic strategies and work-flow characteristics

As Figure 2.6 shows, the *facsimile* organizations are concentrated in the high-coupling, low-autonomy quadrant. *Sequential* organizations are found in both the high-autonomy quadrants, with those operating in volatile consumer markets principally in the high-coupling quadrant. *Independent* organizations dominate the low-coupling, low-autonomy quadrant, and are also found in the low-coupling, high-autonomy quadrant.

Some important caveats

Finally, some important *caveats* to bear in mind when you are trying to link your own organization's requirements with the generic strategies presented here.

Treat business units on their individual merits

If your area of responsibility embraces a group of companies, you should beware of attempting to lump too much together. Differences between business units may be such as to preclude adopting a single architectural approach right across a group. The point is that the nature of the benefits to be derived from end-user systems and from intercommunication have little to do with economies of scale. In the past, large groups could benefit considerably by sharing the resources of large data centres or of tele-communications networks, but nowadays the key benefits are of a different order.

Economies of scale may indeed be available, but thoughtless pursuit of them can easily prove counter-productive. A very experienced tele-communications manager was given the job of devising a strategy for Grand Metropolitan, one of the UK's largest business groups, operating mainly in the leisure and food industries, and he reached this conclusion as a result of his study. Because the individual requirements of the group companies were so different, he decided to provide a basic cost-saving network at group level, and concentrated on encouraging the business units to do their own planning to decide how they should build on this. In other cases, networks or other services provided at group level have failed to deliver the expected benefits because they placed unacceptable constraints on companies in the group. This is not just the *not invented here* syndrome at work. As I have attempted to demonstrate, different types of business do have fundamentally different needs.

Exceptions don't disprove the rule

Within many businesses, there exist groups whose characteristics, and hence whose information needs, are radically different from those of the rest of the business – a research and development group in a process manufacturing company, for example. But these should be treated as exceptions, and not be used as an excuse for adopting no strategy at all. In his influential book *Competitive Advantage*, Michael Porter explains in this way why businesses must adopt one, and only one, of the four generic business strategies that he defines:

> The notion underlying the concept of generic strategies is that competitive advantage is at the heart of any strategy, and achieving competitive advantage requires a firm to make a choice – if a firm is to attain a competitive advantage, it must make a choice about the type of competitive advantage it seeks to attain and the scope within which it will attain it. Being "all things to all people" is a recipe for strategic mediocrity and below-average performance, because it often means that a firm has no competitive advantage at all.[7]

As we should all know by now, corporate success with information systems is only achieved through full-hearted commitment, just as much as success in a competitive marketplace. For this reason and because information technology skills are in chronically short supply, the information systems activities of a business must have a coherent overall theme, orchestrated by a single identifiable strategy. Within that strategy, there must be enough flexibility to cater for the variety of needs which exist within the business. But variety is never a sufficient reason for adopting no strategy at all.

The information business within a business

What I have outlined above is a means of deciding a strategic direction for a business. The objectives of the information systems department (that some see as an information business within the business) may not be 100 per cent aligned with those of the parent organization, since the information systems department has to live within the constraints of budget, authority, and mission defined for it. This may mean that a strategy that is desirable from a business viewpoint is outside the reach of the information systems department without some change in mission or authority, or that the information systems department can only contribute to some aspects of the overall strategy. To avoid complicating the discussion, I do not propose to go beyond making the point that the information systems department must recognize any limits to its own power to deliver, and take action accordingly. Warren McFarlan's four-way classification of information systems environments – *support, factory, turnaround* and *strategic* – is a useful framework for approaching this task.[8]

Decentralization – ends and means

It is important to distinguish between the long term objectives embodied in a strategy and the tactics that may be adopted to bring it about. Sometimes tactics may validly be used which appear to be totally at variance with the strategy. Decentralization and centralization, in particular, can be used very effectively as a manoeuvre to bring about change.

The UK-based chemical group, ICI, for example, decided in the late 1970s to transfer into the control of the operating companies the mainframe computers and development staff which were then controlled at group level. After five or so years, they realized that the inward-looking attitudes which had developed at group level previously, and which decentralization had been intended to destroy, had gradually taken root again, at operating company level. Where once the group had operated a bastion, unresponsive to the needs of operating companies, now each operating company had its own unresponsive bastion. To resolve the problem, group management once again took the mainframe computers out of the hands of the operating companies and installed them in data centres to be run on behalf of the group as a whole. Deprived of their main preoccupation so far, development staff in the operating companies looked round for something else to do, discovered end-user systems and began to channel their efforts in this new direction. The walls of the bastion had fallen once more.

Notes and references

1   The Office Technology Research Group is an association of executives responsible for advanced office systems, based in Los Angeles.
2   A fuller account can be found in Chapter 4 of my book *Business information technology: end user focus* (Prentice Hall, 1988).
3   A brief outline of information resource management can be found on p. 68 of this book.
4   Reported to the Spring 1985 meeting of the Office Technology Research Group; see also John Framel (of Gulf Oil), 'Informational strategies: a concept of change', *Journal of Information and Image Management*, 17, 9, pp. 24-27.
5   Börje Brolin, 'Information as a Resource: from myth to reality', paper at Euro VII, Bologna, Italy, June 1985.
6   Charles B. Handy, *Understanding organizations* (Penguin Books, 1985)
7   Michael E. Porter, *Competitive advantage* (The Free Press, 1988)
8   F. W. McFarlan *et al*, 'The information archipelago – plotting a course', *Harvard Business Review*, Jan-Feb 1983, pp. 145-156.

CHAPTER 3

ENGINEERING FOR THE 1990s

The changing pattern of demand for information systems, reviewed in the preceding chapters, of itself requires us to adopt a new perspective on how those systems should be engineered. External pressures make it all the more urgent that we should do so. While a volatile and increasingly complex business environment demands greater adaptability from business information systems, at the same time powerful technology pressures are operating in favour of distribution of processing power and storage. Both these developments call for new thinking on how information systems should be engineered. They also challenge the methods traditionally used to develop systems, and the role and responsibilities of specialists and end-users within the development process.

In the new systems environment that is now taking shape, the role of the infrastructure is to guarantee, to the maximum extent that is practical, that information systems will have the flexibility and the adaptability that organizations will require from them in the 1990s. At the same time, as technology spreads out into every corner of the enterprise, it provides stability and acts as a vehicle for control, both over the long term and in day-to-day operation.

The pressures for change

Unless we do something about it, the 1990s will be remembered not as the flowering of the information age, but as the period when irresistible forces for change in business practices, originating from changes in the market and whipped up by information technology, met the immovable object of inflexible business information systems. Already there is widespread dissatisfaction among senior and middle managers with the responsiveness and adaptability of existing information systems. In part, perhaps in large part, this is a legacy of our past myopia and the poor tools available to develop systems. Even with today's improved understanding and better tools, however, the task is no easier than it was in the past, because the business environment – markets, regulatory constraints, competition – is becoming more and more demanding, and this in turn increases the pressure for change in information systems.

Business pressures call for flexibility

All the indicators suggest that the rate of change which information systems must absorb is increasing. For many companies, trading conditions are growing more and more turbulent and difficult to predict. Well over half the people who attended focus groups I held in 1986 commented (without being prompted to do so) on the changing business conditions their companies faced and on the planning problem which this posed. To compound the problem, the information needs of individual managers tend to change even more rapidly than do the pressures driving the business as a whole, as they explore and learn how to exploit the new possibilities which information technology puts before them.

These same business pressures are giving birth to new organizational designs. Influential ideas are circulating about how organizations should be restructured in order to remain competitive and effective in the information era. With information technology becoming pervasive in many organizations, its disposition must inevitably be affected by any changes in organization flowing from ideas such as these. In a positive sense, the technology may act as a catalyst and a support for new organizational arrangements. In a negative sense, it may create barriers to the free transfer of information which inhibit change or frustrate the sought-after benefits.

Elizabeth Moss Kanter recently wrote a book called *The Change Masters* that is having a powerful influence on U.S. managers. She pinpoints what she calls 'integrative' organizational structures as the key to innovative attitudes within an organization. She contrasts the assumptions underlying the old 'segmentalist' model of the corporation with those underlying the new model. The fourth of those assumptions is particularly relevant to information technology:

Old Assumption 4. Differentiation of organizations and their units is not only possible but necessary. Specialization is desirable, for both individuals and organizations; neither should be asked to go beyond their primary purposes. ... The ideal organization is divided into functional specialities clearly bounded from one another, and managers develop by moving up within a functional area. As a corollary, it is not necessary for specialized individuals or organizations to know much about the actions of others in different areas. Coordination is itself a speciality, and the coordinators (whether markets, managers or integrating disciplines) will ensure that activities fit together in a coherent and beneficial way.

New Assumption 4. Differentiation of activities and their assignment to specialists is important, but coordination is perhaps even more critical a problem, and thus it is important to avoid overspecialization and to find ways to connect specialists and help them to communicate. Furthermore, beyond whatever specialized roles organizations or the units in them play, they also have a responsibility for the consequences of their actions beyond their own borders. They need to learn about and stay informed about what is happening elsewhere, and they need to honour their social responsibilities to act for the larger good.[1]

Thus, effective organizational design will in turn depend on more flexible business information and communication systems.

In terms of facilities planning also, information systems requirements are far less predictable than they used to be. End-user systems have broadened and diffused the demands placed both on support staff and on shared services, such as telecommunications networks. Previously, demand for such services derived from a limited number of major applications, such as sales order processing or inventory control. Traffic growth was closely linked with business growth and hence was relatively easy to forecast. With services such as electronic messaging, where use is discretionary, growth depends on far less predictable factors. Demand for Digital Equipment Company's electronic messaging service, for example, grew from nothing to over 60,000 accounts and over 1 million messages per week in just nine years of rapid growth, while in other companies electronic messaging has barely got off the ground at all.

The pressures reviewed briefly above raise very clearly a question which is central to the design of an information technology infrastructure in the 1990s: *How can we improve the ability of information systems to absorb change?* Given the huge investment in existing information systems, which it will take many years to replace, this raises a further key question: *How can we overcome the inertia and resistance to change of current information systems?*

Technology pressures favour decentralization

For some time, changing technology cost ratios have been building ever stronger pressures in favour of decentralizing processing power and storage, to locate it close to where the users are. At the end of the 1980s these pressures are already powerful, and they will intensify during the 1990s. To summarize briefly, transmission capacity to transmit digital information – via local area networks, for example – is very cheap on-site, once initial wiring costs have been recovered. Between sites also, transmission capacity is becoming cheaper, as outmoded analog technology in public switching and transmission systems is gradually replaced with digital technology. But inter-site bandwidth will remain relatively expensive compared with on-site bandwidth. With today's data and text traffic, these cost factors already favour distributed switching aimed at keeping as much traffic as possible on the site. Tomorrow's image traffic, and in some organizations video traffic also, will demand much more transmission capacity, and will make that even more worthwhile.

As is obvious from the runaway success of the personal computer, technology pressures in favour of decentralization of computing power are extremely powerful, and they are still growing. In the US, a survey of Fortune 500 companies, carried out in late 1987, showed that personal computers are now rapidly displacing dumb terminals. Already 50 per cent of installed end-user devices were personal computers, rather than dumb terminals. Personal computers themselves, of course, are gaining more processing power and storage as generation succeeds generation; as memory chip succeeds memory chip; and as new mass storage technologies are perfected. Processing power and storage used to be subject to Grosch's Law, which states that processing power increases according to the square of its cost. Not only has Grosch's Law ceased to operate, the personal computer has now stood it on its head. At the time of writing, processing power bought in bulk, in the form of a mainframe or minicomputer, is between one and two orders of magnitude more expensive than when bought in the form of personal computers.

That said, the only meaningful measure of computing power is not what it does – the raw processing power – but what it delivers. This measure brings software into the picture as well as hardware, since any hardware is only as useful as the software – both operating software and applications software – that it runs. In the past, the barriers to distributed computing have not been economic but practical. Many organizations have been deterred from venturing down that path because the operating software did not seem to be reliable or flexible enough to enable distributed systems to be built to necessary standards, or to be managed effectively once in operation.

It would be rash to claim that all the problems have been solved completely, but considerable advances have been made in the software available to support distributed computing, such as for distributed databases and for cooperative processing between free-standing systems. IBM, for so long champion of information systems centred around large mainframe computers, has made a number of product announcements which recognize how the computing world has changed. APPC (advanced program-to-program communication), for example, allows personal computers to intercommunicate across a network without reference to a controlling central computer. APPC has already been adopted by a number of leading suppliers, apart from IBM, and built into their software products.

Advances in software technology also challenge the methods used to develop systems and the traditional role and responsibilities of specialists and end-users within the development process. Personal computers already offer a wide range of easy-to-use application generators and similar tools, which non-specialists can use to build simple applications. For more complex applications, system building tools associated with relational databases are now within the reach of the most computer-literate end-users, and they are bound to improve both in power and in useability. Some suppliers are working on information engineering tools which will generate application systems directly from high-level specification documents.

In the face of these various pressures for decentralization of activities previously under the tight control of a professional information systems department, engineering of information systems clearly is not a straight-forward matter of economics. Indeed, it never has been that. There is an overwhelming trend towards decentralization today, but the extent of decentralization and the methods used to control a decentralized information systems environment vary, and it is these which are at issue. The questions to be addressed are these: *How, in a decentralized environment, will we maintain the quality of systems and the integrity of data? How will we protect management's prerogative to monitor what goes on?*

The infrastructure balances flexibility and control

And so, in engineering the infrastructure, we face a familiar dilemma – control versus flexibility. The same dilemma must be faced when designing an organizational structure, usually expressed as balancing uniformity with diversity. Uniformity has attractions, and particularly for senior management, for a range of reasons – because standard is often cheaper; because standard products or processes can be made interchangeable; because processes can more easily be monitored and controlled; and to economize on scarce specialist resources. Diversity, by contrast, is a product of market and other pressures calling for differentiation, and of the striving of those on the periphery towards disaggregated control; and reflects the need to experiment in an increasingly volatile and unpredictable environment.

For an organizational structure, the solution is to partition the activities of the organization in such a way as to find the optimum blend of uniformity and diversity. Activities are partitioned between centre and periphery, between regions or products, according to the nature of the business, the management culture and other factors. Integrating and co-ordinating mechanisms are then put in place to link activities together. Information systems must model the organizational structure, and, as shown in the previous chapter, the infrastructure that supports them must reflect the preferred coordinating mechanisms. But information systems and infrastructure cannot be an exact *physical* model of their organizational counterparts, because of the particular characteristics of the technologies used to build them. To explain why I say that, I now go on look more closely at the partitioning options in the light of the salient characteristics of systems built with information technology.

Partitioning – the key principle

Since history began, partitioning has been a major human mode of coping with complexity, and for information systems also it is the key engineering principle. Indeed, for purely practical reasons which I explain below, it is an unavoidable necessity. Information systems can be partitioned along two dimensions – horizontally and vertically.

By horizontal partitioning, I mean separation of applications and the information they handle in terms of their purpose. Thus, for example, the operational systems that control business processes and handle business transactions might be separated from the reporting and analysis applications that help managers with their planning and control tasks.

Vertical partitioning, often referred to as distributed computing, means dividing up systems so that organizational units can each control (and sometimes operate) their own part of them. Thus, for example, in a functional organizational structure, each function would have its own systems. More commonly, in organizations some of whose activities are decentralized (by geographical area or by product line), each of those decentralized organizational units controls what is basically a standard system, but which can be modified to meet particular area/product line needs.

There are strict limits to technology-based flexibility

In the early stages of data processing, monolithic applications were developed that were highly efficient in terms of machine performance, but very difficult and expensive to amend, because changes in one part of the application affected other parts also. Consequently, applications were partitioned to separate the main processing functions, as illustrated in Figure 3.1. Each of those functions was designed to have a clear and well-defined interface with its neighbours, so that each could be developed and modified largely independently of the others.

The data files, however, are a rather different case, since by its very nature data cuts across functional and geographic boundaries. Considerable effort has been devoted to building flexibility into data files, and particularly through the application of database management techniques.

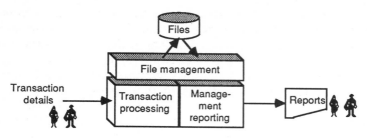

Figure 3.1 Early monolithic systems were partitioned internally

The theory underlying database management is that data can be analysed quite independently of the equipment on which it is to be stored and of the people and business applications that are to use it. Once designed and installed, a database system would enable different users of a company's data to take whatever 'view' of that data they needed, without interfering with other users.

Unfortunately, the theory has proven both demanding and time-consuming to apply in practice. I know of no companies that have made a complete success of database management systems, and quite a few that have failed totally. Many have achieved worthwhile returns, but not what they were hoping for – the promised degree of independence between data and users. For most companies, database management systems have helped to improve the productivity of the information systems department, but have done relatively little to help end-users exploit the company's data resources.

More recently, database management has been absorbed into, or perhaps displaced by, the broader concept of *information resource management* – IRM for short. Whereas data management focuses on the implementation issues, IRM concentrates on the end-product, information. In brief, it calls for a coherent overall approach to managing business information, embodied in the appointment of a Chief Information Officer. The US Paperwork Reduction Act defines IRM as: 'The planning, budgeting, organizing, directing, training, promoting, controlling, and other managerial activities involved with the creation, collection, use, and dissemination of information.' IRM, however, faces the same practical difficulties as database management, compounded by senior management scepticism based on disappointment at past promises unfulfilled. A survey of 35 US companies, reported in *Datamation*,[2] found great confusion about the concept, few companies claiming success, and a range of political and organizational obstacles to be overcome.

The weakness of data management in the past, and of IRM still, is precisely that it is so difficult to involve the end-user in an effective way. Studies aimed at establishing information needs face several barriers.

Senior management support is difficult to secure. Most managers, however familiar with information systems, find it difficult to think through their information needs systematically. The natural way to work these out is step by step, by trial and error. End-users are also aware of the power which possession of information confers, and instinctively adopt a proprietary attitude towards 'their' information.

In short, technology cannot be used to solve a problem with such powerful human implications. The whole history of information systems shows that attempts to build total, integrated systems have the opposite effect of that intended. They become so complex and so difficult to maintain that any flexibility gains available in theory are nullified in practice. I suspect that information systems people for some time have been trying to design systems beyond a 'span of understanding', equivalent to the span of control that defines the limits to any one manager's ability to control staff. You really cannot design flexibility into information systems beyond certain limits. Outside those limits, applications and data must be partitioned, physically or logically, into manageable chunks.

Horizontal partitioning – escaping from yesterday's systems

Figure 3.1 illustrated how processing functions have been partitioned to make operational systems more flexible. Beyond that, the next and most important step is to separate the data needed by managers and professionals for planning and control purposes from the detailed transactional data held on the operational files, as illustrated in Figure 3.2. The main reason for doing this is to escape from the inertia of yesterday's information systems, and I mean that in two senses.

First, escape is necessary is in order to take a different view of the data. Transactional data on, or derived from, operational files reflects yesterday's organization and the trading history associated with it. This means that, without major reprocessing, it may be unsuitable to support new business strategies. A senior planner with Swedish Telecom put it

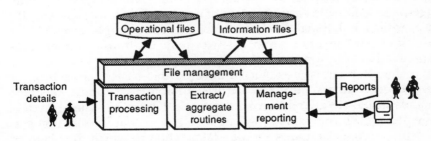

**Figure 3.2 Separate information files are set up to
serve end-users**

very neatly: 'Data processing is for existing business; office systems [which I call *end-user systems*] are for new business.' A manager in ICI's corporate management services group takes a similar view. He summed up as follows the limitations in data processing services, as experienced by staff now able to access data directly using personal computers:

- Focussed on achieved results – rarely on critical 'means'
- Focussed on operational – rarely strategic performance
- Focussed on hard cash – rarely 'soft' measures
- Little emphasis on external data
- Organization- and history-bound and hence unsuitable to support new strategies or organizations[3]

The second sense in which separation of end-user files offers an escape is a purely practical one. In the past, even if logically separated, management reporting routines have been built as part of the operational systems. This was logical, because they were the source of the base data. Experience has shown, however, that this approach has severe practical disadvantages. The point is that end-user information requirements change much more rapidly than the operational systems do. The latter are tied to the fundamental processes of the business, which only change very slowly. End-user information requirements, by contrast, are influenced by a range of both short term and longer term influences, such as customer behaviour, competitive action, legislation, and so on. Building reporting routines as part of the operational systems meant that they had to be modified much more frequently than if the reporting was entirely separate. Most of the changes were minor, which information systems departments generally do not handle very efficiently. This, in my view, was one of the main factors contributing to the heavy maintenance load and the long backlog of development work that so many information systems departments are struggling with.

It also affects the performance of the operational systems. Displacing management reporting routines reduces their load and thus extends their useful life. Both equipment for operational systems and the files themselves can be optimized for throughput, often the key requirement, whereas flexibility and ease of use are of much greater importance for the end-user files. Relational database structures, for example, are ideal for end-user information, but cannot easily provide the transaction throughput demanded of the operational systems.

Further steps must be taken to develop this basic architecture for information systems into a structure suitable to support business demands in the 1990s and beyond, shown in Figure 3.3. The growth of trading networks, mentioned in Chapter 1, shows that information systems are no longer bounded by the organization to which they belong. This point is reinforced by the reference to external data in the list of data processing's limitations given above. Links are also needed to trading

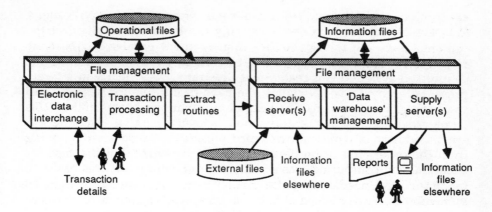

Figure 3.3 Further partitioning increases flexibility

partners' systems, via electronic data interchange, and to external sources of data. Second, the lessons learnt by building monolithic data processing applications apply equally to the applications which will supply information for knowledge workers. They too should be partitioned.[4]

The way to do this is to separate the routines which create and maintain the information database, from the routines that receive information to be added to that database, and again from the routines that supply data in response to requests. I describe these as *receive* and *supply servers*, respectively – I return to the concept of *servers* later.[5] This provides a degree of independence from the technologies that supply and receive the data. The latter in particular – workstation and work-group system technologies – are likely to evolve rapidly. It also makes the structure iterative, since a receive server can call on supply servers elsewhere to call off information not held locally. This is of particular value for organizations operating internationally, where the ability to exchange information across national boundaries might prove crucial.

Vertical partitioning – rote work gives way to knowledge work

As the economics of centralized computing has changed, so the processing logic has gradually been decentralized, first into the terminals and into the network components, later into powerful local systems and workstations. Control of systems, however, has largely been retained at the centre. Generally speaking, this has worked well for transaction processing systems supporting rote clerical work, since all the users worked in basically the same way and exercised limited discretionary control over their work.

Now, however, the business and technology pressures outlined above are combining to separate those aspects of transaction processing applications which benefit from local control from the core applications. The former are decentralized, and only the latter are retained at the centre. Above all, this gives local management greater flexibility to respond to local needs, flexibility that cannot easily, if at all, be built into centralized systems. This reality was illustrated very clearly in a recent presentation by Trevor Nicholas, the head of information systems and resources at Barclays Bank.[6] As head of information systems in the 1970s, he regarded the case for centralization as 'overwhelming'. Then he was appointed head of Barclays' credit card subsidiary, BarclayCard. Looking from the other side of the fence, he came to realize that the case for decentralized computing was equally overwhelming – it was easier to tailor for local needs; created a greater sense of ownership; reduced vulnerability. Now, as head of information systems again, he retains core systems at the centre and everything else is decentralized.

If this is valid for operational systems, then it is certainly valid for end-user systems also. As already reviewed in Chapter 1, knowledge workers' needs are very different from those of the clerical staff that normally use operational systems. They require considerable flexibility to meet *ad hoc* needs and to match fragmented work patterns. Thus, as Figure 3.4 illustrates, they access the end-user files via the knowledge work support architecture developed in Chapter 1.

A final rationalization would be to extend the knowledge work support architecture into the transaction processing area also, as shown

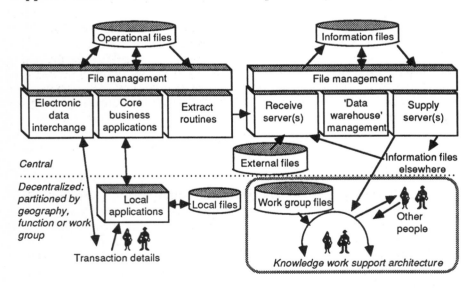

Figure 3.4 Decentralization pressures push functions outwards towards end-users

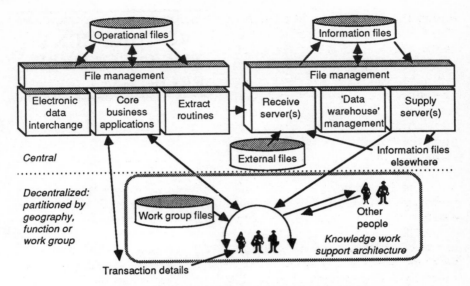

Figure 3.5 The final rationalization – the knowledge work support architecture extended

in Figure 3.5. This adds flexibility by introducing generic services such as messaging and word processing. It also links more closely the systems that support management planning and control with those that support business operations. This can be used to give local management, where appropriate, direct control over operational parameters, enabling the organization to respond more rapidly to events or to change.

This gives us an overall logical architecture, a blueprint for the infrastructure that will give it the qualities needed to survive the stresses and strains that business and technology will place on it in the 1990s and beyond. In Part Two of the book, I will hang some technological flesh on the bones of that architecture.

Notes and references

1 Rosabeth Moss Kanter, *The Change Masters* (George Allen & Unwin, 1985).
2 See Tor Guimaraes 'IRM Revisited', *Datamation*, Mar 1 1985.
3 From a presentation to the UK members of the Office Technology Research Group by Ken Edwards of ICI plc.
4 In this section I have drawn on the work of Malcolm Wicks and his colleagues in DEC (UK)'s information services department.
5 On page 156.
6 Reported in *Computer Weekly*, April 28 1988.

CHAPTER 4

PROCUREMENT – THE INSOLUBLE PROBLEM

Almost since the beginning of business computing, procurement has been a major headache for organizations of any size. This is because there has never been, and is unlikely to be for the forseeable future, any straightforward and reasonably complete solution to the requirement to interconnect, or move applications between, information technology equipment from different suppliers. Those who fail to address the issue risk becoming locked in to a particular supplier whose equipment uses proprietary protocols (computer-speak for the rules governing an exchange of information between two devices). As information technology spreads into more and more parts of the organization, so it becomes more and more important to be able to choose freely from the technology on offer, without needing to worry whether or not it is compatible with the equipment already installed. What compounds the difficulty is the complexity of information technology equipment, which makes it difficult to establish the degree of compatibility of a particular device with certainty prior to purchase.

Experience has already shown all too clearly that there simply is no easy or complete solution to what is often called 'the interconnection problem'. Furthermore, as already explained in Chapter 1, as we move further on into the era of cheap processing power on the desktop and in the department, we will need to think more in terms of (for want of a better term) *open distributed processing* rather than just *open systems interconnection*. In other words, think in terms of the exchange of information between autonomous systems, rather than between components in a single system which happen to be geographically separated. The latter is at least an order of magnitude more difficult than the former, because it involves the matching of formats and meanings, rather than merely the transport of information from one machine to another.

The spread of information technology into more and more parts of the organization, some with highly specialized needs, also forces us to recognize the potential conflict between their immediate needs and a procurement policy aimed at eventual open distributed processing. Any policy that expects to gain acceptance must be sufficiently flexible to accommodate such specialized needs. And, as the variations underlying the four generic strategies clearly illustrate, the preferred forms of distributed processing and of interworking vary from organization to organization. To define an appropriate procurement policy, both these variations and the organization's starting point must be taken into account.

Why no ready-made solution?

It has been a long-standing complaint of purchasers that information technology equipment obtained from different suppliers cannot easily be interconnected. Or, just as bad, if devices can be interconnected physically, information cannot easily be exchanged between them because of incompatibilities in the way the data is formatted or in the way the software operates. In other words, they can inter-*connect* but cannot inter-*work*. Worse still, the same complaint can often be made about different ranges of equipment available from a single supplier, and not least those on offer from the market leader, IBM.

For most major users of information technology equipment, coping with incompatibility has become a constant battle. While they have fought on, hopes of a solution have been kept up by attempts to hammer out internationally agreed standards. Yet even now, despite years of strenuous effort, although considerable progress has been made in some respects, in my judgement there is still no complete solution in sight to the interconnection problem.

Even if you take the optimistic view and see light at the end of the tunnel, you have to face the fact that the transition to the new world of open interconnection will take time and trouble. For all organizations of any size, it simply is not possible to thrust aside the existing huge investment in information technology equipment. The obstacles to doing so are not only the large amount of capital invested in equipment and software. Over and above that, people right across the organization have invested their skills in applications, in procedures and in know-how. Together, these create the huge, and growing, inertia built into corporate information systems. These inertia forces cannot be ignored, they must somehow be accommodated.

No single supplier can cover all the ground

If it were possible to buy a comprehensive range of equipment from a single supplier, then the interworking problem would be easily solved. Unfortunately, no single supplier can cover all requirements comprehensively at present. Each category of supplier starts from a different position of strength, but with serious weaknesses. Personal computers are essentially single-user devices, capable of a wide range of applications, some able to work together in an integrated fashion, many not. Mini-computer suppliers and office automation specialists have developed good multi-user systems which provide work groups with an integrated set of general office services, but these suppliers are relatively weak in the corporate data processing world. Finally, data processing companies are extending their mainframe systems out towards the office, but they still offer relatively little outside their traditional realm.

IBM, with its huge resources, is still battling to escape from the legacy of its proprietary architecture, Systems Network Architecture (SNA), designed when distributed processing was in its infancy and personal computers had not been born. Advanced Program-to-Program Communication (APPC), formally announced along with IBM's token ring local area network only towards the end of 1985, finally enabled personal computers to interwork across an SNA network without the intervention of the mainframe. And IBM still appears to have no mid-range system, designed to operate in a network of distributed machines, that can match the performance and flexibility of those of its competitors.

IBM is, of course, aware that its customers want better than this, and recently announced Systems Applications Architecture (SAA) – 'a collection of software interfaces, conventions and protocols, a framework for the development of consistent, portable applications in the company's three major computing environments – 370, System/3x, and PCs'. By implication, and as information systems specialists know to their cost, at present applications developed for one of these environments are neither consistent nor portable to the others. Thus IBM acknowledges the problem and has laid out its plan for solving it. But SAA is still only a framework rather than a set of products and there are still many hurdles to be cleared. Commentators say that it will be the early 1990s before IBM's products come together in the way SAA prescribes,[1] and to me even that seems optimistic.

'Open' standards – always just round the corner

Those not content to rely on a single supplier have for some years pinned their hopes on the work of the international standards-making bodies, such as ISO (the International Standards Organization) and CCITT (the standards-making body of the telecommunications carriers). Much of their work centres round ISO's Reference Model for *open systems inter-connection*[2] ('the OSI model', for short). This defines a series of software layers, each of which builds on the services of the layer immediately below it (or, in the case of level 1, the communications hardware) and provides a defined level of service to the level above – see Figure 4.1. The standards-makers' task is a formidable one. Not only is their target moving like an express train, it is also splitting up and moving down a number of tracks at once. They have the choice of getting off and seeing the train(s) head off into the distance without them, or trying to standardize the track they are moving on as the train goes along.

The problem they are now facing up to is that the standards have such a profusion of options that a great effort is needed to install them, with no guarantee that any two products which conform to OSI standards will actually work together. Recently, two European nations attempted to integrate the national networks each had set up for its research scientists. Both networks had been implemented according to OSI standards, but they failed to interwork in practice because the suppliers involved had adopted completely valid subsets of the OSI standards, but which proved to be incompatible with one another.

A programme has now been set in motion to define so-called functional standards, that is standards subsets designed to meet a particular narrow set of needs. The most widely publicized among this category of

OSI level	Level of support
Level 7: application	Supports the processing activities appropriate for the application, e.g. • A command sequence to retrieve information from a database • Instructions to send an electronic mail message
Level 6: presentation	Ensures that information is coded and formatted in the right way for processing and/or display in the receiving device.
Level 5: session	Establishes a dialogue or processing session between network users, or between a network user and a service or application, and regulates the flow of messages between them.
Level 4: transport Level 3: network	Provides end-to-end control of the exchange of messages between two network users (level 4) or across a network (level 3).
Level 2: data link	Transfers messages or packets across a communications link.
Level 1: physical	Transmits electrical signals between devices.

Figure 4.1 The layered *open systems interconnection* model orchestrates the standards-making effort

standards are *Manufacturing Automation Protocol* (MAP) and *Technical Office Protocol* (TOP), which were launched initially by General Motors and Boeing to meet what they saw as their requirements. They are now working, along with a number of other organizations, to get these standards adopted by leading manufacturers. In a similar vein, government agencies, including those in the UK and the US, have adopted an architecture called *GOSIP* (Government OSI Profile). Rather than a discrete set of protocols like MAP and TOP, GOSIP defines a number of permitted combinations of protocols. This is intended to be narrow enough to be practicable, but wide enough to satisfy the requirements for government computing.

It will take time and effort before these initiatives result in useable products, but they do demonstrate that organizations or groupings with enough purchasing power might now be able to impose open standards on their suppliers. Smaller organizations cannot do so, although they may benefit indirectly from these initiatives in time. The difficulties for them are twofold. The first difficulty is cost. As I indicated, the OSI Model defines 'layered' protocols, each layer of which receives services from the layer immediately below and provides services to the layer immediately above. It is this which gives the whole structure its flexibility since (in theory at least) any layer can be replaced by another one which obeys the same rules for dealing with its neighbours, as technology changes or to meet a new user requirement. But it also makes the whole structure extremely complex, and therefore costly to implement.

The second difficulty is that standards unavoidably lag behind the technology itself. With a relatively slow-moving technology this does not matter too much, since the benefits of standardization usually outweigh the disadvantages of slightly out-of-date technology. But the pace of change in information technology is so great that this equation may be very different. With information technology used so widely to gain competitive advantage, early access to some new capability may be of strategic importance in particular industries.

'If I were you I wouldn't start from here'

One final point, summed up in the reply of the man (in the English version of the anecdote he was an Irishman, of course) who was asked for directions to a nearby town: 'If I were you I wouldn't start from here'. A large amount of the equipment already in use within business organizations has been left behind by the advance of technology. It is technically difficult and costly to integrate much of this equipment into the new systems which are now being built, let alone those around the technological corner. What is more, end-users have an investment of know-how and applications in this equipment which they are often reluctant to abandon or replace. One of the UK's top confectionery manufacturers, for example, invested early in Wordplex word processors for its senior secretarial staff. These devices were among the best available at the time, but have now been overtaken by personal computers running word processing packages like Microsoft's *Word*. Personal computers both cost far less than the Wordplex machines and, of course, are easier to interconnect with the growing population of personal computers elsewhere. However, arguments such as this do not impress the secretaries who have come to know and love the Wordplex equipment.

For as far ahead as any of us can see, today's systems will have to co-exist with yesterday's. This is a reality which procurement policy cannot ignore. It must not only provide a vision of tomorrow's systems and the methods they will use to interwork. It must also provide for an orderly phase-out of obsolete equipment and for an orderly phase-in of the new.

Today's needs versus tomorrow's integration

Procurement rules inevitably bring out into the open the classic conflict of immediate needs against long term considerations. Expressed in the words of many a disgruntled end-user: 'Why should I go without this equipment, which is exactly what I need to solve my biggest information handling problem, because you say it won't connect to your communications network. As far as I know, I don't even want to do that.' In many cases, in fact, the end-user did not go without the desired equipment, because it was so easy just to ring the local retailer and order it. How can you apply effective control while also catering for legitimate local needs?

Interworking – beyond interconnection

Nearly all large organizations apply procurement policies designed to limit the proliferation of incompatible equipment. Initially, these policies were aimed principally at reducing the future cost of supporting end-user systems, by limiting the range of equipment for which specialist skills were needed. But the emphasis has shifted towards ensuring that end-users have a secure migration path as their requirements evolve. For example, having begun by handling purely local tasks with local information, they want to access corporate files or to exchange information with their colleagues in other departments. In other words, having first used end-user systems mainly to meet their personal processing needs, end-users next want to interwork directly with other people.

Access to existing (usually centralized) data files quickly becomes of crucial importance for the success of end-user systems. Out of more than 60 computer-experienced end-users interviewed in 1986, all of whom were managers or professionals in large European organizations, more than a third regarded access to central files as crucial. Most of the remainder regarded this as important. A significant number also wanted to be able to download data from central files for local processing, this being the best way of achieving the flexibility in handling the data that they needed. In recognition of these requirements, large organizations in Europe and the US began stipulating that end-user systems must be capable of being attached to the corporate network. Increasingly, this is becoming the corner-stone of procurement policy.

Yet attachment to the corporate network may only be a partial solution to the connectivity problem, since it only affects the form of information that is transferred, and not the content. An end-user who produces a budget using Lotus *1-2-3*, for example, will be able to send it to another end-user, but if the recipient is using Microsoft's *Multiplan* rather than *1-2-3*, they will not be able to re-work or consolidate the budget, except perhaps by running a conversion routine first. This means that policy has to specify preferred applications software packages as well, and many organizations have standardized on *1-2-3* for that reason.

An alternative, or supplementary, approach is to adopt general standards for the formatting of documents that are to be exchanged, rather than relying on the proprietary standards set by package suppliers like Lotus. Standards defined by IBM for its own large systems, such as Document Content Architecture (DCA), are attractive for committed IBM users. Other companies have adopted the standards defined for the exchange of trading information via inter-business networks. Some UK companies in food and related industries, for example, have adopted the Tradanet standards originated by the Article Numbering Association.

Diverse local needs demand flexibility

While it is important to anticipate end-users' future needs for inter-connection, it is as important to recognize that local needs vary considerably. Examples of the dangers of too rigid an approach are not difficult to find. In many companies, inflexible procurement rules are simply by-passed. A study of end-user computing in seventeen US companies found that the the four with no controls suffered the worst results, but that the seven with rigid controls 'also encountered huge cost overruns'. As the writer explains:

> The users in these businesses devised ingenious ways to circumvent the controls. For example, purchase control specified IS approval for items that cost more than some threshold amount – usually about $3,500 (the cost of a PC with useful business features). To avoid having to get approval, users unbundled their purchases, buying a basic processor on one order, the printer on another, software on a third.
> Some of them embedded PCs in an existing minicomputer budget, listed them

as terminals, and renamed software 'program documentation'. When one organization conducted an audit a year after implementing hard controls, it was surprised to discover more than 1,500 unapproved PCs.[3]

Knowledge workers' jobs vary from one job to the next, and from one year to the next. Hence, preferred equipment must be able to support a wide range of applications. Ironically, this was a prime reason why so many companies standardized on a single device, the IBM PC. The software industry quickly recognized the PC as a winner, because of IBM's power in the marketplace. Since volume is the key to profits in the personal computer software business, most of the industry's efforts were aimed at the PC and quickly produced a huge range of applications packages. But the IBM PC also suffers the disadvantages of uninspired technology and an economy 'engine' – its operating system, PC-DOS. Its limitations are shown up very clearly in certain specialized applications. Where good text and graphics handling is required, as in a publishing or design environment, a machine like the Apple Macintosh is far superior, and some companies have selected it purely for that reason, despite the much more limited range of applications software which it offers. Casual users, also, such as senior managers, find a machine like the Macintosh much easier to come to terms with than the more conventional IBM PC.

Not only do knowledge workers' jobs vary, so do their attitudes and their ways of working. The machines they use must show some willingness to adapt to these ways of working, if they are to be seen as worth having in the first place. One European bank, for example, set aside the results of comparative tests and decided to acquire office workstations from its supplier of banking terminals, for compatibility reasons. These were installed in the back offices of the branches, but ran into severe operating difficulties, because the staff found them too difficult to use. After strenuous efforts they finally gave up and replaced the workstations with those which had headed the field in the evaluation, but which had been set aside because they were not compatible. Thus, a delicate balance has to be maintained.

High pay-off applications will not be standard

In time, end-users' needs differentiate, and it naturally becomes more difficult to cater for specialized requirements within the scope of an all-embracing policy for procurement. Few major organizations will not have some groups of staff with leading-edge requirements and which might also be crucial to business performance. The choice will often be between delaying exploiting these opportunities, or making exceptions in the interest of speed or successful implementation.

The positive aim of procurement policy should be to encourage the high-payoff applications and, once beyond the exploratory stages of end-user systems, these will not be the 'standard' and standalone activities, such as preparation of budgets on Lotus 1-2-3. As indicated earlier, they will either arise from collective efforts of white-collar staff working more effectively together, or from unique, customized applications which enable the business to differentiate some aspect of its business operations from the competition.

This means that most organizations will have to offer their end-users a priced menu, rather than a set meal. Policy must be driven by their information systems strategy, but must also be sufficiently flexible that it does not stifle local initiative or provoke outright opposition. Restrictions on procurement will have a different force depending on the business requirement with which they are linked. Those which derive from corporate goals will be mandatory. Thus, for example, a multinational whose markets were becoming global imposed mandatory standards for the formatting of documents used by its subsidiary companies to exchange trading information. Below these business-derived restrictions will be further standards or guidelines which identify those approved products which are seen as the best fit with the infrastructure at the particular time, and which the information systems department is geared up to support. Within this procurement framework, or in special circumstances outside it, end-users have the freedom to choose whatever equipment best meets their local needs.

Framework for a realistic policy

Open distributed processing will only be achieved at considerable cost and effort, and will only be sustained by a continuing struggle. Therefore it is essential to be clear about policy objectives, and to prioritize. Once again, the generic strategies help to place the options in perspective.

Policy must cover five dimensions

The discussion of end-users' integration needs in Chapter 1 provides a starting point for analyzing requirements, with a view to establishing priorities. As already explained, integration along each of those three dimensions has different objectives. Those objectives can also be translated into terms relevant to procurement policy:

- In the *information access* dimension, the objective can be expressed as coherent access for end-users to complete, concise, timely information. Different organizational units will possibly have different types of equipment, and will almost certainly have different applications. In this situation, procurement policy is concerned with how the benefit of coherent access to information can be protected, and the way it does so is by specifying how data and documents which might be exchanged should be formatted.

- In the *services* dimension, we are aiming to make applications easier to use, so that a wider range of staff can exploit whatever range of those applications is appropriate for their job. This is achieved by specifying a common interface to applications that guarantees a high degree of consistency from one to the next, and makes it easy to switch between applications, carrying information from one to the next.

- In the *interworking* dimension, we aim to support controlled, timely exchange of data, documents, or information in whatever form. That in turn depends on compatible messaging protocols, and compatible interfaces between the equipment that uses the transmission network – workstations and computers – and the equipment that forms it.

These, if you like, are the three operating dimensions that procurement policy must cover. But there are two additional dimensions, which can be described as enabling dimensions. These reflect the obvious facts that many applications must be developed in the first place, and that the various technology resources must be managed from day to day. Thus the two additional dimensions are the *development* and the *management* dimensions. In the same way as for the three operating dimensions, we can define objectives in these enabling dimensions, and translate those objectives into appropriate terms for procurement policy.

- The aim in the *development* dimension is to produce well-designed and reliable applications that can be used as widely as possible. This means that system building tools should produce applications that can run at least across a range of preferred equipment. The importance attached to end-user development of applications will vary, but where this is given high priority, it will additionally be important that end-users can access and run the system building tools from their own workstations and local systems.

- *Management* of the infrastructure has as its objective effective control and maintenance of the technology resources deployed across the organization, including planning for change and growth. That implies defining a means of access to the applications and services that are provided, such as via standard menus and security procedures; a means of collecting statistics about the use made of key resources; and a means of maintaining control mechanisms such as directories.

The generic strategy defines priorities

As is self-evident, for most organizations it is not a practical proposition to introduce standards covering all five dimensions all at once. Clear priorities must be established, so that chosen standards can be applied as widely as possible, and certainly to all major procurement decisions. The generic strategies are helpful here, since, as already explained, each embodies a distinct approach, relying on particular control and co-ordination mechanisms. These, in turn, will rely for their effectiveness on procurement policy to ensure that the mechanisms mesh with one another right across the organization.

Figure 4.2 summarizes the objectives of procurement policy and the means of achieving them, in each of the five dimensions. It also shows, in the four righthand columns, how important these five aspects of procurement policy are likely to be in the realization of the four generic strategies.

Dimension	Objective	Means	CIE	DIS	OUN	ECE
Information access	Coherent access to complete, relevant information	Standards for identifying, formatting and transmitting items of information	o	•	o	o
Services	Wider and easier use of the technology	Operating software providing a consistent interface to services, and ease of switching between them	o	•	•	•
Interworking	Controlled, timely exchange of data and information	Compatible message transfer and interfaces between devices and network components	•	•	o	o
Management	Effective control and maintenance of the technology resources	Standard and secure means of controlling access to services; and of maintaining control elements like directories	•	•	o	o
Development	Production of well-designed and reliable applications for the widest use	Standard system building tools, producing programs portable at least across preferred equipment ranges	o	o	-	•

Key: • = essential to strategy; o = desirable, perhaps important; - = probably unimportant
CIE = corporate information engine; DIS = distributed information system;
OUN = office utility network; ECE = end-user computing environment

Figure 4.2 Generic strategies and priorities for procurement policy

Notes and references

1 See Peter Purton, 'Totally wired', *Datalink*, Dec 7 1987, pp. 14-15.
2 For a fuller description, see Morris Edwards, 'Universal Architecture Seeks to Oust SNA', *Communications News*, Jun 1984, pp. 50-56.
3 J. Daniel Couger, 'E pluribus computum', *Harvard Business Review*, Sept-Oct 1986, pp. 87-91.

SUMMARY OF PART ONE: PRINCIPLES AND REQUIREMENTS FOR THE INFRASTRUCTURE

To conclude the first part of the book, here is a summary of the argument and of the main conclusions that have been drawn. It is included to serve two purposes – as a reminder for those who have just finished reading, and for quick and easy reference later on.

◊ ◊ ◊ ◊

In order to understand the requirements that should be met, and the design principles that should be applied, we must look at the infrastructure from four points of view:

- From a marketing viewpoint – What are the customers' needs? how should we set out to satisfy them? This in turn breaks down into two – the needs of individual *applications and customers*, and the demands of the *organization* as a whole.
- From an *engineering* viewpoint – What structural qualities should the architecture have? What topology? How should we fit the component parts together?
- From a *procurement* viewpoint – What are the characteristics of the technology components we will call on? Hence, what guidelines or restrictions should we apply to procurement?

I now look at each of these four topics in turn.

Applications and customer needs

Much of the current investment in information systems resides in the central data processing systems (labelled *transaction processing and operational control systems* below), and these also tend to dominate the maintenance effort. But the key growth areas lie elsewhere. Expressed in terms of a simple model of the information flows within a business (below), they are:

A Extended support for staff who deal directly with customers
B External networks to capture transactions at source and exchange trading information directly with customers or suppliers
C Support for professional or technical work groups engaged in research, design, development or maintenance activities
D Support (separated from the operational systems) for management control and planning activities

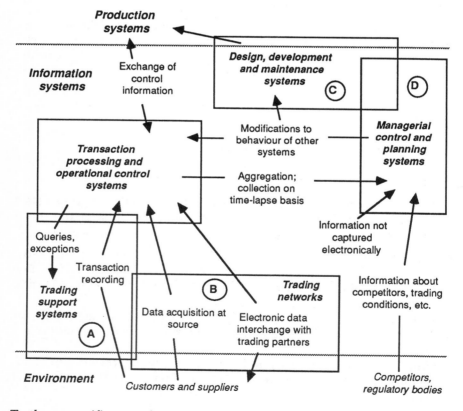

To these specific growth areas can be added two broader trends:

- Systems are being integrated across business functions, as in computer-integrated manufacturing.
- The scope of systems is being extended to handle less structured information – graphics, image, knowledge – as well as data and text.

Leaving aside *trading networks*, which have little direct impact on the infrastructure, the common feature of the growth applications is the emphasis on supporting knowledge work. We still know relatively little about knowledge work. Both usage and attitudes vary considerably from individual to individual and from job to job, but different types of knowledge worker do exhibit characteristic patterns in their computing activity. Knowledge workers' requirements can be best understood by separating them out along three dimensions ...

- In the *information access* dimension, they obtain information from a range of sources.
- In the *services* dimension, they use a range of processing tools to manipulate and present information.
- In the *interworking* dimension, they distribute information to co-workers in their work group or organization, or beyond.

In those terms, the characteristic requirements of different types of staff can be summarized as follows ...

	Information access	Services	Interworking
Executives	Some internal, much external; highly refined	Display options, no manipulation	Mainly via support staff, 'phone and face-to-face
Commercial managers	High volumes of operational data	*Ad hoc* select and present; simple manipulation	Messaging may be very important, e.g. if staff are mobile
Professionals	Varies: internal, external, and self-input; often multiple sources	Complex modelling and manipulation; document preparation	Often localized within work group; perhaps also for rapid distribution
Sharp-end staff	Predefined internal or external data	Display only, no manipulation	Usually formalized and built into application
Administrative support	Predefined internal data, plus some data self-input	Utilities, e.g. word processing, and local applications	Mainly as substitute for telex and internal mail

As well as being individuals with a particular job to do, most knowledge workers also belong to work groups. Work-group systems – combining specific applications with 'office' utilities such as electronic messaging – have been applied successfully to four different types of work group ...

Work-group type	Main payoff derived from
Commercial team a vertical slice of the line activities of a business unit	Faster response to customer demands; better co-ordination of product or other changes; better handling of crises
Critical professional team a team of professionals on the business critical path	Improvements in quality of output and in speed of working; better control & auditing of quality
Professional skill composite a group of professionals united by their common skills	Increased throughput; better handling of peaks or crises; more flexible work as- signment
Senior management team managing a business unit	Supports the setting of a new business direction and acts as a catalyst to change behaviour lower down in the business

Experience so far shows that people operating as work groups can only be supported effectively by providing two features additional to those they need as individuals:

- Applications specific to the work group or department – these tend to provide the key benefits.
- Support for sharing of information within and between work groups.

Work-group systems also provide a wider range of services than personal computers, which means that more applications are used less heavily and with greater urgency for results.

Along each of the three dimensions of their requirements – *information access, services* and *interworking* – knowledge workers need greater coherence, achievable via integration, for two main reasons:

- Partial solutions of the past have erected new 'information frontiers'.
- Today's systems are not easy enough to use – use has barely spread beyond pressed men and enthusiasts.

The upper figure on the right is a summary of requirements and of problems to be overcome. Below it is shown a *knowledge work support architecture* to be embodied in the infrastructure.

Information access

Aim: Make it easier to obtain complete information (rather than just raw data) from computer-based sources.
Gains a) of electronic access:
• Limit re-entry of data and risk of error.
• Extend information reach to improve quality.
Problems: Cost a declining barrier; a minority benefit greatly.
Gains b) of providing complete information on tap:
• Improve management decisions.
• Cut out middlemen and improve professional effectiveness.
Problems: Operational data gives a one-dimensional, incomplete picture of a multi-dimensional reality –
• Managers need refined information, including some external.
• Professionals often draw from multiple sources.

Interworking

Aim:
Promote controlled, timely exchange of information.
Gains:
Lower communication barriers and increase organizational flexibility.
Problem:
Equipment incompatibilities are well entrenched.

Services

Aim: Improve effectiveness of use via
•   A consistent human/computer interface
•   Ease of switching and transportability of information between applications
Gains: • Reduce learning and training time.
            • Draw in intermittent and non-expert users.
Problem: Standard PCs have a wide range of applications and tools, with interfaces to the user varying in design and in quality, while purpose-built 'office systems' lack the range and the 'open'-ness of PCs.

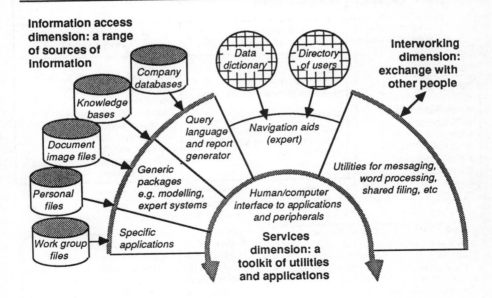

The demands of the organization

The infrastructure must reflect the underlying needs of the organization. Those underlying needs provide a 'strategic direction' that unifies the infrastructure and gives it coherence. Different types of business adopt different viewpoints about the right form of infrastructure to invest in. Their choice depends on two business variables:

1. autonomy   How much freedom should end-users have to develop local applications?

2. coupling   How important is it for end-users to have immediate access to operating data on shared computers?

Taking these variables as the axes of a two-by-two matrix, we can define four generic strategies ...

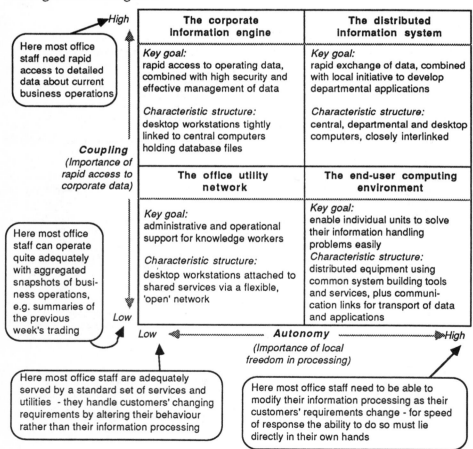

High

Here most office staff need rapid access to detailed data about current business operations

Coupling
(Importance of rapid access to corporate data)

Here most office staff can operate quite adequately with aggregated snapshots of business operations, e.g. summaries of the previous week's trading

Low

The corporate information engine	**The distributed information system**
Key goal: rapid access to operating data, combined with high security and effective management of data	*Key goal:* rapid exchange of data, combined with local initiative to develop departmental applications
Characteristic structure: desktop workstations tightly linked to central computers holding database files	*Characteristic structure:* central, departmental and desktop computers, closely interlinked
The office utility network	**The end-user computing environment**
Key goal: administrative and operational support for knowledge workers	*Key goal:* enable individual units to solve their information handling problems easily
Characteristic structure: desktop workstations attached to shared services via a flexible, 'open' network	*Characteristic structure:* distributed equipment using common system building tools and services, plus communication links for transport of data and applications

Low ◄—————————— **Autonomy** ——————————►High
(Importance of local freedom in processing)

Here most office staff are adequately served by a standard set of services and utilities - they handle customers' changing requirements by altering their behaviour rather than their information processing

Here most office staff need to be able to modify their information processing as their customers' requirements change - for speed of response the ability to do so must lie directly in their own hands

The infrastructure reflects the mechanisms adopted for co-ordination and control in two main ways:

- Via the methods used to manage information.
- Via the methods used to develop applications.

In deciding information management policy, we have to balance the security gained by restrictive control against the flexibility achieved by enabling end-users to respond rapidly to new or changing information needs. In particular, we have to decide to what extent information, and responsibility for it, should be decentralized, and how end-users should gain access to data on central files.

Policy for applications development defines which applications end-users may attempt and how. Restrictive approaches enable the information systems department to maintain the quality of applications, but at the price of slower progress, higher support costs and, often, end-user resentment.

Each generic strategy embodies a coherent control philosophy, in terms of information management and applications development ...

	Topology	Information management	Application development
Corporate information engine	All major systems centralized; local systems limited to *ad hoc* decision support; heavy hierarchical flows of information.	Centralized data management using advanced tools; strict control over downloading to local systems.	Central development shop, also supporting approved PC and 'office' packages; certification of local applications.
Distributed information system	Centralized systems for operational and corporate control, linked to powerful departmental systems; heavy flows of information, laterally and hierarchically.	Central group concerned with directional issues; decentralized accountability for data, backed up by data description and interchange standards.	Central shop for corporate systems; joint projects and end-user computing support for departmental and local applications.
Office utility network	Shared utility services, such as for messaging, with specialized and generic packages used locally; *ad hoc* lateral and local traffic.	Data integrity is local responsibility; low-key, informal management practices, centred round approved application packages.	Small central unit looks after shared utilities and corporate systems, and provides technical support for approved application packages; little local development.
End-user computing environment	Distributed machines used for operational applications and knowledge work support; *ad hoc* access to corporate systems and to system building tools.	Data integrity is local responsibility; low-key, informal management practices centred around approved system building tools.	Centre provides technical support and rapid development service; system building tools used for local applications; design standards to promote application sharing.

It may be possible to associate an organization directly with one of these generic strategies, via the two business variables. If not, there are two other 'windows' through which you can assess them.

Window 1 – IT drivers

Information systems investment falls into three broad areas ...

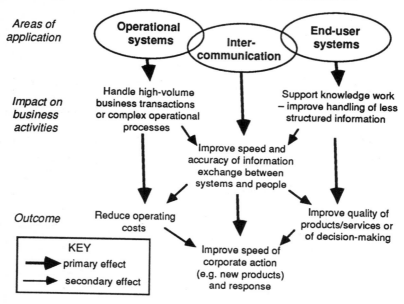

Spending in each of those areas is driven by particular characteristics of the organization's activities – *structure, information intensity* and *linkage*. At present, generic strategies are influenced mainly by the two latter, as shown in the top figure opposite.

Window 2 – organizational work flow

In terms of their work flow, organizations can be placed in one of three categories, each of which relies on a different method of control:

Facsimile   Each part is a mirror image of the others, and control is by rules and procedures.

Sequential   Outputs from one part are inputs to another, and control is by planning and scheduling.

Independent There is no interrelation (except via common services), and control is by personal interaction.

These categories map on to the generic strategies as shown in the lower figure opposite.

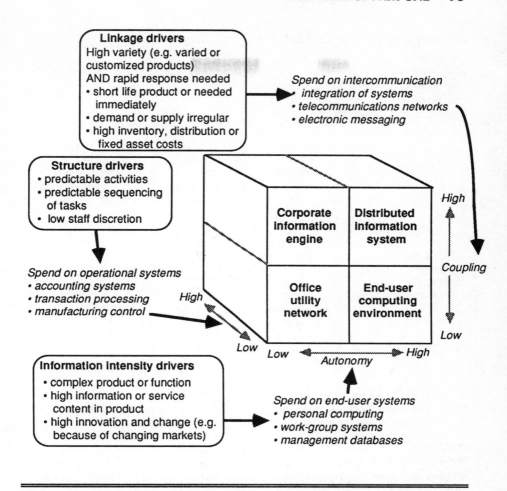

Linkage drivers
High variety (e.g. varied or customized products)
AND rapid response needed
• short life product or needed immediately
• demand or supply irregular
• high inventory, distribution or fixed asset costs

Spend on intercommunication
• *integration of systems*
• *telecommunications networks*
• *electronic messaging*

Structure drivers
• predictable activities
• predictable sequencing of tasks
• low staff discretion

Spend on operational systems
• *accounting systems*
• *transaction processing*
• *manufacturing control*

Corporate information engine

Distributed information system

Office utility network

End-user computing environment

High

Coupling

Low

High

Low   Low   *Autonomy*   *High*

Information intensity drivers
• complex product or function
• high information or service content in product
• high innovation and change (e.g. because of changing markets)

Spend on end-user systems
• *personal computing*
• *work-group systems*
• *management databases*

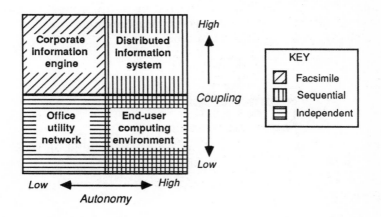

Corporate information engine

Distributed information system

Office utility network

End-user computing environment

High

Coupling

Low

Low ←→ High
Autonomy

KEY
▨ Facsimile
▥ Sequential
▤ Independent

Engineering for the 1990s

Business and technology pressures raise new questions about the engineering of information systems ...

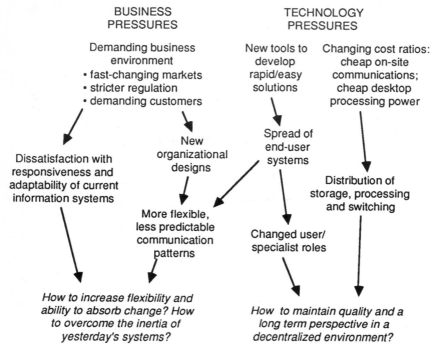

The infrastructure serves to contain and channel pressures for decentralization, in order to balance the need for flexibility in the organization's information systems with management's need to maintain control. As in organizational design, flexibility is achieved by partitioning. The monolithic systems built in the early stages of data processing proved difficult to amend, so they were partitioned internally ...

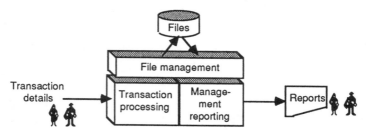

Now, data files are also being partitioned. Separate files are being set up to give end-users information to support planning and control activities. This brings gains in flexibility, and has the additional advantage that it reduces the load on the transaction processing systems and makes them easier to replace ...

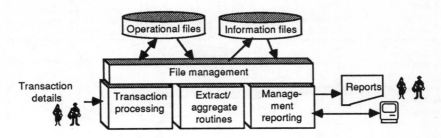

This basic architecture is extended to link in external sources of information. It is also partitioned further to increase flexibility and to make the structure iterative ...

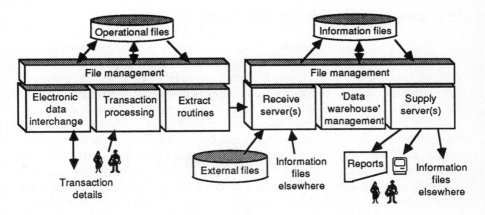

Furthermore, responding to pressures for decentralization, operational systems split into core and local applications, and access to the information files is via the *knowledge work support architecture* (see over).

A final rationalization would be to extend the knowledge work support architecture into the transaction processing area also. This adds flexibility by introducing generic services such as messaging and word processing. It would also give local management, *where appropriate*, direct control over operational parameters, enabling the organization to respond more rapidly to events or to change.

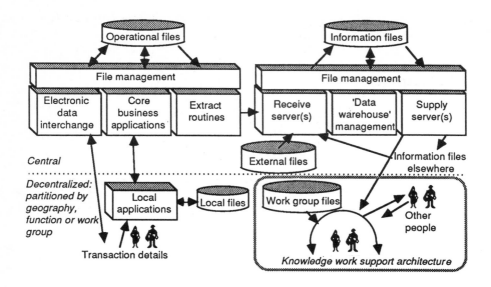

Procurement – the insoluble problem

For all organizations, some degree of compatibility between the various items of information technology equipment that are procured is desirable, so that these can interwork when necessary. For those that place a high priority on integration, compatibility is essential. Hence the importance of looking at the infrastructure from a procurement viewpoint.

Procurement is an insoluble problem in the sense that it cannot be solved completely – it must be managed continuously. This is because no single supplier, even IBM, can cover all the ground, as information technology continues to expand in scope. Nor is there any immediate prospect of supplier-independent interconnection standards that can be applied universally. Organizations or groupings with high bargaining power as buyers may impose suitable standards on their suppliers, but others cannot avoid the disadvantages of relying on international supplier-independent standards:

- The standards will always be some years behind the very latest technology, which may be of strategic importance in certain industries.
- In the short term, the cost of implementation will be high, in terms both of initial investment and of operation.

Additionally, all organizations face the problem of phasing out their existing investment in equipment that does not meet chosen standards.

Rigid rules on procurement provoke resistance, because local needs vary considerably. Not only this, innovative and high-payoff applications will often fall outside the rules.

Open distributed processing (a long step beyond *open systems inter- connection*) will only be achieved at considerable cost and effort and after a long, perhaps never-ending, struggle. Therefore it is essential to be clear about policy objectives, and to prioritize. Procurement policy must cover the three operational dimensions of end-users' requirements – *information access, services* and *interworking* – and also two enabling dimensions – application *development* and infrastructure *management*. The generic strategies help to place the options in perspective ...

Dimension	Objective	Means	CIE	DIS	OUN	ECE
Information access	Coherent access to complete, relevant information	Standards for identifying, formatting and transmitting items of information	o	●	o	o
Services	Wider and easier use of the technology	Operating software providing a consistent interface to services, and ease of switching between them	o	●	●	●
Interworking	Controlled, timely exchange of data and information	Compatible message transfer and interfaces between devices and network components	●	●	o	o
Management	Effective control and maintenance of the technology resources	Standard and secure means of controlling access to services, and of maintaining control elements like directories	●	●	o	o
Development	Production of well- designed and reli- able applications for the widest use	Standard system build- ing tools, producing programs portable at least across preferred equipment ranges	o	o	-	●

Key: ● = essential to strategy; o = desirable, perhaps important; - = probably unimportant
CIE = corporate information engine; DIS = distributed information system;
OUN = office utility network; ECE = end-user computing environment

DEVELOPING THE
INFRASTRUCTURE

This second part of the book explains how to build on the requirements and design principles for the infrastructure developed in Part One, to develop a solution that is both practical and effective. It reviews the specific problems – technical and otherwise – that must be faced, and provides guidance on how to decide an approach that respects the constraints that are likely to be encountered. These include the limitations of current technology and, equally important, the human factors that decide whether solutions are acceptable to the people who will use them, or whether they can be managed effectively. It consists of four chapters, which successively address the following questions.

- How should you work towards the kind of coherence for the end-user at the workstation, described in Chapter 1?
- Picking up from the discussions of organizational demands in Chapter 2 and of engineering requirements in Chapter 3, how should you distribute processing and storage components, and what steps should you take to maintain overall control?
- How should you manage the interconnection problem outlined in Chapter 4?
- Finally, how should you plan the corporate network, the transport system for information?

CHAPTER 5
INFORMATION POWER – THE WORKSTATION

I remember sitting down with a group of colleagues in the course of a market study, a few years ago, to forecast the role of the office work-station in the early 1990s. By extrapolating technology trends, we had concluded that, by 1991, about $2000 would buy a workstation capable of 2 million instructions per second, with 1 megabyte of main memory, a 20 megabyte hard disc, and built-in telecommunications and peripheral interfaces. 'What on earth', we asked ourselves, 'is an end-user going to do with all that power?' The answer was not obvious then, but it is now. Most end-users certainly do not need all the power directly. But the workstation does need a great deal of it to provide an acceptable human/computer interface for a much wider range of people, involved in a broader range of information handling tasks, than those who use personal computers or other desktop devices today.

In the past, discussions of the architecture of information systems have almost invariably started from the mainframe computer or from the telecommunications network. Now, the personal computer, the office workstation in embryo, has turned the topic inside out. It has done this by demonstrating that the workstation plays a key role in making infor-mation systems easier to use. Hence it is the means of opening them up to the majority of office workers whose jobs have still barely been touched by information systems, including middle and senior managers.

As I explained in Chapter 1, many of the difficulties end-users experience with information systems arise because the 'view' of infor-mation provided through the workstation is incoherent, but how, in practical terms, can this be improved? The answer has been obvious for some time – by better integrating the various elements which make up that view. End-users' information handling needs, not only in terms of their job functions but also as individuals, are diverse. Hence, as already explained in Chapter 1, integration possibilities are multidimensional and present extremely complex technical problems. It is this which should give pause for thought, because in the past unmanageable and unwieldy systems have been built in the name of 'integration'. Can the trick really be achieved? Would it not be better just to settle for the simple tools most personal computer users have come to terms with so far, and to pick up improvements as they emerge, piecemeal?

Such an approach, I believe, is misconceived. Experience does not tell us that it is futile to plan for integration, but rather that it is important not to lose sight of the real goals, and not to go too far, too fast. The right approach, therefore, is to be clear about the relative value of different forms of integration in the particular circumstances you face, and selective about where and how you apply the integration 'glue'. In this chapter I explain how to go about that task. I begin by looking in more detail at the three dimensions of integration needs identified in Chapter 1, which I expressed in the form of a *knowledge work support architecture*. This is reproduced in Figure 5.1. First I discuss the ways that requirements can practically be met using current technology, and then I outline how you can go about setting priorities.

Before I do that, I should make clear that by describing features and facilities as provided 'at the workstation', I do not mean that they are things that the workstation, as an item of equipment, should necessarily

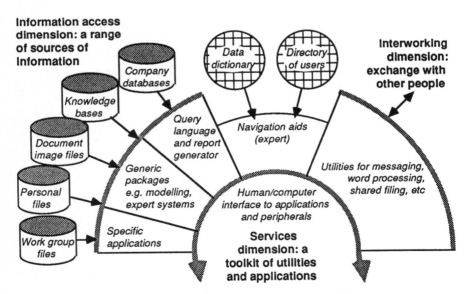

Figure 5.1 The knowledge work support architecture developed in Chapter 1

do itself. Just as many personal computers do at present, office work-stations will often work in cooperation with processors to which they are linked, either locally or remotely via telecommunication lines. Decisions as to which piece of co-operating equipment should do what, and where these should be located, are partly a question of architecture, partly a question of cost/performance. I deal with the architecture questions in the next chapter, and some of the cost/performance issues are covered throughout this book. Others will be specific to particular suppliers' equipment and will be evaluated in the normal course of equipment selection. To reiterate the point, I am talking in this chapter about services which are delivered to the workstation, as the end-user perceives them, not solely about the workstation itself.

Tapping the information resource

As I pointed out in Chapter 1, to give end-users coherence in their access to information, you must think in broader terms than has been necessary in the past. Having recognized, as is usually the case, that existing data processing files are part of the problem, you must also appreciate that, even when these files have been enhanced to meet the new demands placed on them by end-users, they only form part of a satisfactory solution. As well as re-examining the methods used to store data (which I go on to discuss in Chapter 6), we must also evolve new techniques for retrieving data, and for manipulating it to turn it into information. These techniques must better reflect the tasks that knowledge workers, and especially managers, carry out, the skills that they possess, and the circumstances under which they work.

It is already clear from today's experience what the workstation can contribute here, and there can be little doubt that its contribution will increase in the future as its technology continues to improve. Comprehensive and effective solutions will not be built overnight, but they can and must be devised. Now let me try to explain how.

Existing data files cannot provide a total solution

As noted earlier, existing data files generally have serious shortcomings when measured against end-users' requirements for information. In outline, these shortcomings may include any or all of the following:

- They are usually expensive and time-consuming to modify.
- They may not provide the time-lapse data on which many management decisions are based.
- They may not be flexible enough to reflect the fact that the same data, used for different purposes, may be assigned different values.

- They may be divided along the wrong dimensions for decision-making purposes, for example by topic rather than in terms of business processes.

New database technologies, such as those based on the relational model originally propounded by Tedd Codd and adopted by a number of leading suppliers in their latest products,[1] promise to address some of these shortcomings. But even assuming that an organization gains itself enough elbow room to take on the major task of revamping the data processing files using such technologies, some major practical problems remain.

First, 'information at the touch of a key' is costly to deliver. Complex searches of data files can be very expensive in computer power, especially when powerful, and as a result inefficient, query languages are used. End-users are unlikely to be aware of the implications of entering particular queries which happen to be expensive in machine terms. Finding this out when the bill arrives, or when nothing happens for fifteen minutes after a query was entered, is, to say the least, bad for relationships between end-users and information systems specialists. Unrestricted activity of this kind is also unwelcome, since it may interfere with the performance of operational systems. When, as manager responsible for those systems, you have to choose between delaying the issue of invoices and delaying replies to senior managers' urgent requests for information, resignation is probably the only way out.

Despite the continuing reductions in the cost of computer storage, storage cost can also be a serious barrier in the way of an overall solution based on the existing data files. In 1986, American Express Europe assessed the cost of restructuring all their data files to meet end-users' information requirements. They concluded that it would put up their storage costs fivefold. On this basis, it appeared to be much cheaper to leave things as they were, with end-users re-keying data from existing reports into their personal computers to manipulate them. Flexibility costs money, and the kind of flexibility made possible by relational database structures can still prove expensive to realize.

In practice, most organizations are discovering that they need to take action on two fronts. Certainly, something needs to be done to adapt the existing data files and match them more closely to what end-users need, and I return to this in Chapter 6. But, as I now go on to elaborate, the workstation, be it personal computer or whatever, also has an important contribution to make.

Access tools must suit the end-user, not mainly the database

The first respect in which the workstation contributes is by providing tools for accessing and then manipulating data that end-users can master with reasonable ease. (I say *tools for accessing and then manipulating data* because data – facts – only becomes information – facts to which a meaning can be attached – when it is matched with a particular decision or problem, which generally means modifying or combining it in some way. That means that it is wrong to separate access and manipulation.) The point is that the sophisticated enquiry and report generation tools which many information systems specialists see as the way forward do not find favour with most end-users. But they *do* like the straightforward tools available on personal computers, which specialists sometimes dismiss with contempt. A short case example illustrates the point.

One of the UK's largest companies rewrote the suite of mainframe programs used by its corporate reporting group, to run on a mini-computer which they installed within the department. They chose the financial modelling language, FCS, to develop the new systems, specifically so that the accountants within the department would be able to write their own enquiry programs in the future. In practice, very few such programs were developed by the accountants, because they found the language too difficult. The breakthrough came when the dumb terminals installed originally were replaced by personal computers. Although the corporate reporting group was encouraged by their information systems people to adopt the personal computer version of FCS, they rejected it in favour of Lotus *1-2-3*, because the latter was so easy to use. Now, when they need to do new analyses or produce *ad hoc* reports, accountants can transfer data from the departmental machine to their personal computers, where they use Lotus *1-2-3* to manipulate it. Despite the 'minor annoyance' of having to initiate a batch transfer of data, then load it into *1-2-3* before processing, this feature is heavily used and has removed the programming skills bottleneck which constrained them before. It also has the advantage that newcomers to the department (the company operates a policy of circulating accounting staff) usually know *1-2-3* already and can easily pick up the new work.

The problem with the tools – enquiry languages and fourth generation programming languages (4GLs) – available with advanced database management systems is twofold. First, the syntax is difficult for a non-specialist to learn and for any but a regular user to remember. Second, even where end-users can master the tools and where comprehensive data is available in the right form, they face problems in 'navigating' and interpreting that data. Without understanding the structure of the files, and few end-users will, they cannot easily trace the precise information they need, and there is a danger that they will misinterpret what they do find. Enquiry languages that are easier to use, such as those which use a 'query-by-example' approach rather than a complex syntax, are closing the gap, but it still yawns. So far, the evidence is that these tools are suitable for use by trained programmers and by a minority of enthusiast end-users, but not for the generality of office staff. Somehow, power of retrieval must be combined with ease of use.

The workstation links data sources

The second contribution of the workstation is to bring together information from a number of different sources, so that this can be combined or compared. At this relatively early stage of the game, most end-users do need to combine data from at least two sources, and some – professionals doing particular analysis tasks – need to retrieve data from a number of different databases, inside and outside their own organization. In 1986 I carried out a survey of end-users – mainly managers and professionals – in large UK companies who were already experienced in using computer-based tools. I asked them to indicate which were the main sources of the data they processed, and how important it was to them (on a 5-point scale) that the means of access to the data should be improved. Figure 5.2 summarizes the result, showing that, on average, these end-users draw on two separate sources of information, and that, for a minority, access to data from sources external to the organization urgently needs to be improved.

In the same year, ICI conducted an investigation to find out the features which end-users thought essential if they were ever to be confident of effective personal access to a multiplicity of external bibliographic sources. They ended up with a lengthy list:

- One-key automated log-on and log-off
- Automatic re-connection

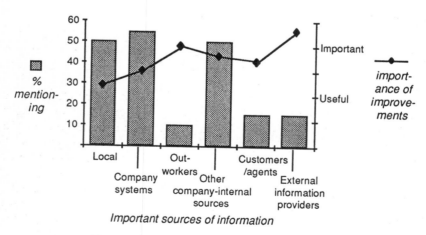

Figure 5.2 Many end-users draw on multiple sources of information

- Expert system to select cost-effective host and database
- Common command language
- Generation of synonyms
- Compatibility with text and graphics software
- Downloading for editing and re-formatting
- Recording and generation of detailed cost information
- Access to up to 30 hosts
- Connection via dial-up modem or autodialler
- Personal file generation

At a more mundane level, but equally important for office staff who have to deal with the messy reality of business activities, the workstation can also provide an escape route when the designers of a system are wrong-footed by unanticipated events. A cost accountant within the corporate reporting group mentioned above had to produce regular accounts for the financial controller based on returns from various parts of the business. These returns were entered by the originators directly into terminals connected to centralized computer systems, from where the cost accountant drew them into the departmental system, first to verify them and then to generate the report. Unfortunately, as a result of the company's policy of dispersal of head office staff, some staff were sent to far-flung parts of the corporate empire, where they did not have the means to enter the cost data directly. So they sent them in on paper and, of course, usually late. Hassle and/or red faces were avoided because the cost accountant was able to use Lotus 1-2-3 on his personal computer to patch the missing data into the report at the last minute.

Data and text are only a subset of information requirements

In the case I have just described, the data concerned should have been captured centrally, but circumstances intervened, as they inevitably do on occasions. But, added to that, the reality for most offices is that the data held on the mainframe computer is only a subset of the information that needs to be processed, because a great deal of information cannot satisfactorily or economically be captured as data or text. This category includes existing paper archives which have to be retained for lengthy periods for legal or other reasons, and for which manual re-keying would take far too much time and be much too expensive. It also includes current documents, generated internally or received from outside, which contain signatures, drawings or pictures, and which cannot be keyed in at all, or those which are simply too transient to be worth recording formally. Before the recent arrival of document image processing, information of this kind, estimated to comprise nearly two-thirds of the paperwork used in business, was partially or completely outside the reach of digital information systems.

By *document image processing*, I mean the capture and storage of information as images rather than as coded data or text. In addition, key information is associated with the stored images, so that they can be retrieved in a flexible manner for examination. These systems do not permit the detailed manipulation of images associated with computer-aided design applications, but they normally allow users to make changes which do not involve manipulation of the images, such as by annotating them or by 'stapling' several of them together electronically. They also assist with comparison and analysis, by enabling users to cut-and-paste portions of images on to different parts of the display screen. Sometimes images can also be drawn down into desktop publishing routines for editing prior to incorporation into documents.[2]

Data processing has always focussed on the more highly structured business activities. Word processing brought information systems into the less structured activities of document handling, and document image processing takes the process a step further. At the time of writing, the cost/performance of document image processing systems is improving rapidly. A number of suppliers are attempting to link the technology into standard personal computers. As the latter grow more powerful, the gap between them and the high-resolution workstations needed to handle images at an acceptable level of quality is beginning to close. This will give the technology further impetus. In fact, pushed in this way by the technology and pulled by the growing difficulties of working with all those paper files, it is reasonable to conclude that document image processing is unstoppable.

I have given space to document image processing because it demon-strates two important things that affect the infrastructure and the position of the workstation within it. First, it shows that some office staff will need very powerful devices on their desks to process information in this or similar forms. The proportion that will need to do so will, of course, vary from one organization to another, but the volume of paper in circulation in all offices is a sign that the potential everywhere is considerable. Furthermore, because of the high bandwidth needed to transmit document images (or similarly unstructured information) between storage devices and workstations, image files will probably be held on files held at department or site level, rather than on a large centralized facility. This makes the workstation, or the work group/departmental computer to which it is connected, the point at which incoming image and data information flows can be expected to converge.

Adaptability – the greatest prize?

The third contribution of the workstation – and, in view of widespread concern about the adaptability of data processing systems, perhaps the most significant one – is to insulate the information handling of end-users from some of the effects of business change. An anecdote will illustrate how it does this. In this particular case, a business team was using a work-group system consisting of advanced workstations networked to a shared processor which provided messaging and shared filing services. The shared processor, in turn, was linked through to the data centre.

At a time when the work-group system had been installed for some time and was in regular use, the data processing manager telephoned the user project manager to warn him that changes were afoot which would disrupt his plans seriously, and advised him to go and talk to his manager about it immediately. He did so, and discovered that a major reorganization was imminent. For the data processing manager this reorganization was a disaster, since he would have to devote many man-years of effort to restructuring data and applications, and he assumed that the work-group system would be hit just as severely. Having thought about it, the user manager realized that the impact was minimal.

What made the difference? Two things – the fact that they had developed their business applications in an evolutionary way, using the generic services provided by their work-group system, which had made these applications open-ended and adaptable; and the fact that they were using small subsets of data, drawn from the main files, then fed down for reprocessing on their work-group systems, which insulated them from most of the effects of the reorganization. Whereas, for example, products on the data processing files were identified by codes which would have to be revised to reflect the reallocation of responsibilities, products on the work-group system were identified by mnemonics, which were translated into codes automatically for transmission to the data centre. (They had done this because people had difficulty remembering the codes.) Thus they only needed to change the translation table, and applications and people were barely affected at all.

Now there may have been an element of good fortune in this, but there can be no doubt that the adaptability of information handling is improved as a result of workstations, and the work-group systems serving them, acting as a programmable buffer between end-users and the operational systems which supply much of the base data.

Steps towards an effective solution

To bring all this together, the situation facing an information systems department can be summarized as follows. The department's goal is to give its end-users access to the information they need to do their jobs – information that is reliable, relevant and complete, available in a timely manner and with a minimum of wasted effort. To achieve that it will probably have to re-structure existing data files, and then link those data files to tools on end-users' workstations which they can master with reasonable ease. Those tools must enable them to find the data they want from the re-structured files, *and* associate it as needed with data from other sources – keyed in from correspondence, perhaps, or retrieved from external data files, or from files of document images held within the department, or whatever. The difficulties to be faced are, first, that the tools available now fall some way short of the ideal and, second, that scarce resources – time, money and skills – will be called on to implement the various changes.

How a particular organization approaches the task will depend, of course, on the particular starting point and the particular requirements of its end-users, but it is possible to provide a framework, showing the main steps to be taken and the migration paths which can be followed, on to which most organization's requirements can be mapped. This is shown diagrammatically in Figure 5.3, and I elaborate below.

I have assumed the not uncommon starting point of data processing files poorly structured to meet end-users' information requirements, and end-users equipped with personal computers running applications packages such as *1-2-3* and *DBase III*, some also able to access the central files by emulating a display terminal. From this point, major progress is contingent on the central files being re-developed using an advanced

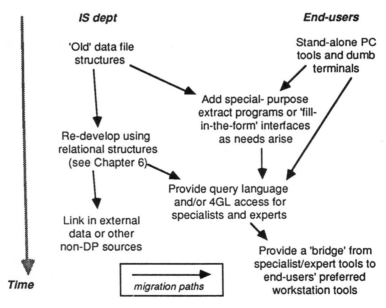

Figure 5.3 Major steps towards coherent access to information

database management system, as further discussed in Chapter 6. But prior to that major step, end-users' needs can be met as they arise by developing special-purpose extract programs to transfer subsets of the central files down to personal computers or to work-group systems, or by providing 'fill-in-the-form' interfaces through which end-users can obtain predetermined items of data.

The job of transferring data, obtained from central files by emulating dumb terminals, into personal computer packages can also be simplified. ICI, for example, has produced an interface routine called *Conductor*, which resides in an IBM PC. It can emulate IBM, DEC and videotex terminals and includes a template program that reformats the screen obtained from any of those sources into the format expected by *1-2-3*. (This also illustrates the role of the workstation as a means of combining data obtained from different sources.)

When the major step of re-developing the central files has been taken, information systems specialists, and those end-users with the motivation and skill to master them, will be able to use the query and applications development languages associated with the database management system to retrieve and manipulate the data. Where those tools prove too difficult for the majority of end-users to master, and this is generally the case at the time of writing, a further task remains. That is to provide a 'bridge' – a means of transferring data to and fro – between the new end-user data files and the tools which they **can** use on their workstations.

Once a satisfactory route has been established between usable data and usable tools for enquiry and manipulation, a further obstacle may be encountered. Different and incompatible tools may be used to obtain data from other sources, or to obtain information in other forms such as image. This brings us into the second dimension of integration – services – which I pick up in the next section.

Matching information handling tools to people

In the services dimension, the central aim of integration must be to make the equipment and its services easy for the generality of office workers to learn and to use. Bringing this about means a great deal more than substituting 'friendly' prompts and menus for the meaningless codes and command strings end-users have been subjected to in the past, although that is certainly a useful start. The human/computer interface must be designed from the ground up to fit the day-to-day working and thinking patterns of all office workers, not just the minority of enthusiasts and computerphiles.

We already have a working model of much of what is required in the form of Apple's Macintosh personal computer, which comes at the end of a long line of research and development that began in Xerox Corporation's Palo Alto Research Centre in the 1970s. The Macintosh at present is *at* the end rather than *the* end of the line of human/computer interface development. As I note later, it, and other established personal computers of today, also has significant limitations in other aspects of workstation performance that it is important to overcome.

Seeing where we want to be and actually getting there are, however, very different matters, and the history of data processing gives us a clear warning as we approach the task. A very old computer joke goes as follows. Question: *What is the definition of an elephant?* Answer: *A mouse with an operating system.* At the time, *mouse*[3] did not have the special meaning information technologists have since given to it, but that old joke could have been designed to remind us now of the danger we face. Try to cram too much into a desktop machine, and the operating system will grow and grow, and the responsive human-computer interface which the mouse helps to drive will quickly take on the clumsiness of an elephant.

Presentation management – the key to easier and wider use

Personal computers in general have turned the spotlight on the qualities of the human/computer interface, but none has taken a more radical and thorough-going approach to that problem than Apple's Macintosh. Attention has tended to focus on the unusual features of the Macintosh interface, such as the windows, the icons, the mouse, and the pull-down menus (which have given rise to the acronym WIMPs), but these in fact only play a part in a whole concept of what has now come to be called *presentation management*.

Apple's *User Interface Guidelines* for the Macintosh[4] explain the concept as follows:

> The Macintosh is designed to appeal to an audience of nonprogrammers, including people who have previously feared and mistrusted computers. To achieve this goal, Macintosh applications should be easy to learn and to use. To help people feel more comfortable with the applications, the application should build on skills that people already have, not force them to learn new ones. The user should feel in control of the computer, not the other way round. This is achieved in applications that embody three qualities: responsiveness, permissiveness, and consistency.
>
> Responsiveness means that the user's actions tend to have direct results. The user should be able to accomplish what needs to be done spontaneously and intuitively, rather than having to think: 'Let's see; to do C, first I have to do A and B and then ... '. For example, with pull-down menus, the user can choose the desired command directly and instantaneously. This is a typical Macintosh operation: the user moves the pointer to a location on the screen and presses the mouse button.
>
> Permissiveness means that the application tends to allow the user to do

anything reasonable. The user, not the system, decides what to do next. Also, error messages come up infrequently. . . .

The third and most important principle is consistency. Since Macintosh users usually divide their time among several applications, they would be confused and irritated if they had to learn a completely new interface for each application.

Consistency across applications is achieved largely through a range of user interface routines which are built into the Macintosh operating system. These include, for example, ways of selecting and editing text; mechanisms for initiating short dialogues with the user, such as to select a file from a list of those available, or to specify the parameters to be used to build a graph; mechanisms for handling 'windows' on the screen; mechanisms for defining and using pull-down menus.

The operating system also supports the transfer of information between applications. Items of information 'cut' or 'copied' from a document in one application are held on a 'clipboard' within the operating system and can then be 'pasted' into another document, either within the same application or in another one entirely. The application sending information to the clipboard can send it in a number of alternative formats – as text, as a picture, as postscript commands (the language used by the laser printer) or in a purely private format. The receiving application will elect to receive the information in whatever format, if any, suits it best. Thus a graphics program may send a text string out both as text and as a picture. Another graphics application might accept this as a picture, whereas a word processing application would take it as editable text. This feature is extremely important since it enables users to choose precisely (well, almost) those applications they prefer for particular tasks, without needing to worry whether they will work together or not. To produce the copy for this book, for example, I have used an outlining package, a word processing package and a drawing package all from different suppliers, transferring information quickly and painlessly between them whenever I wanted.

Two other features of the Macintosh are worth mentioning in the light of points made earlier about end-users' needs. I talked about the fragmented work style of many office workers, and especially managers, and the probability that tomorrow's users will spend less time on a wider range of applications than most of today's users, and wish to switch rapidly between them. A standard pull-down menu is always available on the Macintosh screen, containing a list of what are called 'desk accessories'. (This list can be amended according to preferences.) These are mini-applications that can be called up instantly from within the application that is currently running. They might include, for example, a calculator; a routine for updating a diary; a routine for finding an item of information from a library of 'boilerplate' text or graphics; a routine for sending an electronic mail message. After they have done their job, they disappear from the screen, and the user returns to the main application, which is found in exactly the same state that it was left in.

I also mentioned the need to accommodate both experts and novices. The Macintosh menus are easy for novices to come to terms with and can be accessed fairly rapidly, but a skilled typist, for example, often finds it irritating to have to reach for the mouse and then pick out a menu item, even for occasional operations such as cutting and pasting text. To make that unnecessary, any menu item can be assigned a command key combination (that is, the command key and another key, held down together). This is displayed within the menu alongside the identifying text, and expert users can use the command key option instead of going to the menu if they prefer. Particular applications may provide additional short-cuts activated by various key and mouse combinations.

The aim of the designers of the Macintosh has been to create, in the words of Apple's original sales slogan, 'the computer for the rest of us', a machine which intuition tells you how to drive, rather than an instruction manual. This is reflected in immediately obvious features of the interface – the initial screen resembling a desktop, the windows simulating overlapping sheets of paper, the icons identifying disks and files, the pull-down menus. But the Macintosh is much more than just a computer with a friendly face, its power lies in the way it manages the presentation of information to the user.

Personal computer operating software lacks key features

If the generality of office workers are to come to terms with computers on their desks, it is vital that presentation management features, such as those provided on the Macintosh, should be built into the workstation operating software. To appreciate this it is only necessary to compare the applications software available on the Macintosh with that available for the IBM PC. The PC has a simple operating system designed to operate within the limits of processing power and memory available on the early machines. It specifically lacks any presentation management features. As a result, applications developers have written some of these features into their programs. Much of the success of Lotus *1-2-3*, for example, derived from the mechanisms built into the package which enabled users to switch between its three modules. Other developers, faced with the limitations of the operating system, have chosen other methods to overcome them. The result is confusion for the user. A recent article reviewing desktop publishing compares Macintosh products with those available for the PC and reaches this conclusion:

> Aldus' *Pagemaker* program, which sticks rigidly to the Macintosh interface, ... reveals the deficiencies of the PC.
>
> Data cannot be moved easily from one PC program to another. Virtually every

PC program has a unique interface and, even where there have been attempts to emulate the Macintosh (Microsoft *Windows* and Digital Research *GEM*), interfaces are idiosyncratic and often keyboard oriented.[5]

On the Macintosh, by contrast, not only is a coherent set of presentation management features built into the operating software, it is further reinforced by applications design guidelines published by Apple. In combination, these measures make it difficult for lazy or idiosyncratic applications software developers to cut corners or needlessly invent their own private rules. Furthermore, applications which conform to the rules are genuinely easier to use, so that users are reluctant to adopt non-conforming software. The overall result is that learning times and training costs for Macintosh applications are markedly lower. A recent report from the Gartner Group (commissioned, I should add, by Apple) looked at the learning effort incurred by end-users as they moved from one personal computer application to another and portrayed the difference between PC and Macintosh users as shown in Figure 5.4. They also found that the average Macintosh user had mastered far more applications than the average PC user.

As the quote above indicates, the Macintosh features have been emulated[6] in software products such as Microsoft *Windows* and Digital Research *GEM*, which can be overlaid on the operating system of IBM PCs and similar machines. These products undoubtedly improve the human/computer interface on these machines considerably, but, as we all know, Porsche bodywork on a Volkswagen chassis is no match for a Porsche all the way through. *Windows* has had some commercial success, but few PC applications are designed to operate under it.

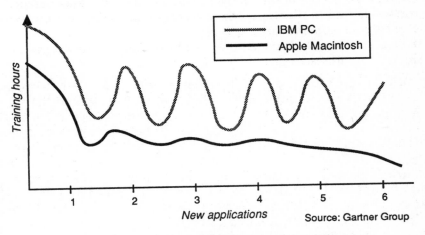

Figure 5.4 A consistent human/computer interface cuts learning effort

OS/2, the operating system (developed in co-operation with Microsoft) for IBM's new range of machines, includes a presentation management module. As with *Windows*, applications developers can decide whether or not to use this. Time will tell how many take the trouble to do so. Corporate purchasers can help them to make the right decision, and help their businesses at the same time, by refusing to endorse personal computer packages that do not conform to a preferred presentation management interface.

Overcoming the single-user, single-task restriction

The excellent human/computer interface of the Macintosh, shared to a degree by popular packages for the IBM PC, such as Lotus *1-2-3*, derives to a large extent from the fact that all the resources of the machine are dedicated to the task in hand, namely serving the user sitting at the machine. In other words, these are essentially single-user, single-task machines. This is the source of their strength, but it is also their weakness. On a strictly single-task machine, an application cannot be started up then left to get on with a lengthy task (such as printing a report) in the background, while the user continues with another task (such as entering more text) in the foreground; nor can data be retrieved from a shared filing system without forcing the user to wait, perhaps for some time, until the reply arrives.

As I explain further below, it is possible to get round some of these limitations of a single-task machine without interfering with its basic mode of operation, and for some users improvements such as these may well be all they will ever need. But the limitations of single-task operation are cruelly exposed in situations where machines are used by groups of end-users to cooperate in shared activities.

We can distinguish three basic ways of overcoming the single-task limitation of a workstation.

- A *virtual screen* routine divides up the memory and shares it between a number of applications, all of which are started up and held in memory, but only one of which controls and occupies the screen and keyboard at any one time. To switch from one application to another, the user either presses a function key, or points at an icon on the screen and clicks the mouse button, whereupon the application in control is 'parked' in its current state, and the newly selected application takes over in whatever state it had been 'parked' in last. This enables the user to switch rapidly between applications when interrupted, for example, by a phone call. This can be implemented on a single-task machine, as it has on the Macintosh, in which case the application in control monopolizes the machine, and the others sit passively waiting to be brought back into operation.

- In *foreground/background* operation, the foreground application controls the screen and keyboard, while another application, previously started up by the foreground application, operates unseen (except perhaps for slowing up foreground operation slightly) in the background, 'stealing' processing power from the foreground application to carry out operations not requiring interaction with the user, such as to drive a printer. This, again, can be achieved on a single-task machine.
- In full-scale *multi-tasking*, more than one application may reside in the machine at a time, with one of them in control of screen and keyboard, as in *foreground/background* operation. In a sophisticated arrangement, the foreground application would control the keyboard plus the active 'window' on the screen; windows belonging to background applications might also be on the screen, overlaid by the active window. Additionally, each application can start up a number of tasks which run under its control in parallel and which can communicate with one another. Thus a file management application, for example, could collect parameters input by the user to update a file, then start up a new task to physically alter the file, returning immediately to the user to continue input. More commonly, multi-tasking is used by applications servicing a number of users at once, as for example a file management routine on a shared departmental machine. Multi-tasking enables it to service requests for access to the files as they arrive and process them concurrently, rather than forming them into a queue and processing them serially.

It is possible to construct multi-user systems, to share access to departmental files for example, by linking a number of single-user workstations to a shared filing system. But problems arise with this arrangement when users need to update shared files concurrently. Mechanisms to guard against the risk of cross-updating (i.e. user A retrieves a record which user B already has, then updates it after user B, thereby obliterating B's update) are difficult to organize, particularly if file structures are complex. Thus transaction processing applications and any other applications which demand intensive access to shared files depend on multi-tasking features in the software managing the files. This will normally reside in a shared processor, with complementary features (such as to activate locks on data records that are about to be updated) built into the software residing in the workstation.

As far as the workstation itself is concerned, however, full multi-tasking can be regarded as a luxury rather than an essential for the vast majority of applications. From the end-user's viewpoint, two things are important, summarized in Figure 5.5. The first of these is presentation management, which enforces consistency across applications and makes it possible to switch painlessly between them. Additionally, network

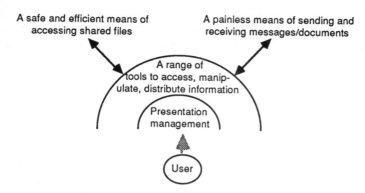

**Figure 5.5 The services dimension – user
requirements summarized**

attachment should be integrated into the operating software, so that
users can send or receive messages, access shared files, initiate long print
runs, or send data files to others, without locking up their workstation for
lengthy periods or invoking clumsy procedures.

Options have varying strengths and weaknesses

If we review the main options available now and in immediate prospect,
against these requirements, we find that they have varying strengths and
weaknesses

THE INTEGRATED APPLICATIONS PACKAGE

As already indicated, the integrated applications package, such as Lotus
1-2-3, offers a limited range of applications designed to work together. Its
weaknesses are apparent as soon as you move outside the confines of
those integrated applications, or of the various add-on products that
extend them. To obtain data from central files, for example, you may
have to leave 1-2-3 and load a data communication application, trans-
form the data into a form suitable for 1-2-3, then reload it and bring in the
data. It is possible, of course, to extend the range of integrated applications, as Lotus indeed did when it produced 1-2-3's big brother,
Symphony. But you are still limited to applications produced by one
particular supplier. Furthermore, there are limits to what can be achieved
through this form of integration, and some people believe that those
limits have already been strained in *Symphony*. The corporate reporting
group mentioned earlier, for example, decided to stay with 1-2-3, rather
than move up to *Symphony*, even though the extra functions were
valuable to them, because they thought *Symphony* was too difficult to
learn. And, even with an acceptable integrated package, you are still left
with the restriction of single-user working. Staff wishing to work jointly

on a shared document or a shared spreadsheet can only do so by exchanging data and working on that data individually and serially.

Integrated applications, then, as their market success has demonstrated, are certainly acceptable as temporary solutions. They can continue to serve well only in situations where there is no great need for close interworking or for frequent access to sources of information external to the workstation, and where the range of functions included is enough to meet requirements.

THE WORKSTATION PRESENTATION MANAGER

I used Apple's Macintosh to illustrate the function of a presentation manager. In the case of the Macintosh, presentation management is fully integrated into the operating system. *OS/2*, the new operating system for IBM's PS/2 range, successor to the PC, also includes a presentation manager, designed as part of the operating system but not totally integrated into it.

The great advantage of having presentation management built into the operating system is that applications from different suppliers can easily be made to work together, and that they present a consistent interface to the user. The cost is mainly incurred by the suppliers of applications software, both because packages that use presentation management are more expensive to develop and because it becomes more difficult for them to lock customers in to their own range of products.

In the case of the Macintosh, some of the marginal disadvantages of a single-user machine remain, in that it is not yet able to communicate with other systems or access shared files as effortlessly as one would wish. *OS/2* promises to remove these limitations also, but only for those applications specifically designed or re-engineered to exploit the new features of the operating software. However, we do not yet know how well *OS/2* will perform. My worry is that the cost of *OS/2*'s extra power will be incurred not by the software suppliers but by the user – the 'mouse with an operating system' syndrome I referred to above. Time will reveal all, but meantime purchasers should be cautious.

THE SHARED 'OFFICE' CONTROLLER

A third approach, represented by products such as Digital's *All-in-1*, effectively takes some aspects of presentation management out of the workstation and places them in a shared computer to which the workstations are connected. This shared machine controls the access of individual workstations to services, via menus displayed on workstation screens; handles communication with remote machines and messaging services; and runs shared applications, such as to maintain departmental files.

From this outline it can be seen that this is a good option for work groups that interwork closely and rely heavily on data and message communication. Since it provides a standard mechanism for accessing the full range of services available, it helps users to find what they want and to switch easily between applications. But users are still left with the problem that individual applications may operate in an inconsistent manner. If a personal computer is used as workstation, for example, the user switches out of the office controller menu into the personal computer operating environment to run standard personal computer applications, then back again when required.

But this arrangement nowhere near matches the presentation management of a machine like the Macintosh. Considerable power is needed to drive a sophisticated human/computer interface like that, and this cannot practically be delivered from a shared machine. Even with the limited presentation management features provided by a product like *All-in-1*, the shared machine can easily run into performance problems. This happens because end-user systems, unlike more predictable transaction processing applications, tend to put sporadic heavy loads on the shared computer. Centering the presentation management tasks in the workstation is both more satisfactory from the end-user's viewpoint, and reduces the risk that the shared machine will become overloaded.

Match sets of services to users, not vice versa

The ideal solution would be a seamless (in other words, the join does not show) combination of the shared controller with a workstation with Macintosh-like presentation management. The shared controller – perhaps a departmental machine, perhaps a large, centralized machine – provides the multi-tasking capability needed to share files and handle message traffic, while the workstation concentrates on looking after the user at the machine. At the time you are reading this book, such a solution may well be available, perhaps out of the cooperation of DEC with Apple, of Microsoft with IBM, or from a specialist in office or departmental systems.

It is certainly right to set such an arrangement as a target and as a model, but for a number of reasons which I come on to, it cannot serve as a universal prescription. I can anticipate a time when equipment costs will have reached a level at which all office workers in sizeable businesses will have a workstation, with a communications link to other workstations and to shared departmental or corporate machines, but most companies are some way short of that point as yet. And I *cannot* anticipate a time when they will all want a workstation of the same type. Office workers have a range of different jobs and, what is more, even those in similar jobs adopt different attitudes to the tools that they use. A manager with DEC's internal systems group describes their experience:

The usual approach to allocating desktop devices was to list the job types within the company and then look at the main characteristics of each job. These characteristics were then matched to the most appropriate desktop device. When this exercise was completed the final list looked something like this:

Job	Desktop device
Secretary	Word processor
Data entry clerk	Display terminal
Salesman	Small PC
Specialist	Powerful PC
Manager	Expensive PC

... Such a list was a useful starting point and identified suitable devices for a large percentage of the user population. However, it caused significant problems for others who found themselves with inappropriate equipment. In many companies – DEC UK included – managers gave their PCs to secretaries and used the secretaries' word processors themselves. Others swapped expensive PCs for simple terminals. All part of a whole range of equipment exchanges and movements – including non-use.[7]

Added to this human unpredictability, certain types of staff will sometimes want special applications which are not available on the standard equipment, and which, for good business reasons, they are reluctant to forgo. This may require a range of different workstations, matched to the needs of different types of staff, to be linked together into a single system. Figure 5.6 shows an example of such a system, installed by GTE in the US.

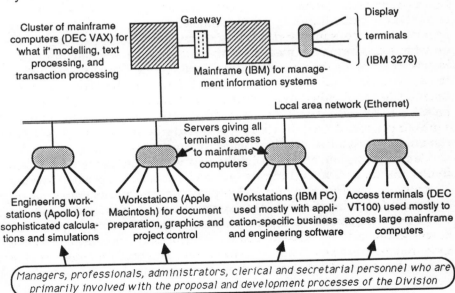

Figure 5.6 A work-group system employing several different types of workstation

We are certainly a long way from the end of the story as far as work-stations are concerned. Many new applications that will give particular types of office workers just what they need are even now being worked on by specialist companies hoping to conquer the market with a new approach. Some of them will certainly succeed.

The moral of all this is that the infrastructure must be a framework which allows you to match sets of services, available via a range of workstations, to different types of user. It should not be a straitjacket based on too rigid a prescription of user requirements. The local area network included in GTE's configuration is one way of achieving this flexibility, and I elaborate on this and other methods in later chapters.

From interconnection to interworking

Every office worker relies on exchanging information in a controlled and timely manner. Interconnection of end-user devices by various forms of telecommunications systems plays a part in this, and, because of its chronic difficulties, has often dominated specialists' attention. But inter-connection alone is not a solution, nor is interconnection a prerequisite for interworking – paper and mail, for all their faults, still serve many communication purposes quite adequately.

Interworking depends not only on a satisfactory connection between two workstations (or between a workstation and a computer system serving as intermediary). It also depends on a common understanding between the parties involved on how information is to be exchanged and on what the information means. If interconnection is the telephone call, interworking is the dialogue between the callers. Here, just as much as in the confused domain of interconnection, different methods of represent-ing information handled by computers have created a potential Tower of Babel.

As the protracted efforts of the standards-making bodies have shown, to define universal interconnection standards is a mammoth task, and for user organizations to implement those standards no less so. Interworking, as I have indicated, is another long step even beyond interconnection. The only practical approach, therefore, as I elaborate in this section, is to be selective. A universal form and level of service right across an organization is neither necessary nor desirable. Support for interworking must be tailored to suit the particular community involved – the nature of the exchanges between the members and the benefits derived by changing today's communication habits.

Technology extends the business communication options

The term *electronic mail* was coined in the early excitement about office automation and its potential for improving office productivity. Since then, we have seen the economic obstacles in the path of providing such a service at a corporate level steadily decline. Costs, reflected in the price of communications bandwidth and interfacing equipment, have not yet reached an insignificant level, but at least they have shrunk to a secondary element in the equation. But while the straight cost barriers have declined, other technical barriers, associated with the problem of interfacing equipment from different suppliers, have proved far less tractable. 'If only we could solve the interconnection problem ... ', office automation and telecommunications specialists have been intoning tragically for years now. What they sometimes seem to imply is that, were the interconnection barrier to fall, we would sweep onward into the new era of integrated information systems.

Meantime, it has become clear that the term *electronic mail*, like the term *office automation* which it grew out of, does not do justice to the possibilities. It suggests that our aim is to replace physical mail with an electronic, and therefore faster and cheaper, substitute. This indeed we can do, and those benefits are always welcome, if often less than mind-blowing. But, by supporting the methods office workers use to communicate, we can gain other benefits of a different order. We can improve the effectiveness of their exchange of information, particularly within close-knit working groups. What is more, by linking mechanisms for the exchange of information in electronic form with mechanisms for electronic storage and retrieval, we can reduce paper handling and enable people to use information more effectively to carry out their tasks.

I must make the important proviso that organizational culture and a number of other non-technical factors determine how and whether people within an organization communicate with one another.[8] That said, technology can help them to do so, when they are so minded. Communication is the backbone of all business activities, and information technology is becoming a pervasive presence, not only in data centres and on desktops, but also on the shop floor and in warehouses. Hence there are a growing number of situations in which technology can usefully be adopted, and a variety of ways in which it can contribute. But, in planning how to support business communication, we must be careful to view it as a whole, and avoid falling into the trap of seeing it solely in terms of opportunities for souping up existing media.

Business communication can conveniently be divided into two categories. There is informal communication, which I deal with later, and formal, documented communication, which provides a record of business transactions, decision-making processes and decisions. This category can be further divided into real time (relatively speaking) transfer of information, such as by mail or telex, and deferred information transfer. The latter is achieved through records management that retains information on file for retrieval later when it is needed. Since information technology has been heavily involved in one way and another with formal business systems, its main contribution so far has been to formal communication. Predominantly, this has been achieved via printed computer reports, often generated as a by-product of transaction processing, sometimes requested and produced *ad hoc*. The main drawback of these reports is that the end-user has only limited control over their content and presentation. Too often, the result is 'too much data, too little information' – the proverbial foot-high pile of printout that has to be searched to glean a few items of information. More recently, new modes of communication have been developed which overcome this limitation and add new capabilities. In summary, these are as follows:

- *Transfer of data files*, either electronically or by physical exchange of storage media such as floppy disks. This is a step toward overcoming the problem of 'too much data, too little information', since, given the right tools, the receiver can manipulate the data to produce precisely the information that is required.

- *Electronic messaging*, serving as a cheaper, faster, and more convenient substitute for mail and telex. The two methods of communication mentioned above – printed reports and file transfer – are essentially one-way, and therefore unhelpful where two or more people need to interact with one another. Electronic messaging, by contrast, is a conversational medium which can support a degree of interaction, although not of the same intensity as can be achieved via the informal communication systems outlined below.

- *Electronic bulletin boards* – whereas electronic messaging supports communication one-to-one or one-to-few, these support one-to-many communication. They are used for volatile information which many others need to refer to, such as booking availability details or lists of consultants on call in a hospital.

- *Shared filing*, enabling a work group jointly engaged in a common set of tasks to both enter and retrieve information relating to those tasks – for example, a team of repair engineers maintaining a shared log of repair calls, diagnostics and details of repairs carried out. Here, the interactive quality of electronic messaging is combined with the records management power associated with data processing systems. To date, shared filing has mainly been used for keyed information – data and text. Recently, however, a number of systems have been installed that store and retrieve visual information, such as page images of documents, signatures, maps and street plans.

Office workers rely heavily on informal methods of communication –

face-to-face meetings and telephony – to deal with many of the challenging problems they face. It is easy, in the excitement of discovering the new options for formal communication which information technology opens up, to lose sight of this reality. So far, at least, information technology support for informal business communication is in its infancy. This is partly because the technology is less mature, partly because poorly understood sociological factors condition acceptance. This category includes:

- *Computer conferencing*, enabling a large number of contributors to establish a meeting of minds, non-synchronously and perhaps over an extended period of time. The system keeps a full record of all public contributions, indexed by topic, that can be referred to by participants when they wish.[9]
- A range of *meeting support* tools is being experimented with, which provide support either at or between face-to-face meetings.[10]
- *Voice mail* – electronic messaging using dictated voice rather than keyboard-entered text.[11]
- *Video conferencing*, as a substitute for face-to-face meetings. There is a growing number of variants and sophistications, including full-motion or the much cheaper freeze-frame, and options to integrate foreground or background visuals with the video image.[12]

Only a limited number of organizations are achieving worthwhile benefits from technologies such as these at present, but I have no doubt they will become a great deal more important in future. However, there is still much to be learnt about their application. They also stand apart from the family of technologies supporting formal communications outlined earlier, and from the established data processing systems, which means that their influence on the infrastructure is peripheral. For these reasons, I leave them aside from now on and concentrate on formal communications.

Before I do so, it is worth noting a key difference between these recently arrived business communication technologies and the one we are all familiar with – the telephone system. The telephone instrument is a relatively simple device, serving firstly to establish a connection and then as a passive transmission medium. In the formal communication systems outlined above, the role of the instrument used for access – the workstation – is much greater. It provides the flexibility necessary to make the communication system usable in a variety of work situations. (Some of these facilities can be, and sometimes are, built into the computer system that provides the service, rather than performed by the workstation, but this is a hangover from the time when terminals lacked the necessary intelligence. The workstation is the logical place to put them.) The key tasks it performs are as follows:

- It provides a 'scratchpad' – a private area in which messages or documents can be assembled, checked and edited before they are committed to the system.
- It provides the link with personal or departmental applications, enabling data or text extracts to be transferred to and from these without undue effort.
- It gives the user the freedom to decide the best means of distributing or filing the information received – in softcopy or hardcopy form; in a different format, such as a graph or histogram.

Messaging is the key to formal communications

An electronic messaging service is the foundation on which support for formal communication is built. It serves not only as a vehicle for exchanging messages such as have been carried for years via telex, but also as a vehicle for exchanging documents. This is because documents rather than messages are the basis for a great deal of internal business communication. The reasons for providing a messaging service are now widely appreciated, but it is important to see it as a building block in an overall scheme for interworking, rather than just as a messaging service. First, let me summarize briefly what its contribution is.

A range of software products are available on personal computers to support communication of text or data. To use these for communication between two such machines, you have to go through an elaborate procedure something like this:

- First you ring the other user and ask them to start a communications program on their personal computer.
- You then ring up their personal computer to establish a direct tele-communications link between the machines.
- Next, you start up the communications program in your machine to initiate and carry out the transfer.
- On completion of the transfer, the recipient may then have further work to do to get the message on to the screen or into whatever form is appropriate to act on it.

The first and most obvious contribution of the messaging service is to co-ordinate such a process automatically, and, by acting as intermediary, remove the need for the communicating parties to synchronize their activities. Normally, users of a messaging service adopt the discipline of looking in their electronic mailboxes two or three times a day, just as they might look in their in-tray. Some services (often relying on special-purpose equipment rather than standard personal computers) can additionally put up a warning signal on the screen as soon as an urgent message is received.

On top of that, the messaging service may act as an 'honest broker', so that messages can be exchanged between unlike devices. It is common for a messaging service to be linked, on a two-way basis, to the telex service, which is still the medium of choice for urgent external business communications. A link to the telex system also enfranchises those within an organization who do not have workstations and/or a means of connecting to the messaging service, but who are within reach of a telex machine. Similarly, an in-house messaging service can be linked to external, public services.

From an organizational point of view, an electronic messaging service has the further advantage that the users themselves can collect messages from anywhere that suits them, provided of course that they have access to a workstation and a telecommunications connection. This removes a constraint on staff mobility, which may be invaluable in special circumstances, and, in general, increases organizational flexibility.

Gains such as these, together with straight cost savings, often provide the initial justification for a messaging service, but they are only the beginning. In those organizations that have made a success of messaging, the service eventually becomes the vehicle for access to a range of other services. DEC, for example, whose in-house electronic messaging system is one of the largest in the world, built its initial service as purely an internal messaging service, with links to telex. Before long, the limitations of the service became apparent, and it was upgraded.

> The new mail products ... opened up new paths of communication. For example, ... the mail agent can be used not only to transmit and receive ordinary messages, but also to transmit compound documents containing colour graphics, word processing, or even entire data files, and with no limitations on size. The mail agent can even be used to start up jobs on remote computers, and then mail the results back to the originator or to anyone else on the mail system.
> ... To be successful with electronic mail it is vital to integrate it into current and future computing and telecoms services, rather than treating it as a stand alone service.[13]

The nature of the 'future computing and telecoms services' into which electronic messaging is integrated naturally varies, from organization to organization and over time. But two particular features of the service serve to keep the vital options open. One of them is that the messaging service does not differentiate between messages and documents. To do so creates artificial barriers between communication activities that are basically similar.

The second feature is that it should be possible for users to send blocks of information to one another across the messaging service transparently. A user sending such a block specifies the addressee in the same way as for a text message, then sends the block using an error-checking protocol of some kind that is completely independent of the contents of the block. The receiver collects the block in the same way. The purpose of this is to free users from whatever information handling constraints are built into the communication protocols used by the messaging service. At present, these generally expect commands and messages to consist of printable text characters, so that special arrangements such as I have outlined are needed to send, for example, program code or a document image. The constraints built into messaging protocols will ease as standards advance, but they are always likely to be behind the latest generation of equipment and software in use somewhere within an organization.

Document retrieval is not the same as data retrieval

As suggested above, shared filing opens up the opportunity to improve the handling of business information, rather than just its distribution. Moreover, the potential scope of shared filing systems is extending to include new forms of information, such as page images and maps. Data processing systems, of course, have provided facilities for shared access to data files for some time. Some shared filing in the office will be data processing writ small, and in those cases the data processing experience is entirely relevant. Much of it, however, will be different in an important respect. While data files are highly structured, and can be searched using precise search criteria, many of the electronic shared files that are being established in the office now, and that will be established there in the future, are less highly structured. Their structures will approximate more closely to the structures of the manual records management systems that they are beginning to replace.

The difference is apparent if you consider the nature of access to data files, as compared with access to document files. A data retrieval system directly answers an enquirer's question, for example: *What were total sales of widgets in Brazil last month?* Document retrieval, by contrast, is more indirect, for example: *What reports do we have which discuss our main competitor's marketing posture?* The system responds by finding those documents which *might* satisfy the enquirer. The differences are summed up in Figure 5.7, taken from a paper by an academic specialist in document management.[14]

Techniques such as associative (for example, ICL's Content Addressable File Store – *CAFS*) and free text retrieval (for example, IBM's *STAIRS*)have been developed to help to meet the novel requirements posed by document management, but they only help, they do not entirely bridge the gap. It remains for the designer of a system to think through (and perhaps verify in a prototyping stage) just how users will want to retrieve information, so that the most helpful information can be included in the title and other primary key fields used to identify

Data Retrieval	Document Retrieval
Direct retrieval that answers the enquirer's question: typical query is specific ("I want to know X")	Indirect retrieval that provides or refers to a set of documents which will *likely* contain what the enquirer wants: typical query is general or topical ("I want to know about X")
Necessary relation between the request and the correct answer (hence, data retrieval systems are deterministic)	Probabilistic relation between the request and a satisfactory answer (hence, document retrieval systems are non-deterministic)
Criterion of successful retrieval: *correctness of answer* (Objective: "Does the system answer the enquirer's question correctly?")	Criterion of successful retrieval: *utility* (Subjective: "Does the system answer the enquirer's need?")

Figure 5.7 The differences between data retrieval and document retrieval

documents. In document image processing systems, for example, all the identifying information must be captured explicitly, so this task is vital. The paper from which Figure 5.7 is taken gives an example which illustrates the point:

> ... a document retrieval system was developed to keep track of the substantial number of documents (engineering drawings, purchase orders, subcontracts, correspondence, receipts, etc) which were generated during the course of a large construction project. Since the major documents (drawings, orders, receipts and subcontracts) all had unique numbers associated with each of them, the system designers felt that these numbers should be the primary access points to the documents on the data base. Unfortunately, after the the system was built, it was discovered that the users could rarely remember (or find) the exact number associated with a desired drawing, order, receipt, or subcontract. In fact, over 80 percent of the searches were based on subject descriptions - an access point not well developed in the system.

Document management skills needed to deal with design issues such as these are often possessed by records management specialists dispersed throughout the organization. But these are people who have been brought up in a paper-oriented world. Both their skills and those of information technology specialists must be brought to bear on shared filing projects. Often, an educational programme will be needed to upgrade skills on both sides and bring them together.

Importance of the directory

As electronic methods of exchanging information spread, so the directory function becomes more important. In preparation, it is very important to define all the addressing rules clearly and to agree on the one source of directory data. Two factors bear on how this is done – the size of the organization and of its electronic messaging community, and the diversity of the computing environment.

DEC, claiming the largest electronic messaging network in the world, believes that the ease with which a message can be addressed is a significant factor affecting the level of use. They have developed a world-wide addressing scheme, based on DEC's *Message Router* software. The sender of a message types the recipient's first and last name, followed by a three-character location code, and the network does the rest, including looking up in the directory which type of mail system the recipient would like his message delivered to. This makes it possible to send messages via external messaging systems, such as *Dialcom* in the US and *Telecom Gold* in the UK. The location code is essential within DEC because of the scale of the system – 60,000 accounts worldwide, including 36 J Smiths! In a smaller system it would be quite practical to hold an organization-wide directory on every messaging computer.

DEC, as an information systems supplier itself, does not not have to face the problem that bedevils many organizations – the problem of catering for equipment from a number of different suppliers. Where a number of different operating environments are in use, the only practical approach may be to establish a directory within each operating environment separately, and then progressively link these together, rather than to attempt to establish an organization-wide directory in one go. I go into the mechanics of this in more detail later, in Chapter 7,

Start with services aimed at identified groups

So far, I have tried to summarize potential rather than actual requirements. Most office workers have some need to exchange information electronically, but only a minority have a regular and frequent requirement such as justifies the initial installation of electronic messaging or the related services outlined above. This does not only affect how the cost of installation is justified, it also raises the practical problem of getting the service used. The value to an individual of a messaging service, or any other means of supporting interworking, depends on the number of other people that he or she can usefully communicate with via that service. The problem is to make sure that a critical mass of users is established at an early stage. Thereafter momentum can be maintained by extending the service to other users, and by enhancing the service itself to increase intensity of use.

Both experience and common sense suggest that it is best to pick out those groups that can gain great value from electronic communication, and target services specifically at them, rather than to attempt from the outset to provide a uniform level of service on a wider front. Once a number of the targeted groups have become confirmed users, they are likely to constitute a critical mass for a wider service. How do you pick out the target groups? Figure 5.8 gives a weighted list of characteristics of

Characteristic of group	Weight
Nature of their work patterns { Complex relationships	Important
High competitive/external pressures	Important
Widespread geographically or mobile	Important
High and regular intercommunication	Important
Nature of the information they exchange { Volatile	At least one of these is crucial
Time-sensitive	
Need to match information	
High administration costs	Important
Nature of the environment { Suitable terminals already in place	Influential
Easy to extend beyond initial service	Influential

Figure 5.8 Characteristics of work groups that imply a need for electronic messaging

work groups that make them potential targets for electronic messaging and related services.

Setting priorities

For organizations that have already made good progress in building an infrastructure around the workstation, such as I have just described, the next step they should take may well be obvious. But those not so far advanced, faced with what is obviously a major and protracted effort, may justifiably ask *where do I start?* Not only is this a big job in itself, it is usually complicated by the need to wean end-users off the equipment they have learned to live with, often at considerable personal effort. To be saleable both to the end-users affected and to senior management, it must be seen as driven by business needs and not as indulgence in technology for its own sake.

The task demands all the technology management skills, technical judgement and political adroitness that information systems departments, and other staff involved with information systems in business, have built up over the years. I cannot hope to convey all that accumulated wisdom through the pages of this book, but I can give you some guidelines, based on my experience and that of leading-edge organizations, and here they are.

Target highly motivated work groups

When embarking on a difficult and high-profile task, such as this certainly is, it is natural to look round for a low-risk entry point. Low-key experiments may appear to be a less risky way of building expertise, but experience shows that projects involving knowledge workers are most likely to succeed where they are driven by genuine business problems.

The main reason for this is that success depends heavily on a sustained commitment from end-users. The point is that end-users themselves must discover the potential of the new systems, because they change procedures, communication patterns and working relationships in ways that cannot easily be predicted beforehand. Where a new system is seen as a tool for dealing with a particular business problem *and* is an appropriate vehicle for dealing with it, this process of discovery usually takes place, and the system succeeds.

Where the system is seen only as a more efficient substitute for existing support systems or, worse still, as a practice run, there is no drive on the part of the principals concerned – professionals, managers, clerical supervisors – to discover its potential. Often the initiative is delegated early on to support staff. In these circumstances, not surprisingly, their priorities come to dominate, and the opportunity to achieve something more substantial than shave a few per cent off administrative costs is lost. Often, all concerned console themselves with the thought *it was a useful pilot exercise*, and office operations, if they ever diverged from normal, return to the familiar groove.

This means that, whatever line of attack you decide on, you must choose your targets for the key projects carefully. By *key projects*, I mean those that advance the state of the art within the organization and, if successful, form a model for others to emulate. You should look particularly for groups of knowledge workers under pressure to improve performance, such as those I described in Chapter 1. Initially, you should go for those work groups also needing ready access to structured data, because here you are likely to find specific applications with clear business benefits that today's technology can handle comfortably.

If the people in the work group are enthusiasts for information technology, that is an extra bonus, but this is not an essential ingredient. Provided at least that they are not actively resistant to change, their enthusiasm will grow out of understanding what the technology can contribute to business and personal objectives. This does, however, demand a major education and training effort at the outset of any project that breaks new ground.[15]

Prioritize dimensions and concentrate on one at a time

As I explained in Chapter 2, the four generic strategies for information technology reflect the distinct forces driving businesses of different kinds. These same driving forces influence the priorities different organizations attach to making progress along one or other of the three dimensions of integration requirements.

The information access dimension is the key to everything else. Unless knowledge workers can obtain the information they need to do their jobs, all the rest is futile. So all organizations must make an effort here. The effort should be targeted where success and business benefits are most likely to be attained, as I have just indicated.

Beyond that, high-linkage companies should give priority to the interworking dimension, so that they can improve co-ordination across functional boundaries and increase the responsiveness of the business as a whole. For information intensive companies, by contrast, the services dimension is critical. Their priority should be to improve their ability to manage complexity, by making sure that the best possible information handling tools are available to those that require them.

The generic strategies, then, provide a simple framework for assigning priorities that correspond with underlying business needs. To avoid being overwhelmed by the complexity of the task, it is advisable to concentrate development efforts on one dimension of integration needs at a time, so building up the infrastructure step by step.

Beware the Swiss army knife principle

Finally, a warning to avoid the ever-present danger of going too far, of over-engineering solutions to the extent that they become unusable.

Mitch Kapor, former Chairman of Lotus Development Corporation, originators of 1-2-3, spoke to the Financial Times' Personal Computer Conference in 1984 about the limits to integration. Referring to Lotus' successor product to 1-2-3, he said:

> I believe that a product like *Symphony* illustrates that there is some reality to the Swiss army knife principle. Let me explain what I mean. The Swiss army knife, at least in the US, is one of these pocket knives that has about 42 blades in it, little scissors and a tiny magnifying glass, a tooth pick and a few other things. There does come a certain point at which trying to stuff all possible applications that everybody is ever going to want into a single product is not going to take over the world. *Symphony* illustrates the reality of that because, fortunately ... 80 per cent of the product is coherently focused on doing the best possible job in an integrated fashion for the quantitatively-oriented user. That is why it is successful – because it is successful in integrating the right thing.

The moral is to include no more blades on the knife than the organization really needs. In other words, go for the simplest solution that integrates 80 per cent or so of the most important needs.

Notes and references

1   For a succinct review of database technology and product trends, see Robert M. Curtice and William Casey, 'Database: what's in store?', *Datamation*, Dec 1 1985.
2   For an introduction, see Connie Moore, 'Image processing offers MIS a new view of information', *Computerworld*, Jun 23 1986, pp. 69-84.
3   *Mouse* is the term used to describe the device that is rolled about on the desktop to control the cursor and to access pull-down menus. It is one part of the intuitive human-computer interface that I am about to describe in more detail.
4   *Inside Macintosh Volume I* (Addison-Wesley)
5   Phil Manchester, 'Macintosh – made to measure?', *Computer Weekly*, Jan 14 1988, pp.36-37.
6   To avoid phone calls from litigious lawyers, I should make clear that I take no position on who copied whose interface. I say 'emulate' because the presentation management concept is similar.
7   Malcolm Wicks, *Management Workstations – Myth or Magic* (Digital Equipment Co Ltd, 1986).
8   See, for example, Rosabeth Kanter's *The Change Masters* (George Allen & Unwin, 1984) for a description of the differing internal communication patterns in what she terms 'integrative' and 'segmentalist' organizations.
9   For a succinct summary, see 'Computer conferencing lets users have meetings of the mind', *Information Week*, July 21 1986, pp. 48-51.
10   See Robert Johansen, *User approaches to computer-supported teams*, CISR Working Paper No. 155 (MIT, 1987).
11   See Johanna Ambrosio, 'Electronic and voice mail: they're no match for each other – yet', *Computerworld*, May 19 1986, pp. 53-55.
12   See 'Internal "market research" program is yielding successful video-conferencing for ARCOvision' and 'Exploring the various technologies used for video-conferencing', *Communications News*, Feb 1986, pp. 48-54.
13   Malcolm Wicks, *DEC's experience with electronic mail* (Digital Equipment Company Ltd, 1986).
14   David C. Blair, 'The Management of Information: Basic Distinctions', *Sloan Management Review*, vol. 26, no. 1, pp. 13-23.
15   For more on techniques for success with work-group systems, see Chapter 6 in my book *End user focus* (Prentice Hall, 1988).

DISTRIBUTING PROCESSING POWER AND INFORMATION

Chapter 3 pointed out that flexibility is achieved by partitioning information systems, in recognition of the diverse needs of different parts of an organization. It then developed a logical architecture, reflecting powerful pressures for decentralization of processing power. This is reproduced in Figure 6.1. The way such a logical architecture is expressed in terms of physical equipment does of course reflect various physical aspects of the organization, such as site geography, but it is also heavily influenced by the methods adopted for control and co-ordination of information systems. Since the infrastructure serves as a unifying framework for the information systems, naturally enough these same factors influence its physical structure also.

Even in a small organization, there are a large number of different ways in which information systems can be partitioned physically, and in a large one the permutations are almost infinite. Therefore, it is helpful to break the problem down and to think about information systems as a hierarchy of three levels:

- *Information* – the resource to be exploited.
- *Services* – the means of capturing, accessing, manipulating and distributing that resource.
- *The network* – the physical transport system, linking users with the various services they use, and linking services to one another.

Information, at the top of the hierarchy, is the key resource, and the two other levels are only there so that it can be exploited. It can be partitioned in two ways – into vertical slices, by business function or by geography; and into horizontal layers, separated by type of use. It is

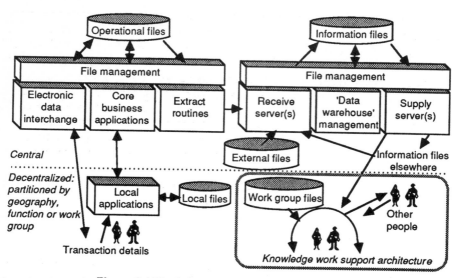

**Figure 6.1 The information handling architecture
developed in Chapter 3**

usually operational files that are partitioned vertically, and this is often referred to as distributed data processing. I begin by looking separately at each of these partitioning options, then consider the services that operate on the information resources. I deal with the communications network later in the book.

Partitioning operational files

Because of the complexity of business operations even in small companies, data has to be partitioned vertically, by geography or by business function, so that applications meeting the needs of particular organizational units can be developed within a reasonable timeframe. Originally, this was done by developing separate applications, each with their own files and held on centralized computers, to meet different departmental needs. More recently, database design techniques have been used to develop databases containing data organized around a subject area, such as customer or product, rather than oriented towards a particular application. These subject area databases can then be used by a number of applications serving different areas of the business.

Sometimes, the equipment supporting these applications and files has been decentralized, to meet management demands for additional control and to reduce reliance on an often unresponsive central information systems department. Decentralization gives end-users greater freedom to handle information in their own way and to set their own operational priorities. It also disperses the impact of equipment failures, sabotage, industrial action and disasters. Furthermore, it allows accountability for information, and for the applications that process it, to be aligned with accountability for business results.

Justifiably, problems of security and control have always been advanced as arguments against decentralized computing, and the cost case for decentralization has not, until recently, been overwhelming. Now, with such powerful pressures in favour of decentralization as outlined earlier and with the tide already running strongly in that direction, the question to be answered is not 'Should we decentralize or not?', but rather, 'How should we decentralize processing power and information, and yet still retain adequate control?'

Reliable foundations are essential

Whatever technological solution is adopted, adequate control can only be retained by building reliable logical foundations for the data that is to be held on computer files. So before I look at the options, it is worth spending a little time reviewing why such foundations are needed, and how they can be built and maintained.

The two reasons for partitioning data, and thus the information systems that capture and process it, are to minimize costs and to increase flexibility. But, over the long term, the functional and geographical boundaries along which the information systems are partitioned can be expected to change, and corporate strategy may shift attention to new indicators of performance. Unless information systems can be adapted with relative ease to follow these changes, clearly organizational flexibility and business performance will suffer. For this reason, architectural foundations for the data must be built, based on a corporate view of requirements rather than on a narrow functional or regional view. How should this corporate view be formulated? It would take another complete book to give a comprehensive answer, but there is space here for some general guidance, derived from recent experience.

The traditional approach is exemplified by planning techniques such as IBM's Business Systems Planning (BSP) and updated variants such as James Martin's Strategic Data Planning.[1] These techniques, often referred to generically as strategic data modelling, attempt to link the acquisition and use of data with business objectives. They produce a blueprint or map of the systems and/or the information that the business needs, based on a methodical process of analysis. The drawbacks of this approach are that the analysis process is very expensive and difficult to organize. It demands the commitment of senior managers who really understand the business, which is often difficult to obtain. Even where this difficulty can be overcome, the blueprint that is produced can easily prove so complex and unwieldy that its value as a strategic corporate overview is obscured by a mass of detail. And, since analysis invariably focuses on today's operations, it is always vulnerable to unanticipated changes in markets or in organization. I know of far more organizations that have developed a strategic data model, then shelved it or adopted only a small part of it, than have successfully carried a substantial part of the model through to implementation in the form of databases and applications. In summary, then, a technique that has some influential proponents and that has given useful results in the past, but that can, according to the evidence, be relied on only by relatively simple businesses enjoying stable trading conditions.[2]

Many leading-edge organizations have tried strategic data modelling in the past, but now find it wanting.[3] As an alternative to a rigorous, but expensive data planning method, many are adopting more pragmatic approaches which seek to identify a bounded subset of the data the organization handles, for which an agreed structure can be derived within a limited timescale. The subset may consist of a key corporate-wide subject area. An electronics company, for example, where top management had made improved product quality a top priority, concentrated on designing a corporate-wide database for product quality.

An alternative approach, appropriate where business priorities are not so clearcut or do not point directly to a subset of corporate data, is to identify a limited number of important data elements, and focus design effort on these. A computer company, for example, formed a task force to identify critical problems of data definition within the organization. They asked information systems groups in different parts of the business to nominate the important cross-functional data elements. This gave them a long list of about 200 elements, which was later reduced to a short list by focusing on those elements for which a specific business impact could be identified. Common data definitions were then developed and agreed.[4]

Accurate and robust definitions of data elements or of databases are a necessary part of the architectural foundations for decentralized information and processing, but they are not sufficient on their own. As suggested earlier, to underpin the definitions, responsible staff within the organization must assume responsibility for the information itself. Increased user involvement has become a common feature of the work of designing applications, such as in the use of task forces with joint user/specialist involvement. But, with the continuing growth of end-user systems, it is now clear that end-users must also assume greater accountability for information. Indeed, as they spread, end-user systems tend to force these ownership issues out into the open, as end-users discover the value and the pitfalls of making available to others data collected on their own systems, initially for their own use.[5]

Recognizing the importance of addressing these ownership issues head on, advanced and successful organizations define firm rules about the ownership of information and the accompanying responsibilities. Any 'set' of data held on a computer system is assigned to an owner, usually a manager or the leader of a work group. The owner is responsible for the integrity and security of the data, and decides who may have access to it and on what terms. Rather than acting as custodian of data on behalf of the corporation, the information systems department operates in a supporting role. It operates the machines on which centralized data resides, and administers mechanisms (such as data dictionaries and directories) and procedures (such as for registration of ownership) which help end-users to meet their ownership responsibilities.

As accountability for information decentralizes, all the more reason for someone somewhere in the organization to take a 'corporate view' of requirements. Suppose, for example, that senior management recognizes long term changes taking place in the market. So that the organization can follow those changes, it may be necessary gradually to adapt the organization of the sales function. This implies changes to the methods used to code products into groups, that in turn affect a number of other data elements 'owned' by different functional groups. Such a change could most easily be put in hand by a central group equipped with specialized data analysis skills. The information systems department is the logical candidate for such a role. DEC (UK), which has gone further down the road towards decentralized accountability for information systems than most organizations, has established just such a group within the corporate information services department. Responsibilities within the group are allocated by business process (customers, logistics, services, people and finance), rather than by function, because the boundaries between processes do not change as the business changes.

Three partitioning options

Once the foundations are in place, how do you decide how to build on to them the partitioned file structures that will be needed? First, we know that there is little problem with distributing relatively static information such as price lists or product descriptions, because a master copy can be held and updated at any single convenient location, and new versions can be sent out periodically or whenever the information changes. The serious problems arise with the capture and updating of volatile operating information, versions of which will be required at a number of different points for a variety of purposes. There are three basic options for decentralizing information of this type, which I term *dispersed, distributed* and *replicated,* respectively. These options are not mutually exclusive, and different ones could be used for different categories of information. One

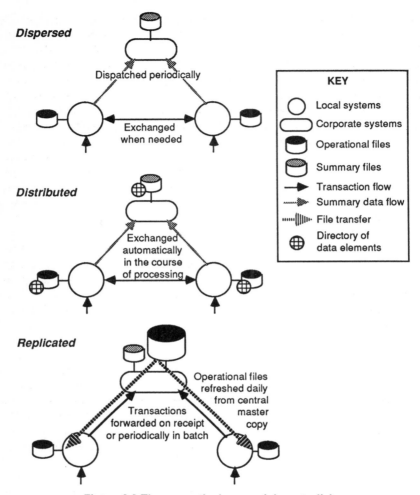

**Figure 6.2 Three practical ways of decentralizing
the operational files**

method could be used for information used by sales and distribution units, for example, and another for those involved with production. As I explain below, each method (illustrated in Figure 6.2) has characteristics which makes it appropriate for supporting business operations of a particular type.

DISPERSED

I use the term *dispersed* to describe an arrangement in which all updating of information is carried out locally, as near as possible to the point of capture of data. Systems and information will be partitioned by business function or by project, or in whatever way best matches the way work is organized. Summary data, needed for control purposes, is sent periodically or when required to the corporate systems. This may be done by direct connection between the systems concerned or by exchange of storage media, and often manual intervention will be needed to dispatch it on its way. Similarly, data needed to co-ordinate functions or projects is exchanged directly between the partitioned systems when necessary.

This arrangement suits organizations that do not depend, or depend very little, on any time-critical co-ordination of activities across functions or across business areas, which means that the rather relaxed measures that I have outlined are adequate. Low-volume custom manufacturers and professional services firms are typical examples. Harking back to the three work-flow configurations mentioned in Chapter 2, it obviously suits organizations whose work flow is *independent* and that rely on personal interaction for co-ordination and control.

In terms of technical feasibility, the key requirement is that there should be high locality of data, so that the majority of updates originate where the information affected is stored. Frequent forwarding of transactions for processing elsewhere is inefficient in terms of manpower and telecommunications costs, and is also likely to lead to problems in validating and controlling data.

DISTRIBUTED

In what I term a *distributed* arrangement, capture and updating is again carried out locally. The difference from the *dispersed* arrangement described above is that the relationships between elements of data stored in the various partitioned systems and, if required, at the centre are maintained automatically. As well as being maintained automatically, relationships may also be kept up-to-date automatically in real time, or at least only with a short delay between transaction and update of affected data elements. This process is normally controlled by means of a directory of data elements, of which a complete copy is held at the centre. Partial copies may also be held elsewhere both to minimize unnecessary traffic and to reduce dependence on the central directory. Mechanisms built into the software ensure, as far as possible, that users need not concern themselves with where data is stored. They merely identify the data elements required, and leave it to the software to find out where these are stored and to retrieve and present them.

In other words, the whole collection of distributed information continues to behave, and to appear to the user, as if it were a set of discrete logical databases. In theory this makes it possible to partition information and systems according to the logic of the work they are supporting, but in practice current technology has performance limitations that demand a more cautious approach which I talk about later.

As you would expect, this *distributed* arrangement is far more demanding from a technical viewpoint than the *dispersed* option. It is favoured by organizations that do depend on time-critical scheduling and sequencing of activities, in other words organizations whose work-flow can be characterized as *sequential*. High-volume engineering or process manufacturers fit this category.

To be practical in terms of today's technology, it again depends on reasonable locality of data in terms of where transactions originate. A high volume and variety of enquiries on data held elsewhere would bring the cost effectiveness of a distributed arrangement into question, particularly where systems are distributed across large geographical distances.

REPLICATED

I describe as *replicated* an arrangement where a full database is held centrally. Periodically, for example every workday morning, subsets of the data are distributed to the locations where transactions originate. Here, the subsets (sometimes called *memo files*) are updated. One of two alternative methods can be used to keep the central database up to date. Where no significant business penalty is incurred if it is up to a day behind, either the updated subset data or the day's transactions are returned at the end of the working day and are applied to the central database overnight. Otherwise, for example where the central database must be up-to-date to service queries from locations other than that holding the data, transactions are sent on to the central site immediately they are raised, so that both central and subset databases are updated more or less in parallel.

This arrangement marries the proven and familiar technology of centralized database management with some of the advantages of distributed processing. For it to work, the subsets of data must not overlap, such as for example where the database can be divided up by geographical area. Hence it suits organizations described in Chapter 2 as *facsimile*. It also suits organizations with time-critical centralized functions, such as purchasing in a supermarket company.

Once again, performance depends to a considerable extent on locality of data, and ideally this should be 100 per cent. It would not work for a clearing bank, for example, where each branch handles transactions on accounts held at other branches as well as those on the accounts it manages itself.

Making decentralized processing work

Decentralized processing of information raises, or to be more accurate, intensifies, certain operational risks that are more easily contained at a central site. I dealt above with the issue of information integrity – clarity about ownership and accountability with regard to data elements is an essential prerequisite. Once the associated management disciplines are established, then supporting tools such as data dictionaries can be introduced. Data dictionaries specify the meaning of data elements and summarize the uses to which they are put. Both programmers and would-be users of data may refer to the dictionary to help with their respective tasks.

Data dictionaries provide a static view of data, but in practice, of course, the use of data is highly dynamic. It is normal for centralized systems to keep an audit trail of transactions that modify data files. In a decentralized environment, equivalent arrangements are needed, so that owners of data elements can directly control access to data via their systems, where this is necessary, and can reconstruct what has happened retrospectively, where direct control is not appropriate. Such measures are essential if they are to be in a position to vouch for the integrity of the data for which they are accountable.

Security is a rather different case. For some organizations, operating highly sensitive industrial or military processes, for example, breaches of confidentiality can prove very expensive. Whether a single, highly visible central installation or a number of smaller decentralized installations are more vulnerable is, however, arguable, since operating procedures and hardware/software mechanisms, such as encryption, can be established to minimize the additional risks incurred by decentralizing information. Security, then, is perhaps best treated as a cost issue, rather than central being regarded as inherently more secure than decentralized.

But decentralized systems do have a distinctive drawback, namely that recovery from errors is much more difficult to organize. Errors may be caused by bugs in the software, by operator mistake, or by equipment failure. As with all computer systems, the error may not be noticed, or corrective action may not be possible, until some time after it has occurred. With decentralized systems consisting of a number of independently operating, but interdependent systems – especially the *distributed* case outlined above – backtracking to a known state in order to recover is much more difficult than with a single centralized system.

Fred Withington, writing on the lessons of experience with distributed systems,[6] recommends that all transactions should carry status tags, in other words codes indicating the last operation through which the transaction has passed. Since only transactions that are currently in the middle of a processing operation will be lost, this makes it possible to reconstruct the precise extent of any failure. For this to work under any failure conditions, transactions must be physically rewritten to storage whenever a status code is changed, so there is a not insignificant cost in terms of processing power and storage loading.

Status codes are a way of tracking how much work the computers have done, but it is equally important to track the work the people using the systems have done. If data supplied from a number of decentralized sites is to be consolidated centrally, clearly there must be some means of verifying that all the expected input has arrived before the consolidation takes place. Checks built into the receiving application can verify that the expected input has arrived, but cannot vouch for its quality – completeness and currency, for example. There is no substitute for assigning responsibility for the operations at each site to one individual, who can certify when necessary that processing is up-to-date and make sure that routine housekeeping and security procedures are followed. As I return to later, this can be a significant cost factor.

Building the data warehouse

Many organizations have begun drawing data from the operational files held in their data centre computers to create secondary databases intended specifically for use by managers and by professional staff. Often, this is an essential step to escape from the inertia of yesterday's data processing systems and to provide systems which can genuinely support the management of the business, rather than just its operations. It is also implicit recognition that the information world is broader and more diverse than as represented in the operational files. This process of creating separate, secondary databases – for which I use the term *data warehouse* – is a practical illustration of the layering principle. Evidence is growing that it is the cornerstone for attempts to improve the supply of information to management. But how exactly should it be constructed?

At this stage it is only possible to give a partial answer, since managers' information requirements are still poorly understood and leading-edge organizations are only now beginning to gain practical experience. But we are beginning to find answers to three key questions – *what data should be selected from the operational files? how should it be aggregated for storage?* and *in what format should it be held?*

Taking the question about selection first, clearly the safe approach is to store all the information that is likely to be required over the longest likely timescale. Unfortunately, this is still prohibitively expensive, despite the continuing reductions in the cost of storage. American Express estimated that doing this would increase their central site storage requirements sevenfold. This being so, it started to look economically attractive to do nothing and ask managers to continue rekeying data from existing reports into their personal computers! What this shows is that flexibility costs significant sums of money even in the age of cheap computer power.

Other organizations that have tried to assess their managers' requirements have come to the tentative conclusion that only a small proportion – 10 per cent or so – of the data held on operational files is of value to managers. I say *of value* deliberately, because essentially it is a value judgement by managers, based on past experience and their knowledge of where the business is going, that says what information they will want to refer to and analyse in the future. Given that funds to create and maintain a data warehouse are finite, it clearly is vital to face managers with that question and require them to make the judgment. A pharmaceutical company, planning a management database to support its research and development staff, ran workshops for the staff mainly affected. During these workshops, they were required to estimate not only the frequency of access to different types of information, but also the value to them of having the information available in electronic form. As a result they decided to exclude legal data altogether from the initial version of the database. Including it would have made the database much more complex, and they believe the decision to exclude it made an important contribution to their eventual success.

Having decided which data to include, you next have to decide how to aggregate it. Aggregation refines information and reduces storage requirements. But also, of course, it closes off options. When the Centre for Information Systems Research at MIT studied data management efforts in a sample of large US corporations, they found that most were creating information databases consisting of selected and aggregated data drawn from the operational files, to be held over a much longer timeframe than the more detailed data held there. This formed a simple two-block model – operational files feeding an information database designed for end-users. However, as Figure 6.3 illustrates, some added a third block, by

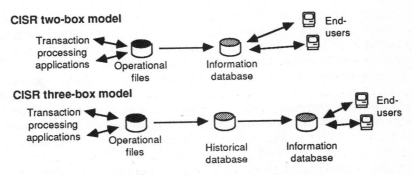

Figure 6.3 Two alternative ways of building the information database

interposing an historical database between the operational systems and the information database. As the CISR report points out:

> This two block model requires either that we know in advance what detailed historical data managers will be interested in, or that we download to the information database all detailed data purged from the transaction database, or that we accept that some future questions will go unanswered.
>
> The three block model [bottom of the figure] . . . recognizes that questions of interest to managers querying the information database will change over time, in ways that cannot be predicted in advance. Therefore it adds the historical database which is intended to carry *all* data about company transactions *at the lowest level of detail* available. Extract programs to feed the information database can change as needs change, and if it is necessary to view data in a new configuration, both current and historical data can be put into that form.[7]

Obviously, the historical database will become very large, but the performance demands placed on it are light, since it is the information database which services end-users' queries. This technique can be applied selectively to those types of information where future requirements are uncertain, and where the anticipated time or cost of reconstructing the (probably partial) picture from other sources justify the additional cost of the historical database. For example, detailed data on sales might be captured in an historical database because it is likely that marketing structures will change, whereas information on purchases is aggregated, and detailed manufacturing data is purged altogether because it is presumed to have no historical significance.

The third question is how to format the data. This has two aspects – one is to do with the content and identification of data fields, and the other with how the data should be structured for ease of use. Beginning with the former, it is clear that, as far as is possible, data held in the warehouse should be corporate in scope, and should be structured to serve the organization as a whole, rather than individual application requirements. Otherwise changing organizational structures and changing information systems will render it obsolete or unuseable. It might be important to ensure, for example, that product data could easily be regrouped to follow the logic of a long term marketing strategy.

Turning to the structure, it is now widely accepted that it is valuable to apply relational database principles, because these have conceptual simplicity and guarantee great flexibility in how the data is used. We can also learn some valuable lessons from the user-friendly data management tools available on personal computers. Whether out of the necessity of respecting the limitations of personal computers or by design, these impose simple structures on data, and this in turn is the key to their ease of use. You should think in terms of only one item per field, and only one field per item; fields should be one of a short range of well-understood types – for example: text, numeric, integer, date, logical; and each should have a single validation criterion.[8]

Locating the shared services

Previously, sharing of computer resources was dictated by the need to husband expensive processing power and to economize on the skills needed to operate and maintain the equipment. Now, as explained earlier, Grosch's law has been reversed and other pressures are now running strongly in favour of decentralization. This does not mean that the practical lessons of the past are no longer valid, but it does make it important to rethink policy on location of shared equipment.

What determines where equipment is located?

One of the primary considerations when deciding where to locate equipment is the cost incurred to attain the required level of performance. The cost implications of the technology trends reviewed earlier in Chapter 3 can be summarized as follows:

- To exploit cheap processing power available in small units, it is advantageous to break information systems down into component parts that can co-operate with each other.
- To exploit changing ratios of communications and processing costs, it is advantageous to distribute services, together with any associated switching and communications equipment, so as to localize traffic and keep it on the site.

But equipment cost is not the only consideration. Turning from cost to performance, the move of information systems to support knowledge workers and staff who deal directly with customers brings two particular aspects of performance to the fore. First, systems must be responsive. That does not always mean an instant reply to a request, although it may if a customer or a senior manager is waiting impatiently. But it always implies an instant acknowledgement, bringing with it a reasonable certainty that results will be available within a predictable timescale and in a controlled way. The right analogy is the secretary, albeit a supercharged one in terms of information handling capacity, rather than some kind of button-operated dispensing machine for information. That familiar sales slogan 'Information at the press of a button' does us all a disservice here. I emphasize this point because it bears on methods used to link users with services, which I return to shortly.

Second, as information systems come to support everyday work and dependence on them grows (and it inevitably does grow if they provide value), it becomes increasingly important that systems should be readily available. That means that they should be available rapidly and promptly whenever the task in hand requires it, because disruption of knowledge work can be very expensive. It also means that they should be available whenever people choose to work, rather than just during the normal working day.

Neither responsiveness nor ready availability are novel requirements altogether, since on-line transaction processing systems demand the same qualities, but they are novel in the context in which they are occuring now, both because of the rapid and continuing growth in the range of services available directly to knowledge workers and because of the strong move towards decentralized systems.

So far, I have dealt with cost and performance factors, which are changing in the ways I have just outlined. But location is also heavily influenced by operational considerations. As equipment costs fall and business dependence on information systems grows, so the cost and effectiveness of human operational support grows in importance, even while the equipment is being designed to require less human intervention to operate, maintain and repair it. Here we find pressures pulling in both directions – into the centre where the specialist professional operators are normally based, and out towards the periphery where more and more end-users are coming to depend on the support of the equipment.

Beginning with the pressures for centralized operation, the *status quo*, for good economic reasons features are increasingly being built into systems that enable a small team of specialists to monitor a network of equipment from a central point. Very high availability also may imply centralization. Equipment is inherently more reliable than it used to be, but very high levels of availability, such as is required for example for a dealing system, can only be achieved, at a substantial cost premium, by adopting equipment with high levels of redundancy and backup power supplies. A more economical alternative is to locate a cluster of compatible machines in a shared machine room. In the event of an equipment failure, systems requiring very high availability take precedence over those with a lower requirement until all the equipment is functioning again. A large London teaching hospital, for example, installed three compatible machines to hold a patient index, a messaging service, and a program development service, respectively. If the patient index machine or the messaging machine failed, the program development service was withdrawn so that these higher priority services could continue on that machine.

At the same time, however, a whole range of new administrative support tasks is being created as equipment spreads out across the workplace, and these create pressure for decentralization. As more sophisticated work-group systems supplement personal computers, administrative staff take on regular housekeeping tasks such as making backup copies of files or running 'garbage removal' routines; distribute output from shared printers; and possibly provide first-line support when users get into difficulty. Additionally, systems of any degree of sophistication require day-to-day management. The responsible manager must keep up to date directories of users and security controls; supervise the allocation and use of system resources; schedule repair and maintenance activity; and assign operating priorities. These tasks do not necessarily require that all the equipment should be on the site and in the office of the staff affected, but they certainly cannot practically be carried out by specialists at the other end of a building, let alone on another site altogether.

Four types of shared service

With this as background, let me review the different types of processing service that need to be provided, and for which decisions on the location of equipment must be made. The starting point is a simple model of information systems, as seen from the user's viewpoint, shown in Figure 6.4. Immediately to hand, the user has a *workstation* that provides access to a range of shared services. The shared services, consisting of *applications* and *utilities*, are in the next layer, as it were. The difference between applications and utilities, as I use the terms here, is that applications are developed to perform specific operations on particular files of information, while utilities are general-purpose, open-ended tools. Some

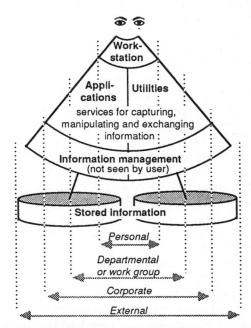

Figure 6.4 Information systems from the end-user's viewpoint – a simple model

people use the term *generic computing* to refer to the latter. The importance of making the distinction will become clear shortly.

The applications and utilities provide various means of recording, searching, extracting and distributing information. Beyond this layer again are the files of *stored information* – data, text, image, knowledge or whatever – together with the logic for identifying, retrieving and updating specified records, which I term *information management*.

This is a different view of the three dimensions of knowledge workers' integration needs described in Chapter 1. The layers nearest the user represent the *services* dimension, with the *information access* and *interworking* dimensions extending out below it on the left and right hand sides respectively. This implies that applications belong to the information access dimension, and utilities to the interworking dimension. That is not quite true, although they are dominant in those dimensions, but it is an simplification that will serve for my purpose here.

As the figure illustrates, both information and the associated applications and utilities may be partitioned and located at corporate, work group/departmental, or personal level. Some information, additionally, is stored externally to the organization. The left-hand side of the *stored information* layer – mainly structured data and text, perhaps in the future structured image files also – has just been discussed. As I have already explained, technology places constraints on the freedom with which information can be partitioned. Also, information tends to be drawn in towards the centre because of the need to co-ordinate and control updating.

The associated applications, by contrast, will be driven outwards (or up in terms of the figure) towards the user by decentralization pressures, to reside at what I call their *administrative span*. The administrative span of an application or utility is the span of people using it. Thus a company-wide messaging utility has a corporate span and, all other things being equal (I explain below why I qualify this), would reside at corporate level. Similarly, a personnel management application has a departmental span and would reside at the level of the department.

The constraints which apply to structured information do not apply to the information held on the right-hand side, handled by the shared utilites, because these are unstructured systems to which no external controls need be applied over and above making sure that privacy and access authority are respected. Therefore, both information and the associated utilities together are driven outwards to reside at the level of their administrative span.

Having established the general principles that *a)* shared applications and *b)* shared utilities **plus** information are driven out to the level of their administrative span, let me explain why I added the qualification *all other* *things being equal,* or in other words deal with the factors that might interfere with that general principle. These factors are different in different cases.

LARGE-SCALE SHARED APPLICATIONS

The first category to consider consists of the familiar large-scale transaction processing applications operated by most organizations of any size. As I suggested earlier, many of these will evolve in due course into the co-ordinating component of distributed or replicated application systems, as information and processing power decentralize. Some, no doubt, will be displaced altogether.

As this process unrolls, however, the cost and disruption of redevelopment will inhibit major changes to these centralized systems, regardless of the changing economics of large and small machines. Progress can, however, be made with minimal redevelopment and disruption. A public utility serving a metropolitan area with over a million customers, for example, decided to insert a new system into the stream of transactions from the accounts offices to the central transaction processing system. This new system processed transactions to provide the additional enquiry and analysis facilities which management needed, and also forwarded transactions to the unchanged billing system.

A more common arrangement, as explained earlier, is to draw data from the operational files to produce a separate information database, or *data warehouse,* designed specifically for use by managers and professional staff. In both cases, reporting routines are progressively displaced from the transaction processing systems. This extends their life by reducing their load. It also simplifies them, so that they are easier to replace when the time comes.

As suggested above, operational considerations also play a part in deciding where large-scale applications are to be located. High availability can be achieved at limited cost by clustering compatible machines at a single location, so that high priority applications can displace lower priority applications when equipment fails. However, this policy must be pursued with caution, since it also increases vulnerability to disasters (a burst water pipe over the machine room, for example), sabotage and industrial action. A very large chemical multinational has dispersed shared services and shared applications across a number of regional centres, interlinked by telecommunications lines, to counter this risk, while it is common for organizations whose business is heavily dependent on continued operation of their transaction processing systems, such as banks and supermarkets, to duplicate their data centres and arrange to switch the traffic from remote systems and terminals in the branches rapidly from one to the other when needed.

SHARED UTILITIES

In this category I include shared communication utilities, such as electronic messaging and free text filing services, but I exclude application development services, which are covered below.

The key point to make is that utilities such as these need not be located and operated right at the top of their administrative span, that is normally at corporate or business unit level. Provided that they are perceived by users as a single, integrated service, they may be physically partitioned and separate equipment installed on each major site. The criteria are whether this minimizes equipment costs (that is, reduces telecommunications costs, offset by any additional hardware costs) and improves operational support. DEC's electronic messaging and general communications service, EASYnet, for example, operates worldwide as a single entity, regardless of geographical and functional boundaries, but it is also partitioned into more than 40 areas, the equipment in each managed by a local manager. (Operational support for networked services such as these is discussed further in Chapter 8.)

Operational considerations play a part in deciding where utilities are located, in the same way as they do for shared applications. Generally, though, utilities need less operator attention, and user dependence on them is lower than on shared applications, so the pressures for centralization are weaker.

APPLICATION DEVELOPMENT SERVICES

With application development languages and system building tools, there is a trade-off between ease of use and flexibility. Sophisticated and powerful tools which combine both qualities, sometimes called fourth generation languages, are very expensive in their demands on processing resources and often require skilled support. This means that, even in this age of cheap processing power and end-user emancipation, it is worthwhile to provide a centralized, shared service, which both central and decentralized development staff can access when needed.

Whether development is approached in this way derives from the strategy for development that has been adopted. In terms of the four generic strategies introduced earlier, it is clearly most valuable in the *end-user computing environment* appropriate for high-autonomy, low-coupling companies. (Powerful system building tools are, of course, used by specialist development shops, but then they need not be networked as a common service, so do not affect the infrastructure.)

Similar considerations apply for very powerful modelling systems, which also demand considerable processing resources and are, in effect, non-procedural program development tools of specialized application.

WORK GROUP SYSTEMS

Moving down the size scale, we come to applications and utilities belonging at departmental level, which I refer to as work-group systems. The key lesson of experience with these systems is that pressure from users to operate the equipment themselves should be resisted. Work-group systems, among other things, do offer users an escape from complete dependence on the information systems department. Unfortunately, users sometimes equate physical possession of the departmental machine with the ownership and control of their information systems that they really want. Here I am talking only of major system components, such as the shared processor, and obviously do not include passive shared equipment such as printers and network interfaces that have to be installed close to the users.

At more than one site I have seen, users began by operating the equipment themselves, but soon learnt the lessons learnt years ago by the specialists – about the value of false floors, the need for storage space for spares, etc. Perhaps more important still, before long they ran into problems with staffing, discovering that operation cannot be restricted to normal office hours. As user dependence on the system builds up, so weekend and 24-hour operation becomes more and more difficult to avoid. At one site, for example, users had to persuade operators from the central machine room to come in and check batch programs which they left running overnight. At another, it became progressively more difficult to close the system for maintenance or upgrading during working hours.

There may well be circumstances in which it is not practical to install a work group's machine in a machine room staffed by professional operators – for example where the cost of remote telecommunications access is very high. What is more, some equipment is already able to operate with little, if any, operator attention for 24 hours a day, seven days a week. Clearly, decisions must take these factors into account, but the principle to be followed is that users should make a positive case before major components of work-group systems are installed within their premises for them to operate themselves.

The principle of minimum coupling

As computer power has spread and as information systems have been applied to knowledge work, so the characteristics, both of the equipment available to users and of the work those users do, have changed compared with the data processing era. Therefore it is important to rethink how users should be linked to the services they use, as well as rethinking where those services should be located. My advice is to adopt a principle of *minimum coupling*. I now explain what I mean by *minimum coupling*, and outline some of the key concepts associated with the principle.

Device relationships and patterns of use are changing

When online terminals were first introduced, they were 'dumb' in the sense that they responded slavishly to prompts received from the central system and took no decisions themselves based on the nature of the dialogue between user and system. While terminals have become more intelligent since then and are able, for example, to control local printers or format the screen without explicit commands from the controlling system, to this day most transaction processing systems work on the basis that the central system exercises tight and continuous control over the terminals through which users gain access to applications. Once signed on to a transaction processing system or to a timesharing system, a terminal is effectively owned by that application and is expected to do things in the sequence and in the manner that application requires.

More than vestiges of this philosophy are still apparent in IBM's blueprint for networked systems, SNA. Until the recent announcement of APPC (Advanced Program to Program Communications), nothing moved in an SNA network without the knowledge and consent of one of the mainframe computers acting as host to the central control software. The devices on the network are tightly controlled from the centre, and normally they can also be described as tightly coupled with the central system, in that there is close synchronization between the activities of the terminal and its human operator on the one hand, and of the logic in the central transaction processing system on the other.

Now, and indeed for some time past, it has been economic to use as terminals programmable devices intelligent enough to operate autonomously from the centralized applications and to conduct, where appropriate, a peer-to-peer rather than a master-slave relationship with those applications.

Not only has the relationship between terminals and applications changed, so also has the relationship between users and applications. In the past, the clerks who were the typical users of transaction processing systems were able to give constant attention to the terminal, and typically their work was organized into discrete transactions, each of which was completed and the results tidied away before the next one started. While this arrangement may not always have delighted the clerk, it certainly suited the transaction processing software.

Now that managers and professionals are using information systems directly to support their work, the assumption that the user is at the terminal continuously is no longer valid. Furthermore, some of their transactions, such as complex enquiries for information or requests for reports, may take too long to satisfy to expect the user to wait patiently before getting on with the next task. Unfortunately, however, the systems they are expected to use too often are still designed on the old basis.

Recently I came across a perfect illustration. A project manager entered an enquiry to an information system installed at the regional office. As she knew, the enquiry would take a couple of hours to answer, so she did not wait at the terminal. When she did come back, she found that the enquiry had been satisfied and that the information system had then asked, helpfully, whether she would like a printout of the results. On getting no answer within what it regarded as a reasonable time, not so helpfully it had given up and thrown away the results. The project manager had, in fact, acted in a natural and reasonable way for a busy manager or professional, entering the request while s/he goes off to a meeting or to lunch and expecting to find the results, or at the very worst a request for a further decision, awaiting on return. As this example shows, tight coupling built into the design of an information system requires users to conform to the pace set by the application, rather than leaving them free to adopt the pace that suits them.

Minimum coupling maximizes flexibility

As we know, human resources are the valuable resources now, certainly where expensive knowledge workers are concerned, and probably where humble clerks are concerned also. Sometimes, of course, tight coupling is in the nature of the application, because application and user must interact directly to agree precisely what is required or because a customer is waiting impatiently for a response. But where this is not the case looser coupling can profitably be used. The next step downwards on the scale of coupling is exemplified by messaging services. Messaging services act as intermediaries between calling and called parties, thus enabling both to communicate non-synchronously, at the price of a delay – which may be short – in the transfer of the information. The next step beyond that is to make the transfer completely offline, in the form of a file transfer. And beyond that still, there is the option of producing hard-copy output delivered by mail.

The advantage of loose coupling is that it increases flexibility both as far as people's work patterns are concerned, and as far as the equipment is concerned. With a tightly coupled arrangement, changes to the way the application works will almost certainly affect the terminal and *vice versa*, and any such changes must be made in close synchronization. In a loosely coupled arrangement, by contrast, it is easier to match the activities of the communicating parties because this does not have to be done 'on the fly'.

Thus you gain flexibility by applying the principle of minimum coupling whenever you must decide how to link users with the applications and services that are on offer via the infrastructure. The principle is also embodied in two key design concepts – the *agent* and the *server*.

THE AGENT CONCEPT

I can best illustrate the *agent* concept by describing how it might have been applied in the example given above of the enquiry program that would not wait. The user would start up the enquiry by means of the normal dialogue, then, assuming that an electronic messaging service or equivalent was available, would specify that service as agent for collection of results, for example by passing over a mailbox number. When processing was complete, the enquiry program would send the results (or, if something went wrong, an explanation) to the mailbox. Later, whenever (and perhaps from wherever) was convenient, the user would retrieve the results.

The agent concept can usefully be applied within the infrastructure wherever one system or one user passes responsibility for progressing an information handling activity to another. Figure 6.5, for example, shows the model embodied in the CCITT X.400 standard for electronic messaging services. The user agent serves the purpose illustrated by my example. The message transfer agent is included because a message may pass through the control of a number of different networks in its journey from sender to recipient. Each of them assumes responsibility for a message while within their territory, and hands over to the next when the message has passed safely through.

THE SERVER CONCEPT

A *server* is a system, usually attached to a network at a known address, that provides a defined task for other devices on that network (its *clients*), on demand. Servers are used:

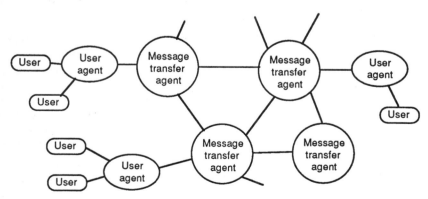

**Figure 6.5 The agent concept within the CCITT
X.400 standard for electronic mail**

- To provide services that are inherently shared, such as managing the files shared by a work group.
- To share relatively expensive resources, such as laser printers.
- To provide a single, managed point of access to a resource, for example a communications server (sometimes known as a *gateway*), linking a local area network to the outside world. It may choose least-cost routes for outgoing traffic, check the identity of incoming callers, and so on.

The server concept arose with the local area network, and contributes to its particular advantages as a means of interconnecting computer-based devices within a limited geographical area. Effectively, a local area network allows a system to be split down into component parts, each of which retains its own autonomy and can be positioned where most convenient, but is also able to communicate at will with other components of the system attached to the local area network, to exchange information with them or to call on their resources. In other words, the local area network with all its attached systems operates as a single coherent system. Figure 6.6 shows a typical configuration of a small departmental network within a large organization.

As must be clear from the description, the local area network confers greater flexibility than the traditional approach of a discrete shared computer system. Its particular advantages are:

- *Incremental growth*: new resources can be added to the network when they are needed or when they become available.
- *Redundancy*: this can easily be built into the system by providing stand-by servers or duplicate copies of files.
- *Location flexibility*: workstations and peripherals can be placed where they are needed, and can be relocated with limited disruption.
- *Operational autonomy*: control and administration of resources can be assigned to those that use them.

These are very much the qualities that are needed in the knowledge work environment that I have already described. The server concept complements local area network technology, but a similar concept had already been applied over public networks before local area networks made their appearance. Public information retrieval services such as Dialog and public messaging services such as Dialcom operate in much the same way as a file server or a messaging server on a departmental local area network. The concept can usefully be adopted within the corporate infrastructure for any shared resource at corporate, departmental or work group level. Figure 6.6, for example, shows laser printers attached to a print server, and the file server shown there could be used (in conjunction with a high-speed local area network) to hold operating

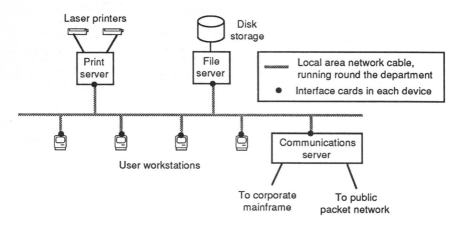

Figure 6.6 Configuration of a typical departmental local area network

and applications software for the workstations, so that they do not need to have individual hard disks.

Notes and references

1   James Martin's *Strategic data planning methodologies* (Prentice Hall, 1982) provides a comprehensive description of these techniques.
2   That does not mean that these techniques are not valuable in other circumstances. But their value lies more in clarifying today's requirements for information systems, rather than in pointing the way ahead.
3   See Cornelius H. Sullivan, 'Systems planning in the information age', *Sloan Management Review*, 26, 2, pp. 3-12.
4   These examples are drawn from a study by Dale L. Goodhue, Judith A. Quillard and John F. Rockart of the Center for Information Systems Research at MIT, reported in *CISR Working Paper no. 150*, Jan 1987.
5   For a cautionary example, see 'The case of Joe Smith: deciding who owns the data', *Management Technology*, Dec 1983, pp.32-34.
6   'Four rules of DDP you can't break', *Datamation*, May 15 1987, pp. 105-108.
7   Dale L. Goodhue, Judith A. Quillard, John F. Rockart 'The Management of Data: Preliminary Research Results', *CISR Working Paper No. 140*, May 1986.
8   See Tasker, 'In search of fourth generation data', *Datamation*, July 1 1987.

CHAPTER 7

MANAGING THE INTERCONNECTION PROBLEM

The reason why the 'interconnection problem' causes such difficulty is, first, that the problem itself is extremely complex. Second, short-term pressures to deliver working systems, using proven technology, are very powerful, and that proven technology often does not fit within a plan to solve the interconnection problem. Every organization would like to build open systems, to maximize freedom of equipment choice in the future, but how do you actually achieve this without substantial, and risky, investment, and without imposing unacceptable restrictions in the short term?

Certainly, the problem has to be attacked step by step, rather than than in one big leap. To help you decide which steps to take first, Chapter 4 gave some guidance on setting priorities for procurement standards. Equally certainly, you must have a clear sense of direction – a strategy – to make sure the steps lead in a direction that is both desirable and sustainable. This chapter begins by discussing strategy options, then talks about the key components within any strategy for managing the interconnection problem. Finally, it outlines some measures that can be used to keep the strategy on course as technologies wax and wane, and as short-term pressures threaten to subvert it.

Deciding a strategy

Given that reliance on today's *de facto* standards is unavoidable, and that your long term objective is to solve the problem of interconnection, there are effectively three ways you can work towards a solution. In outline, these are:

1. *Divide and link*: a low risk, pragmatic approach, relying on well-established protocols and treating the support needs of different groups within the organization on their individual merits.
2. *Proprietary architecture*: relying on the so-called network architectures developed by major computer suppliers, which are both more mature and more comprehensive at present than products conforming to open interconnection standards.
3. *OSI intercept*: a commitment to adopting open standards as soon as practical.

Each of those strategies has different merits and involves a different level of investment and risk. After outlining some of the background, I go on to explain in more detail what the three strategies entail.

The old standards die hard

Despite all the efforts to define open standards, and then to establish them in the market for information technology equipment, the reality is that the long-established standards are still not only alive, but kicking. Figure 7.1 shows the protocols for data communications being adopted by a sample of large US companies surveyed in 1986, both within their private networks and to link with public services off their sites. The figure shows widespread use of three quite different categories of protocol:

ASYNCHRONOUS PROTOCOLS
These protocols are described as *asynchronous* because no attempt is made to synchronize sending and receiving devices, so that each knows when one transmitted character ends and the next one starts. Instead, each character is 'framed' by preceding it by a start bit and following it by one or more stop bits. For this reason, these protocols are also referred to as *start-stop* protocols and also, since they were originally adopted by teletype terminals, as *teletype* protocols. These protocols have been used for many years by basic keyboard and screen terminals to access time-sharing services and to retrieve information from public databases. They have since been adopted, with refinements, by minicomputer suppliers, and are now almost universally supported by personal computers.

Their limitations are threefold. They incorporate limited flow and error-checking; they can only be used at relatively low speeds (up to 2400 bit/second on public networks and up to 19200 bit/second on a short direct connection), and only on dedicated point-to-point links (which can, of course, be multiplexed with others using appropriate equipment); and they can only handle character-based information using the ASCII 7-bit character set. They can, however, be used to dial up remote computers over packet-switching networks, via packet assembler/disassembler

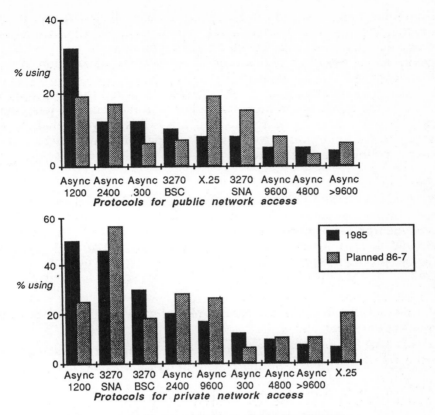

**Figure 7.1 US companies' actual and planned use
of data communications protocols**

(PAD) routines built into access nodes. This partially compensates for the
first two of these limitations, because they now only apply over the
relatively error-free link between terminal and node. Recently, new
protocols (*Kermit* and *XModem*, for example) have been added to the
family to transport binary information such as software programs over
the telephone network, with full error checking and error correction built
in.

IBM'S PROPRIETARY PROTOCOLS
IBM's BSC (binary synchronous communication) protocols, now super-
ceded by the bit-synchronous protocols used within SNA, were designed
for intelligent terminals operating within a data network centred on a
mainframe computer. The best known of these are the 3270 family for
screen terminals, and the 2780/3780 family for bulk transfer. By comparison with asynchronous protocols, they use more effective flow and error
control procedures; can operate at higher line speeds and over shared

communication lines; and can handle binary as well as character information. BSC procedures only work with the message contents in a particular character code, but this code-dependency is removed altogether in the bit-synchronous procedures, so that information in any format whatsoever can be carried.

One serious limitation of IBM's protocols is that they use coaxial cable as the transmission medium, rather than the standard telephone cable that can carry asynchronous traffic. It is this above all that makes access to IBM mainframe computers from personal computers such a costly and inconvenient business.

X.25

X.25 was originally the standard interface to public packet-switching services and has since been assimilated into the OSI standards. It uses a bit-synchronous protocol like those used within IBM's SNA, but goes beyond them (but not beyond the SNA concept as a whole) in that it defines procedures for establishing connections across a network and for controlling the flow of messages, as well as procedures for controlling a link.

Figure 7.1 shows three separate areas of growth in the use of communications protocols:

- In higher-speed *asynchronous* protocols, reflecting the personal computer boom, the continuing penetration of minicomputers, and the arrival of cheap modems.
- In *3270 SNA*, reflecting the continuing migration of IBM's customers (in a substantial majority among large US organizations) from BSC protocols to the full SNA architecture.
- In *X.25*, now the universal standard for public packet-switching networks, and also being adopted for electronic data interchange networks and within large corporate networks.

This graphically illustrates the diverse requirements that have somehow to be accommodated within an interconnection strategy.

Strategy 1: divide and link

The *divide and link* strategy rests on the principle that it is better to optimize the interconnection mechanisms for different categories of network use, than to adopt an organization-wide universal standard that suits some categories but not others. For each category, you select a well-established protocol (or combination of protocols). Thus, for example, you might select an asynchronous terminal protocol (such as Digital's VT100) for conversational applications such as electronic messaging and information retrieval; a mainframe computer supplier's protocol (such as

IBM's 3270) for transaction processing; and the X.25 packet-switching standard as the basis for external communication with trading partners. Many organizations, in fact, start from a situation in which their information systems are already divided along similar lines. In many manufacturing companies and public utilities, for example, DEC is the supplier of choice for technical groups, while IBM or another mainframe computer supplier serves the administrative groups.

Links between the different categories are established via common access points, such as an electronic messaging system, or via special gateways. For example, when Mountain Bell moved to a new headquarters building, they decided to rationalize the diverse networks that had been installed. Within those various networks, four different operating environments predominated – DEC *All-in-1*, Wang *Office*, IBM *Profs*, and *Unix System V* on a variety of machines. As a first step, each of those environments was required to have a standard directory of electronic addresses, the ability to update that directory, a file transfer format and consistency in software revision levels. Then a gateway was developed to permit the Wang systems to interface with those using *Unix* so as to share directories and exchange messages and documents. Further gateways were to be developed to link the other operating environments.

The weakness of the approach is that direct interworking across the different categories, rather than merely transfer of messages or data between them, may be cumbersome, and may not even be possible at acceptable cost. Its strength is its practicality and low cost, since it uses well-established technologies.

Strategy 2: adopt a proprietary architecture

Organizations that rely on close interworking between many of their staff – in terms of my generic strategies, tightly-coupled organizations – are likely to find that a pragmatic *divide and link* approach does not provide the degree of control that they need. For such organizations, there may appear to be no practical choice other than to adopt a supplier's proprietary architecture as the basis for interconnection strategy. The advantages and disadvantages of standardizing on a supplier's proprietary architecture have been much debated and are now well recognized. The key advantages are greater stability, reduced risk and a reduced requirement for support skills in-house. The main disadvantage is limitation of equipment choice.

Obviously, the chosen supplier has to be well-established, and command the resources to keep his architecture up to date as both the telecommunications infrastructure and application needs evolve. For most large organizations that criterion probably reduces the choice to the two market leaders – IBM or DEC. For obvious reasons, the option is most attractive to organizations with a heavy existing commitment to the chosen supplier and not under pressure to innovate in areas outside that supplier's main-line equipment strategy.

Choosing to adopt a proprietary architecture does not settle all equipment decisions, but only defines the protocols which equipment must conform to. Not even IBM is readily able to meet the whole range of information systems requirements of a major organization, so equipment conforming to proprietary protocols often has to be acquired from other suppliers.

Many major suppliers are committed, in more or less emphatic terms, to eventual conformance with OSI protocols. Those who decide to base their strategy round the proprietary architecture of a supplier that has made such a commitment can take some comfort from it. They should not, however, deceive themselves into thinking that this is the same as my third strategy, of tracking OSI directly. When the time comes to convert to OSI, the cost of transition and the cost of operation may well prove much higher than if the interconnection problem had been tackled from the outset from outside the confines of the proprietary architecture. The plain fact is that OSI is not in the short term commercial interests of the established major suppliers, although it may prove so in the longer term. In the short term they can only lose business to smaller suppliers who take advantage of the lower entry barriers created by open standards. The longer term gain will only come if open standards expand the market enough to compensate them for that initial loss.

Strategy 3: intercept OSI

It is not yet possible to adopt OSI standards across the board, both because the standards are still evolving in some critical areas and because of a shortage of products that conform to the standards. Some organizations, nonetheless, have opted to stay as close behind the evolution of OSI standards as they can, and accept the short term cost and the risk that this entails. This approach is favoured by organizations committed, for political reasons, to promoting OSI standards, such as bodies responsible for government procurement and the European Commission, and it is also being pursued by some very large private sector companies who have come to see open standards as of great commercial importance to themselves.

Because of the multitude of interconnection possibilities allowed even by the standards defined so far, an essential preliminary is to choose a well-defined subset of the standards, so that the conformance of products to the standards can be verified. This is the basis of the efforts of General Motors and Boeing respectively to establish Manufacturing Automation Protocol (MAP) and Technical & Office Protocol (TOP) as standards within their industries.[1] Similarly, a Government OSI Profile (GOSIP) has been defined, consisting of a small number of permitted combinations of OSI standards that are believed to cover adequately the needs of government departments.[2] This has been adopted by several government bodies, including the US Department of Defence.

For practical reasons, the transition to OSI standards can only be achieved gradually. The best tactics are to pick communities of users with similar needs and well-defined limits, and implement chosen OSI standards within those communities. Additionally, you need a number of universal standards that can be adopted across all communities of users before or as they are drawn into the developing open architecture. As the chosen standards become stable, you progressively link the various communities together, using conversion routines to link in those which have not or cannot be converted to OSI. The European Commission has adopted a variation on this principle for the development of information systems within its own administration, and has produced a set of guidelines explaining how it will be achieved:

> The deployment of informatics resources proposed in the guidelines is based on a distributed architecture which reflects closely the way user communities are organized. ... Essentially this is a two-layer architecture which distinguishes, within an Institution, between Local Support Units (LSUs) dedicated to a local user community with a close working relationship and Common Support Units (CSU) dedicated to the Institution as a whole.
>
> LSUs are intended to cover flexibly the different user requirements of different user communities. CSUs are used for services that cannot be practically distributed (e.g. common databases), or are centralized by definition, such as common accounting, communication between institutions, etc.
>
> ... The guidelines ... recognize the fact that transition from a manufacturer oriented architecture to an open one allowing full interworking cannot be achieved overnight. The guidelines foresee an evolutionary plan which will gradually attain the intended goal. Eventually the user should access the proposed architecture through a single multi-function workstation ... . In the first instance emphasis is placed on such services as file transfer, Teletex [intended to become the successor to telex], access to the packet-switching network etc, which form mandatory features of any equipment to be purchased.[3]

The framework – the integrating components

Having chosen a strategy for interconnection, how precisely do you set it in motion? Which standards, among the many you could adopt, should be made the centrepiece of the effort to turn strategy into reality? Certainly you will need standards at the level of the communications network, but I believe that these standards are secondary. What should drive the strategy along are requirements of end-users, reflected in the hardware and software products they use to meet their information handling needs. Unless they can see that the pieces are gradually coming together, they are unlikely to give the strategy full-hearted support. Without that, it will certainly falter, if not fail altogether.

I have already talked in earlier chapters about the dimensions of end-users' requirements for integration. Interconnection plays a key role, depending on the strategy adopted, along four or more of those dimensions. In each of those, we can define a key component, or key components. When translated into standards and guidelines for procurement, these become the 'glue' that holds the infrastructure together along the various dimension. Since the standards and guidelines are to form the basis for actual projects and actual product decisions, they must be, or be reflected in, real products. There is no point adopting paper standards before they have resulted in useable products.

Obviously, the decisions on standards and guidelines are important ones whose impact will be felt for many years. Good timing is essential. You should expect to have to make some interim choices, and you should expect to back some losers occasionally. All the more reason, as I suggested above, to organize the whole strategy so that end-users, and senior management, can see the results as well as the restrictions on choice.

Now I look briefly at each of the five dimensions, explaining what the components are that are candidates for standardization, and what are the main options, if any.

THE INFORMATION ACCESS DIMENSION

If you refer back to the architecture for information storage introduced in Chapter 3 and developed in Chapter 6, you will see that the key components in the access dimension are the server routines used to bring data into the data warehouse, and to distribute extracts to wherever they are needed. These will normally be developed using the tools associated with the database management system used to maintain the data warehouse. By implication, the choice of that system is the key decision.

Beyond that, you may also be able to specify the preferred end-user tools, used to manipulate information at the workstation. This will enable you to choose or build the 'bridges' that will carry information over from those tools to the data warehouse. In some organizations, personal computer packages such as Lotus 1-2-3 have already become the preferred choice. We are still a long way from the end of the evolution of the personal computer, though, so care is needed to choose for this purpose a standard that will survive by evolving along with the personal computer.

THE SERVICES DIMENSION

In the services dimension, what is needed is a standard framework to support the various applications and utilities available to end-users. It should show end-users a consistent and friendly face, and enable them to carry information between services with reasonable ease; and it should also provide links into the information access and interworking dimensions. I say 'a framework' but, as suggested earlier, complex organizations – possibly following the *divide and link* strategy – will need such a framework for each of the divisions that they carve out within their information systems.

After discussing the options in the Chapter 5, I suggested that the 'ideal' framework would consist of a workstation operating system, incorporating both presentation and communications management, in combination with a multi-tasking 'office controller' to handle the shared files. Many undoubtedly will see IBM's promised *OS/2* as the most likely candidate here for both roles. Never underestimate IBM, but my suspicion is that *OS/2* will take some time to stabilize and even then prove too unwieldy, and that by the time its problems are solved others will already have stolen the prize of acceptance in the marketplace from under IBM's nose.

There is also a substantial lobby for *Unix* as a standard operating environment, fitting all systems from workstations up to large shared computers. Whatever its merits as a portable operating system, however, unadorned *Unix* (designed nearly twenty years ago, and looking like it) comes nowhere near meeting my criteria for presentation management. *Unix* is designed so that a 'shell' can be written to accept commands in any format and translate them into the commands expected by *Unix* itself. This feature could be used to give *Unix* similar qualities to those enjoyed by the Macintosh, but this implies choosing (or, in the unlikely event that you have a few hotshot programmers to spare, producing) a version of *Unix* with an acceptable shell, then making sure that only that version is used. Otherwise, of course, the whole advantage of a consistent approach to presentation management is lost.

Apart from this possibility, the candidates here are few at present. They include Apple's Macintosh, of course, growing more acceptable as a corporate option as its ability to communicate with other suppliers' equipment improves; Microsoft's *Windows*, close relation of the presentation manager in *OS/2*; and *GEM* from Digital Research, tipped by some pundits earlier, but not looking very convincing now. Alternative candidates for the office controller role would be DEC's *All-in-1*; and Wang's *Office*, and equivalent products from other major suppliers.

A rather messy picture, and likely to remain so for some years yet. This, after all, is the battleground where positions for the big information technology markets of the 1990s will be established. Few organizations, however, can afford to wait until those positions are established. In the meantime, how can you make sense of the options?

The key to the problem, I believe, is to decide whether to emphasize the workstation itself, and the qualities of its human/computer interface, or the shared controller, with its relative strength in handling shared applications. Having made that decision, you first standardize on an operating environment for the chosen component – *Macintosh, OS/2, Windows* or whatever for the workstation; *Unix, All-in-1* or possibly a mainframe product such as IBM's *Profs* for the shared controller. Having thus cleared the ground somewhat, you can then in due time choose a complementary and compatible operating environment for the remaining component.

Returning for a moment to the generic strategies, it would be logical for low-autonomy organizations – *corporate information engine* and *office utility network* – to start with the workstation, while high-autonomy organizations – *distributed information system* and *end-user computing environment* – would need the power of a shared controller to run the local applications and manage the shared work-group/departmental files.

THE INTERWORKING DIMENSION
A number of organizations have got themselves into a position where different work groups have come to rely on the interworking mechanisms – messaging services and the like – built on the operating environment used within their own work group. To link through into other operating environments involves tedious and inconsistent procedures, so in practice it rarely happens. Better to take your chance with the internal mail, or resume the familiar game of telephone tag. In the interworking dimension, then, the key component is a universal (or as near as you can make it) mechanism for messaging and information exchange. It should have the attributes I outlined in the previous chapter.

For those looking for a universal standard, the CCITT standards adopted for OSI – X.400 for message handling and X.500 for the directory – are the obvious solution, although these standards are probably over-engineered for use privately rather than as a public service, except within very large organizations. Those already committed to more than one messaging product, in terms of use if not standards, may follow the approach taken by Mountain Bell described earlier. They defined a standard means of exchanging and accessing directory information, then went on to link the different operating environments together via gateways.

At workstation level, the messaging service should be complemented by a word processing package (or word processing packages) that can be used to prepare messages before sending, and to manipulate them for whatever purpose is appropriate on receipt. Obviously, this must link well with messaging routines, and for that reason it is important that it should not differentiate between messages and documents. A message, after all, is merely a short document intended for reading from a screen rather than from a printed page. Why introduce artificial distinctions, as some products do?

The comments made above on the problem of choice of standards apply here also, so again you must take a pragmatic line. Obviously, standards to promote interworking will assume higher priority for tightly-coupled organizations – *corporate information engine* and *distributed information system* – than for loosely-coupled ones.

THE DEVELOPMENT DIMENSION

System development is a large and complex topic, and in a particular ferment at the moment with the debate among specialists about new tools such as IPSEs (integrated programming support environment), as well as the arrival of system building tools that can be used by non-specialists. So I must make it clear that I am dealing here with only a small part of the total problem – the use of advanced system building tools outside the central information systems department on a widespread basis, and the impact of that use on the infrastructure and on procurement. The widespread use of system building tools is central to the generic strategy I call *end-user computing environment*, and of considerable importance in the *distributed information system* strategy also.

By *advanced* system building tools I mean toolkits such as *Mapper* or *Focus*, usually associated with database management systems and requiring a sizeable machine, rather than the application generators available on personal computers, such as *DBase III*. The latter can be treated in the same way as any other personal computer tool, whereas advanced tools demand a whole-hearted commitment from the organization, and, as I outline below, affect both the human and the technology infrastructure. Different tools have different merits and can be applied to different types of application. Those like *Focus*, *Nomad* and *Ramis* that are good for management information or decision support applications are of particular interest in this context, and also those families of tools that include both tools for use by end-users or analysts out in the business, and tools for specialist programmers in the information systems department. The reason for excluding tools used by information systems departments alone is not that this is unimportant – it certainly is – but that the department's needs are highly specialized and best met by special arrangements that do not affect the infrastructure as a whole.

To use advanced system building tools effectively, the information systems department must change radically the way it operates, and the transition can create some painful problems. They also affect the way support skills are deployed within the organization. With appropriate training, both end-users and business analysts without programming skills will be able to exploit the straightforward features of the tools, but they will need to call on specialist support to use the more sophisticated features. Also, applications built with these tools usually demand much more computing power and memory to run than applications developed in the conventional way, and may lack adequate security or recovery features. For short-life applications this may not matter too much, but critical applications or ones that are to be used regularly may need to be tuned by specialists to improve performance or security.

These are essential tasks for the human infrastructure – the training and support arrangements that underpin the tools themselves. As far as the technology infrastructure is concerned, the chosen tools will constrain equipment choice, since they will run, and the applications they generate will run, only on a specified range of equipment. Depending on the organization's starting point, then, either the existing information systems environment (and particularly the computers hosting the main business applications) will define the range of tools from which a choice can be made, or the chosen tools will define the range of equipment that can be used. The chosen tools will also have to be assimilated into the knowledge work support architecture, so that they can be accessed from authorized workstations whenever needed, and this will in turn constrain the choice of equipment or standards in this area.

THE MANAGEMENT DIMENSION

Management of the infrastructure involves a number of maintenance and planning tasks that will rely on the collection of statistics about end-users' activities and about traffic. For a large organization, it may well be worthwhile to build appropriate mechanisms into the infrastructure. But for organizations of any size, access security is the most critical aspect and also the most often neglected. As workstations and other systems spread out across the business, it becomes both more important and more difficult to prevent unauthorized access. The infrastructure must therefore incorporate a security system that polices access, if not to all applications and services available from the workstation, at least to those provided on a shared basis and that need protection.

Access to workstations can be controlled physically by electronic badges or keys, and by controlling access to the premises where they are kept. Measures such as these are vital to protect information held locally,[4] but will have to be supplemented by logical controls built into the infrastructure, whereby users identify themselves on first access, by means of passwords or by some other secure method, so that their authority to use various shared services can be checked. This is commonly implemented by having a standard sign-on screen, linked to a central directory of users and the services that they are authorized to access. This means that the initial menu, displayed after the user has identified him- or herself, can show only those items that are available, rather than cluttering up the screen with those that are out of bounds and saying 'no entry' later. As a further convenience to users, they should also be able to customize the initial menu to exclude those items they have no intention of using even if authorized to do so. The sign-on screen is either called in automatically whenever a workstation starts up, or as soon as a user attempts to access any shared services.

The use of a central directory also means that users do not need to be at their normal workstation to take advantage of the services on offer – they can work from wherever they can find a suitable workstation, including from home. The price of this flexibility, however, is vulnerability to hacking. The password protection system must be foolproof, and the use of passwords must be policed to make sure that people do not get sloppy and use obvious passwords, or thoughtlessly give their passwords away to others.

A growing range of security products, hardware and software, are available for personal computers, and larger machines have security features built into their operating systems and into applications packages that can be tailored to meet installation needs. The difficulty is to weld these together into a coherent and effective organization-wide security system. Work on standards in this area, unfortunately, is not very far advanced, so those not content to limit themselves to a single major equipment supplier have no real alternative at present. They must choose from the proprietary security features available on preferred equipment and software, and then do whatever extra work is needed to integrate them.

Keeping on course

It need hardly be said that the starting point from which all organizations approach the interconnection problem is a long way from perfect. If given the option, most organizations emphatically would not launch their assault on this intractable problem from where they now stand. Even given an ideal starting point, transition and change are unavoidable further downstream as technology creates new turbulence. Here are three practical measures you can adopt to increase your chances of keeping the boat pointing in the right direction.

Assimilating new technologies – the chinese walls policy

Any newly-arrived technology brings with it the threat of future incompatibility as standards evolve. At the time of writing, document image processing is an excellent example, and I use it to illustrate the problem and the solution, which I call the *chinese walls* policy.

At this stage, there are no widely-accepted industry standards for document formats or for document interchange that extend to document images as well as coded text. In terms of the format of the document image itself, digital fax standards are obviously relevant and have been adopted. In terms of the format of documents as a whole, often including both image and coded text, there are no definitive standards other than those set by individual suppliers. IBM's influence cannot be discounted - Document Content Architecture (DCA) envisages compound documents including image. The OSI X.400 standard for electronic messaging does so also.

Thus there is a battle ahead to set standards. What is more, document image processing systems will certainly provoke a re-think on network structures, because of the enormous additional traffic load they can be expected to create. Using the best compression techniques currently available, a one-page image document occupies at least 250,000 bits at a typical scanning density. This is an at least an order of magnitude greater than a page generated by a word processor. To provide the sort of response users are likely to expect from an electronic system (much faster, of course, than they put up with when their secretaries retrieve the same documents by hand), line speeds in excess of those now normally provided are certain to be needed.

Unfortunately, despite these problems, organizations that stand to gain a great deal from document image processing may have no choice but to proceed, whatever the uncertainties. Offering the advice 'We think you should wait until the standards firm up' or 'We need a year or two to get the network up to scratch' is likely to cut little ice with a manager with a serious records management problem who has just seen an impressive demonstration.

A certain amount of muddling through is unavoidable, but what I call the *chinese walls* policy helps to limit the muddle. (If you have not come across the term, *chinese walls* are imaginary barriers between departments in financial services firms, erected to avoid potential conflicts of interest between business activities.) In this particular case, what you would seek to do is to separate image traffic from existing network traffic, until you are in a position to integrate those traffic streams properly using standards that can be relied on to survive. You can do this, for example, by carrying image traffic on separate lines, which converge at the workstation. You also keep the coupling between a document image processing system and other systems as loose as possible, for example by dumping data files which it accesses out into the system itself or into a separate server, rather than handling data access requests online.

Market pressures do not help, because established suppliers, naturally enough, try to make it as easy as possible for users to add new features to their existing equipment. Already, for example, inexpensive document image processing add-ons to personal computers are available. This makes the *chinese walls* policy difficult to enforce completely, but it will always contribute something in the long run.

The safety net

Using a safety net can be seen either as a sign of weakness or as a wise precaution. In view of the uncertainties surrounding interconnection, the use of a safety net can only be construed as wise. What it consists of in this context is a set of minimum standards – basic standards to which most equipment, including what is already installed, can readily conform. These minimum standards bring all devices down to a common level at which they can interconnect, although possibly with penalties in the form of inconvenience or loss of function. One manager referred to these minimum standards as 'levellers', which neatly sums up their purpose. Such standards only restrict freedom of choice to a minimal extent. Thus they can easily be applied to all purchases of information technology equipment.

One way of defining the safety net standards is to see them as the highest common factor, in terms of interconnection, between two things:

- The equipment already installed in significant numbers and not on the verge of being replaced.
- The preferred products and standards adopted as part of your inter-connection strategy.

Thus you define them by comparing the interconnection methods supported by the former with those supported by the latter, to identify the lowest point at which they coincide. (This exercise may reveal some equipment that you should phase out because there is no satisfactory way of interconnecting it.) Alternatively, or if the above exercise reveals no commonality whatsoever, you can adopt suitable standards that are in widespread use. Some organizations have adopted those used by public messaging and information retrieval services, such as asynchronous protocols for conversational applications; ASCII text-only formats for documents and data files; and XModem as a secure file transfer protocol.

Equipment which meets safety net standards but not those of the interconnection strategy pays a price. Because interconnection is at a low level, the user will normally have to put up with inconvenience or loss of function or both. The inconvenience may consist in having to print out and re-key the information. The loss of function might be that transmitted text is not formatted correctly, or that equipment is unable to participate in access security schemes or use certain services.

'Soft' control via conformance levels

A number of studies, as well as common sense, tell us that controls that link restrictions to the benefits gained by accepting them are more likely to prevail than those that are merely presented as rules to be followed. With interconnection, that principle can be followed by defining different levels of attachment to the infrastructure and its services, tied to different levels of restriction on procurement. Such a scheme enables end-users evaluating a particular project or a particular purchase to make an explicit judgement about the relative advantages of a higher level of service via the infrastructure, as against the merits of particular items of equipment or methods of procurement that may not fit the inter-connection strategy. For example, they might have to choose between an off-the-shelf applications package running on equipment that did not fit into the strategy, and developing from scratch a bespoke system to run on approved equipment.

One public service organization that was pursuing a radical policy of decentralization of equipment defined three levels of service to be provided by the network they installed. At the highest level, users' equipment would be able to access all the shared services easily, via interface routines provided and maintained by the information systems department. The *quid pro quo* was that choice was restricted to the range of equipment of one particular supplier. At the two lower levels, access to shared services either was not possible at all, or would demand devel-opment effort for which the user took responsibility, but choice was extended to a much wider range of equipment.

Notes and references

1   See Jennifer E. Beaver, 'TOP: new standards for the office?', *Computer Decisions*, Jan 28 1986, pp. 46-47, 80 and Stan Kolodziej, 'Will TOP take off?', *Computerworld Focus*, May 14 1986, pp. 31-33.
2   See Adrian Stokes, 'Talkin' bout Gosip', *Communicate*, Nov 1987, p.22.
3   Based on a paper given by Dr Ir W. de Backer to the Benelux members of the *Butler Cox Foundation* in 1986.
4   For some useful checklists, see Joel S. Zimmerman, 'PC security: so what's new?', *Datamation*, Nov 1 1985, pp. 86-92.

CHAPTER 8

THE CORPORATE NETWORK

If information systems are the nervous system of the organization as a whole, then the corporate telecommunications network is the nervous system of the infrastructure that underpins those information systems. Microelectronics has transformed cost structures in the computing world, and it is also working a revolution in telecommunications. Switching and transmission systems, both public and private, are adopting digital technologies for all forms of traffic, not just for digital data and text. This has opened up the attractive prospect of the integrated all-purpose network, flexible enough to handle all forms of traffic and, of course, inexpensive. This, in the marketing jargon of the telecommunications authorities, is the Integrated Services Digital Network (ISDN).[1] Digital technology has also increased the economies of scale that can be gained by acquiring high-speed lines – bandwidth in bulk – to link major sites.

When fully operational, digital networks such as ISDN will certainly be a major step forward in public communications. But while telecommunications engineers get to grips with all the problems associated with introducing such a major new technology, the advances in information technology reviewed earlier in this book are complicating the issue. End-user systems are creating more volatile traffic patterns and higher rates of change, and are bringing new forms of traffic – such as image – on to corporate networks. When evaluating the considerable cost and performance advantages of new digital telecommunications technologies, the network manager must be careful not to lose sight of the new demands his internal customers will be placing on the network. A few per cent shaved off annual operating costs are unlikely to count for much against the fury of managers who cannot gain access to their information in the middle of a crisis.

The question the network manager must address is this: *How should I plan and configure the corporate network to support the information systems activities of the 1990s, while also taking advantage of new telecommunications technologies?* In this chapter, I offer some guidance. First, I describe a way of taking a fresh look at requirements, by picturing these in terms of what I call *information communities*. By so doing, you can see the relationships between information flows, but without losing sight of the practical implications of transporting and combining these over a corporate network. Then I look at the changing role and structure of the network, linking this with the generic strategies described in Chapter 2. Next, I deal with the operating philosophy of the network – how it is to be managed in the end-user systems era. Finally, I review the pros and cons of integration.

Information communities – uncovering the requirements

In the past, it was relatively easy to forecast the volumes and patterns of information traffic within business organizations. Traffic could be associated with a limited number of major applications – telephony, order processing, shop floor data capture, or whatever. Growth was normally predictable and uniform, and could be associated, for example, with growth in headcount or in business volume. Now, demand for access to shared services or for telecommunications support is much more diverse and far less predictable than in the past. Thus an essential preliminary to any decisions on the form that the corporate network should take is to view the likely traffic patterns within the organization as a whole, to visualize how they interrelate and overlap. The concept of *information communities*, helps to do just that. I now explain what *information communities* are and why it is helpful to express requirements in that way.

What are information communities?

Information communities are defined as groups of network users who share a need to communicate or to exchange information via an organization's corporate network. That shared need may take one of two forms. The first of those was the normal pattern in data processing in the past, and is still widespread. It occurs where users of computer terminals share the use of a large centralized computer system, which holds a corporate database, a transaction processing application, or a timesharing system. Clearly, the shape and even the existence of this form of information community is contingent on the location and the design of the application that is shared. As processing power and storage decentralize, driven by the pressures reviewed in Chapters 3 and 5, the shape of many information communities of this form will change radically.

The second form of information community has the pattern typical of telephone communication and increasingly of communication in other forms also, such as text and image. Here, network users are united by a set of common tasks that depend for their effective completion on electronic communication of some kind. For example, they may be a project team working on a time-sensitive project, and forced to communicate by telephone or by electronic mail because they are highly mobile.

But the definition of information communities does not end there. They have a further distinguishing characteristic, and that is the type of information, and hence the type of traffic on the network, that flows within them between the members of the community. So, for example, the members of a department using a shared system for electronic messaging constitute one information community. Those people in the department who are specialist engineers and exchange engineering drawings electronically with their peers elsewhere in the organization constitute a second information community, overlapping the first. As this example makes clear, any individual or group may, and often does, participate in more than one information community.

Sometimes, people will participate in a particular information community only very occasionally, especially in the case of telephony but also, for example, in the case of a market analyst who now and again calls up external databases. In both these instances, access is achieved via easily-available public services, so it is not too important to take such occasional use explicitly into account when planning the network. There may, of course, be circumstances when occasional participation *is* important – the US President's hot line, for example – but, for planning purposes, it will normally be enough to concentrate on those information communities which generate regular and/or intense traffic on the network.

I will elaborate later on the characteristics that distinguish different types of traffic, and which in turn define separate information communities. But, first let me clarify and illustrate the point I am making by insisting on distinguishing forms of traffic in this way. I am not saying that it is always undesirable to bring these together, rather that it is important to be sensitive to the difficulties involved. The history of telecommunications in business to date illustrates how stubbornly resistant different forms of traffic are to being assimiliated into new integrated schemes. Within data processing, each of the three main modes of data communication – timesharing, transaction processing and bulk data transfer – originally had their own protocols, each incompatible with the others. These have been gradually brought together by means of the bit-synchronous protocols (such as IBM's SDLC, incorporated in SNA, and the public network equivalent HDLC), but it has taken the best part of a decade for that to happen, and a great deal of traffic still uses the old tried and tested protocols. Now, of course, we have to concern ourselves not only with telephony and with growing volumes of data and text traffic, but also perhaps with image and video.

Different types of traffic have very different characteristics

Let me restate the key point – that information communities must be distinguished by the type of traffic flowing across them – in slightly different terms. The reason types of traffic must be looked at separately is because currently available technology cannot easily overcome the functional differences between them, so that the traffic flows can be integrated together. Or at least, technology cannot easily do so in a manner that makes economic sense *and* that provides an acceptable level of service to the end-users or machines relying on the telecommunications service. Therefore, it is prudent to focus on the information communities first, and come to the integration options later. Too many telecommunications specialists have come to grief by doing it the other way round.

There are three particular aspects of telecommunications traffic which have a key impact on the performance and the features of the network that carries them. Hence, differences in these three parameters define the types of traffic that we need to distinguish. Those three parameters are *burstiness, connectivity,* and *bandwidth.* Now let me explain what I mean by those terms, and why it is important to take account of them.

BURSTINESS

Voice traffic occupies the transmission channel across a network at a constant level for the duration of a telephone call. Most non-voice traffic, by contrast, occupies the channel in very short bursts. This 'burstiness' is often expressed as a peak-to-average ratio – the higher the ratio, the more bursty the traffic.

As far as the network is concerned, bursty traffic must be concentrated (or, to use a telecommunications term that means much the same, multiplexed) on to fewer channels than there are devices generating that traffic, if transmission and switching capacity is to be used at all efficiently. Concentrators and multiplexers, you will infer, channel the traffic from many devices on to fewer transmission channels, by exploiting the gaps between bursts of traffic. Two recently introduced telecommunications technologies, packet-switching and local area networks, have precisely this attribute, being capable of concentration ratios in the hundreds with highly bursty traffic. Conversely, they are less well suited to telephony, which requires a continuous channel for the duration of a call.

Although expenditure on data concentration and network management is catching up steadily, transmission charges still form the dominant cost area in large organizations' corporate data networks, representing about half an average US budget in 1987. Hence the burstiness factor cannot safely be ignored. More often than not, it will be economic to treat bursty traffic differently, and separately, from continuous traffic such as telephony or full motion video. A comment by the manager of one of the largest corporate networks in the UK graphically illustrates the point:

> We found the average phone call lasted something over two minutes but the average data call took around 15 minutes. This meant that if we were to set up one site for, say, 1000 phone calls a day and we added 10% in data calls we would have to virtually double the number of lines out of the building.
>
> It was therefore sensible to separate voice and data traffic and send data down multiplexed links ... .[2]

CONNECTIVITY

Some users operating over a corporate network require to intercommunicate with a large number of other network users. Other users, by contrast, deal only with a restricted number of other users or services, and sometimes only a single one. This is normally the case, for example, with transaction processing terminals. In other words, the degree of connectivity required by different network users varies widely. Telephony, quite obviously, depends very heavily on connectivity, whereas most computer applications demand a very limited range of connections. If it were possible to provide all users of computer workstations with the same level of connectivity as the telephone system at acceptable cost, then this would not be an issue. But, for reasons I go into later, that is not yet the case and is unlikely to become so.

It costs money to provide high connectivity, and it also affects the level of service users get. Providing a very wide addressing range, as the telephone does, can be inconvenient for users, because it means that they have to remember or find out (or use a secretary to do so) lengthy addresses. Unless the network operator devotes considerable effort to building and maintaining directories and interface software, it imposes unnecessary tasks and unnecessary complexity on those network users who do not need the connectivity. Anyone who has keyed in the five or six fields, each at least six characters long, necessary to connect to a public information retrieval service via a packet-switching network, will have no difficulty appreciating this point.

Even more important in some circumstances, high connectivity makes it much more difficult to maintain acceptable levels of access security. The lurid tales in the media of hackers gaining access to US military computers make very clear how great the risks are. The risks are there within corporate networks, and are even greater when the network can be accessed from outside via a public network.

BANDWIDTH

The bandwidth, or carrying capacity, of a transmission line does not only determine how much traffic that line can handle in a given period. It also determines, when combined with any delays introduced by switching devices, how long a message takes to get from source to destination. What the user at the workstation perceives, of course, is the time from despatch of the message to the arrival of the reply – the response time. As more and more office workers have their own workstations, and as more and more of the information they handle finds its way on to computer storage, so the bandwidth required to give them an acceptable level of service, including acceptable response times, increases dramatically. And, as with the motorways, that bandwidth must be configured to handle the rush hour peaks, not just the average level of traffic.

Continuing the motorway analogy, it should further be noted that improved methods of handling information electronically increase end-users' expectations, just as new motorways increase drivers' expectations. Now the M25 motorway round London is in operation, many commuters have much shorter journeys. However, this does not stop them from complaining when the South-West section clogs up every morning. Similarly, some managers will expect electronically filed documents to appear on the screen within a few seconds of the request being entered, whereas they accepted without question delays of minutes when their secretaries had to go and rummage in filing cabinets.

The bandwidth required to transmit a unit of information depends on how densely compressed it is. Figure 8.1 compares the average number of bits needed to represent an A4 page in the highly compressed form used by word processors – a string of coded text characters – with that used to represent a page as a bit-mapped image. Clearly, if documents are to be stored as bit-mapped images rather than as coded text, then the demands on the network will be substantially greater.

For bursty traffic which is to be multiplexed, bandwidth requirements, very roughly speaking, are something more (because 100% loading is not practical) than the product of number of devices and the bandwidth requirement of a single device, with the peak-to-average ratio determining how many devices can share a single line. Bandwidth requirements directly affect on-site wiring and switching options. While telephone wiring, switched via a digital telephone exchange, can handle 64K bit/second, a similar line or a coax cable, switched via a local area network, can handle between 500K and 10M bit/second, depending on the technology used.

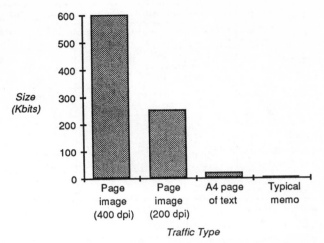

Figure 8.1 Comparison of compression densities of
image and coded text

For inter-site transmission, to put it in a nutshell, constraints are more acute and costs are higher. As a rule of thumb, cost/performance will vary inversely with the degree of variation in bandwidth and in peak-to-average ratios a single transmission and switching system has to handle. Or, as experience has always told us, versatility (which means extra complexity) costs money.

What do information communities reveal?

To define the concept of information communities more closely, Figure 8.2 tabulates different types of traffic, along with typical characteristics for each, expressed in the terms discussed above. The telecommunications characteristics given in the table indicate, at a summary level, what demands that type of traffic will place on the corporate network. These types of traffic, or whatever subset is relevant, should be used to distinguish information communities. Where you are dealing with a known situation, you can substitute exact values for the typical ones given in the table. You may also wish to add new types to cover special requirements.

To use the concept of information communities to analyse network requirements, you should first of all draw up a chart of the geographical and functional structure of your organization. That chart should show the boundaries – between sites, buildings and countries; and between major organizational units, such as operating companies or divisions – that information will cross, along with the rough distances involved. On to this chart you should then map the organization's information

Telecommunications Characteristics						
Type of Traffic		Burst-iness	Connectivity			Band-width
Name	**Description**	Typical peak/aver-age ratio	Inter-connect flexibility	Access security	Links to outside world	Typical require-ment (bit/s)
Video	For conferencing or instruction	1:1	Predefined, limited	Not important	None	2M
Telephony	Switched telephone service	1:1	High	Usually un-important	Essential	64K
Image	Bit-mapped facsimiles of documents	10:1	Usually modest	Usually un-important	Often	64K
Convers-ational	Eg text messaging, information retrieval	10:1	Modest	Important or critical	Essential	2.4K
Transaction processing	Eg order processing, credit clearing	100:1	Predefined, limited	Usually important	Usually none	9.6K
Bulk transfer	Of data files or documents	2:1	Can be high Ad hoc	Usually un-important	Sometimes	48K
Resource-sharing	Eg CAD work groups, PCs with shared files	1000:1	Predefined	Important	Sometimes	200K

Figure 8.2 Characteristics of different types of traffic

communities, both for existing traffic and for all new traffic that you are able to forecast with reasonable confidence, showing approximate numbers expected to participate in each. You should also mark the location of major shared resources, such as processing centres, telephone exchanges or messaging services. These, of course, form the hub of some of the information communities. If you are able to compute traffic volumes on major routes , then it is helpful to include these as well. For very large organizations, you may need an overview chart, plus detailed charts. For simplicity, it helps to take the telephony requirement as read, rather than complicate the chart by marking it in.

When you have completed this exercise, what can you learn from it? Two things in particular, each of which are important because of the changing demands on the network reviewed earlier:

- Opportunities for integrating network services arise where information communities overlap. Seeing these opportunities in terms of information communities with a given set of characteristics helps to focus on the differences between types of traffic which an integrated network must reconcile effectively. As well as looking at the potential cost savings arising from integration, you must also take on board the performance implications – how will an integrated network cope with the characteristics of the information communities? how will service to users be affected?

- Organizational and geographical boundaries, and particularly the boundary between the private on-site domain and the public off-site domain, are significant break points, where the degree of control that the network operator can exercise over costs or over procedures changes, sometimes radically. For this reason, it is important to focus on these boundaries, and the methods that are to be used to carry traffic across them. Those methods determine how much control is retained by the network operator. For example, an intelligent interface device at the point where traffic leaves a large site and enters the public domain can optimize the packaging (for example, sending messages in bursts rather than individually) and the routing of traffic (for example, choosing least cost routes), and thus protect against future changes in the carrier's tariff structures. It can also control access authorization for traffic entering the site from the outside world. Without such an interface device, any such control would have to be organized individually by the various devices participating in the information community concerned.

To illustrate how the information community concept can be applied, here are some examples.

EXAMPLE A: A HEALTH AUTHORITY
The organization represented in Figure 8.3 consists of two large hospitals run by a London health authority, one of them a teaching hospital. The figure shows very clearly that the organization has, or anticipates having, a number of information communities. Apart from the ubiquitous

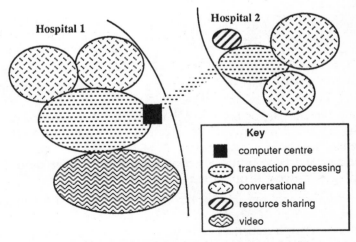

Figure 8.3 Information communities in a health district

telephone system, there is very limited overlap between them. They are:

- A community of dumb terminals, linking users to a processing centre for applications such as patient records and supplies (*transaction processing*).
- Various small communities of professionals using closed networks for *ad hoc* non-voice interworking (*conversational* and *resource-sharing*).
- A planned computer-aided instruction network using fixed and dynamic frame TV communication (*video*).

Looking at the different characteristics of these communities, the organization decided that the best option would be to implement a number of dedicated networks for each community. This also helped to meet their concerns about security. Traffic between the two main sites would be channelled on to a number of high-bandwidth leased lines, allocated separately for voice and non-voice traffic. Until such time as voice switching equipment was intelligent enough to allocate bandwidth dynamically, allocation would be controlled manually by a supervisor.

EXAMPLE B: AN INTERNATIONAL BANK
This international bank was preparing to move its operations staff out of its city centre office into a new out-of-town location, to make room for anticipated expansion. The computer centre also was to relocate. Figure 8.4 represents the position it anticipated in 1990. Ignoring telephony, five types of traffic are shown on the figure:

- Word processors and personal computers, requiring *ad hoc* links to one another and to services at the computer centre (*conversational* and *bulk transfer*).
- Terminals accessing transaction processing and enquiry applications at the computer centre, from both of the bank's major locations and from customers' premises (*transaction processing*).
- Message traffic between the bank and other banks, branches and customers, distributed via the bank's own international message network and via telex (*conversational*).
- Facsimile terminals, usually associated with word processors, transmitting uncoded documents, for example for signature verification (*image bulk transfer*).
- Full video or freeze frame videoconferencing to overcome the disadvantages of two-site operation (*video*).

International banking is a highly integrated form of business, and this shows in the high degree of overlap between the communities. Where there are high densities of non-voice terminals used for varying purposes, such as occurs at both sites, local area network technology comes into its own, so the bank decided to install local area networks at

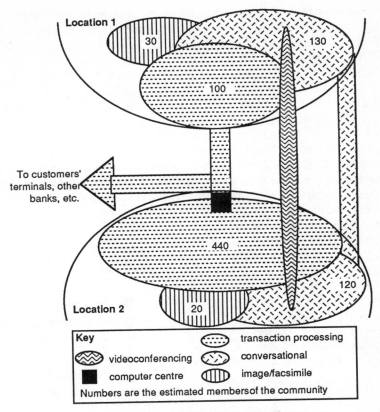

Figure 8.4 Information communities in an International bank

both sites for all but the transaction processing terminals, with separate telephone exchanges for voice traffic. The transaction processing terminals would remain on the established multiplexed data communications network, with *ad hoc* extensions provided by the local area network. Inter-site traffic would be channeled over a number of high-bandwidth leased lines, with manual switching of capacity so that, for example, video traffic could be allocated capacity when needed. There would also be a 'gateway' system providing an entry point for external terminals and an access point for external networks such as Reuters and SWIFT.

EXAMPLE C: A MANUFACTURING GROUP
This group manufactures and distributes footwear and clothing. It has two head offices, serving manufacturing locations in the north and south of the country respectively. The position anticipated in 1989 is shown in Figure 8.5. At the head office sites, they expect rapid growth in the use of terminals linked to the computer centres, and of word processors and

personal computers. They considered using integrated voice plus data exchanges for both head office sites, to support both telephony and 'office' applications, but found this option to be more expensive than specialist data switching technologies, such as local area networks.

Major manufacturing locations have their own information systems for manufacturing control and for distribution, so traffic between them and head office is modest, consisting mainly of bulk data transfers. Consequently, traffic between major sites is insufficient on its own to justify dedicated leased lines, and cannot be multiplexed with voice traffic to share voice lines. Longer term, the growth of point of sale transactions exchanged between manufacturing locations and their customers may justify installing a corporate network, or adopting a third-party data network, to carry both this traffic and the bulk data.

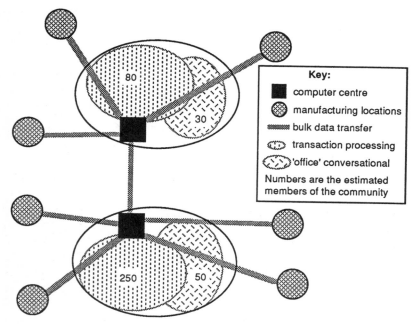

Figure 8.5 Information communities in a manufacturing group

Deciding network structure

The role of the corporate network has changed. It is no longer mainly a means of limiting telecommunications costs, as it so often was in the past. Now, its main *raison d'être* is to facilitate the exchange of information, and increasingly that means non-voice as well as voice, by the organizational units and the individuals within the organization. Those responsible for planning the network, therefore, must be wary of an excessive concern with traffic volumes and with the cost of transporting bits, important though those are. In terms of its role – what it seeks to do for its users – and its overall structure, the corporate network today is shaped more by the strategy you adopt to distribute information and processing power and by the means you choose to support interworking, than it is by traffic volumes. Hence, as I now explain, these are the issues you should focus on. Once again, the generic strategies introduced in Chapter 2 are a valuable guide to the best approach.

Desktop power demands new structures

Cheap processing power and storage has already arrived on many desks in the shape of personal computers equipped with hard disks, and the pace of improvement in cost/performance shows no sign of slowing yet. As already explained, the arrival of these powerful workstations, combined with other factors, creates strong pressures in favour of distributing processing power and information out into the business. Even in the heartland of data processing, personal computers are rapidly displacing the dumb terminals which have been the mainstay of online transaction processing so far. In this emerging environment of cheap desktop power, the structure of the corporate network will increasingly reflect information structures, rather than the disposition of shared technology resources such as mainframe computers.

Powerful workstations also generate more complex, more *ad hoc* traffic patterns than the dumb terminals which they are now beginning to replace. These more complex traffic patterns arise partly because the machines are more versatile, but also because they are increasingly being used by knowledge workers such as professionals and managers. The information handling of these knowledge workers is different in kind from that of most clerical staff. Knowledge workers tend to synthesize information from a variety of different sources, while clerical staff typically specialize in a narrow range of information-related tasks. (This, of course, is what has made clerical staff easier targets for automation via computer systems than knowledge workers.) These different work patterns imply a different network structure than that required for information systems oriented toward clerical work.

Typically, today's corporate data networks funnel traffic inwards, either directly to a data centre, or to a limited number of nodes sited near the data centres that concentrate the traffic. These structures are inefficient and inconvenient for powerful workstations and decentralized computers to use. When more and more of the traffic comes in to the nodes in order to be switched out again to remote sites, they quickly turn into serious bottlenecks. A private telephone system, which has switching systems (PABXs) on every site, linked by direct lines between them or by the public switched telephone network, is a much better model for the type of structure that will be needed.

A new role - to facilitate interworking

While the telephone network is a good structural model for the corporate network of the future, it is less suitable as a model in other important respects, because of the differences between types of traffic that I outlined above. Telephone networks, naturally enough, are designed to support telephone conversations, which require lengthy, continuous channel connections, or in other words circuit-switching technology, rather than the packet-switching technology appropriate for much non-voice traffic. These separate requirements can be reconciled in a single piece of equipment, but the cost of doing so narrows, and often wipes out altogether, the margin gained by sharing equipment and wiring between voice and non-voice traffic.

Equally important, the telephone network is designed to support essentially passive terminals which require very little control from the network. Once a connection has been established between two telephones, the network becomes transparent, concerning itself only with transmitting voice signals from one end to the other of the connection. Data devices such as screen terminals and personal computers, by contrast, need what is normally referred to as *end-to-end control* to ensure that dialogues are conducted in an orderly and secure manner. Paradoxically, the use of a transparent telephone network to support non-voice dialogues tends to hinder, rather than help with this task. An example illustrates the problems that emerge when the worlds of voice and data collide in this way.

As a pilot exercise, Aer Lingus installed a digital PABX to switch voice and data between its buildings, scattered about Dublin airport. It was in fact the geography of its buildings that made an integrated voice plus data solution so attractive, because the cost of separate wiring to support the growth of data traffic would have been very high. As well as all the telephone traffic on the Dublin airport site, the PABX was to handle enquiries from data terminals and personal computers to a common database containing information on topics such as crew rostering and unavailability of staff due to leave, and to a shared 'office automation' system (based on DEC's *All-in-1*) to be used for word processing and electronic mail. The pilot revealed a number of problems:

- Calls to the new applications were set up via the PABX, then users logged on to the service they required. However, if a call was terminated by the PABX, the application to which the user was connected was not aware of this, and the terminal was left logged on. Another user could then dial in to the same port that the previous user had occupied, and be surprised to find him- or herself in the middle of that user's half-finished session.

- To avoid the inconvenience of setting up calls and logging on, users tended to log on for the whole day. This defeated the purpose of having the PABX as a switching system, and reduced its effective carrying capacity.

- Because the computer hosting the 'office automation' system could not dial out to shared printers, they had to be permanently connected using separate lines and modems. Again, this reduced the value of having a voice plus data switching system.

The results of the pilot were mixed – a reasonable level of user satisfaction overall, but little use of 'office automation' services apart from word processing. Although many other factors are involved, it is more than likely that the inconveniences introduced by the presence of the PABX helped to inhibit use of services such as electronic messaging. Because of the geographical spread of buildings on the site, electronic messaging should have been of particular value.

To sum up, the key difference between telephone communication and communication between computer-based devices is that the former is mediated by people – the telephone users – while the latter has to be mediated by the devices themselves. Computer-based devices are much less adaptable than people, so they need a much higher level of support from the network. They require this support not only to operate efficiently, that is to make good use of transmission capacity, but also to operate effectively – to establish contact with the application they wish to use, to ensure an orderly flow of information, and so on, and all with a minimum of manual intervention by their users or operators.

While the telephone network is not an ideal model for what is required, nor are the networks designed for transaction processing. They do provide the kind of control features which computer-based devices require, but they tend to be too rigidly organized to support the more complex, more *ad hoc* traffic patterns that I referred to above. In transaction processing networks, the host computer acts as master, with the terminals as its slaves. Nothing exists in the network that the control software in the host does not know about, and nothing moves without its knowledge and consent.

The new role required of the corporate network is an amalgam of the desirable features of the telephone network and of traditional, centrally controlled data networks. The network must provide the discipline and the support which computer-based devices and their users need in order to interwork effectively, and to access their varied sources of information. But it must also have the flexibility appropriate for an information systems environment containing growing numbers of powerful work-stations and work-group systems that operate independently of the central systems and exchange information on a peer-to-peer basis, rather than as between master and slave.

How intelligent should the corporate network be?

Given that the network must do more for its users, it is not immediately clear how much more it should do. For network managers, the Catch-22 clause runs: 'the more you try to do for network users, the more you will look like a spendthrift and power maniac whose main aim in life is to extend your own empire'. Not only do intelligent networks cost more than the basic variety everyone built in the past. Additionally, because of 'the interconnection problem' referred to in Chapter 4, the more intel-ligence you build into the corporate network, the more assumptions you have to make about the protocols and procedures devices attached to the network will use, and hence the more constraints you place on user choice.

Thus network managers can easily find themselves caught between a rock and a hard place. Do too little for your users, and they build their own networks or buy in services from outside suppliers (assuming, that is, that they are allowed to do any such thing; if not, they pressure senior management to give them the option). Do too much, and they react in exactly the same manner, complaining that money is being wasted building a complicated network that does not even meet basic require-ments. More than a few network managers have gone to the wall after failing to find a tenable position between these two dangers. The trick is to get the role of the network just right – enough help to make a differ-ence, but not so much as to deter use. Both from a technical point of view and in terms of corporate politics, this is a very difficult trick to bring off. I am certainly not going to give you a foolproof formula for success, but I can give you some pointers.

First, a way of looking at the objective – of supporting interworking and access to information – in a structured way, so that you can gauge the impact of providing different levels of support. We already have a framework for doing this, in the form of ISO's OSI Reference Model. This breaks down the task of interconnecting devices across a network into seven levels. As summarized in the lefthand column of Figure 8.6, each level builds additional function on to the levels below it to provide a certain level of support to applications or to network users.

Clearly, if a network and/or the devices using it are incompatible at any of the levels, either nothing useful will be achieved at all, or alternatively some cost will be incurred because someone or something somewhere has to do extra work to bridge the gap in compatibility. By

OSI level	Level of support	Cost of limited/no support
Level 7: application	Supports the processing activities appropriate for the application, e.g. • A command sequence to retrieve information from a database. • Instructions to send an electronic mail message.	Some application functions are inaccessible; operating procedures are clumsy or confusing, e.g. function keys or commands do not have the effect the screen or manual tells you they should.
Level 6: presentation	Ensures that information is coded and formatted in the right way for processing and/or display in the receiving device.	Information is presented badly or has to be reformatted or converted before use, e.g. formatting instructions for a word processing document have to be re-entered.
Level 5: session	Establishes a dialogue or processing session between network users, or between a network user and a service or application, and regulates the flow of messages between them.	It is difficult to establish connection to, or change between services, e.g. you have to sign off completely from one service, then re-connect and sign on again to another related service. Conversely, it is too easy to gain access to services, with consequent risk of fraud or sabotage.
Level 4: transport Level 3: network	Provides end-to-end control of the exchange of messages between two network users (level 4) or across a network (level 3).	Ineffective error handling, leading to loss or duplication of information; inefficient performance.
Level 2: data link	Transfers messages or packets across a communications link.	Undetected corruption of information; inefficient performance.
Level 1: physical	Transmits electrical signals between devices.	Poor diagnostics; no communication.

Figure 8.6 Interconnection levels and the probable cost of incompatibility

analogy, if two people who do not share a common language wish to communicate, they can hire an interpreter, or leaf laboriously through a dictionary or phrasebook, or even (eventually, no doubt) use an automatic translation machine. Each of those solutions has its own merits and demerits, and an associated cost. Returning to the OSI model, the nature of any cost that is incurred depends on the level at which the incompatibility arises, and the right-hand column of the figure shows the likely cost at each level of the model. Bear in mind in looking at this that incompatibility at lower levels can imply some or all of the costs incurred at levels above, as well as at its own level.

My analogy with language communication suggested that there is usually more than one way to solve an incompatibility problem, and the same is generally true for interconnection of computer-based devices, particularly at levels 5 and above, where the basic communication tasks dealt with by lower levels give way to tasks which have more to do with the application in hand. This is the second pointer – be aware of the several ways in which many interconnection problems can be handled, including by the corporate network, and of the pros and cons of each.

In essence, these problems can be handled in one of three ways:

- By building extra intelligence into the systems running the *shared services*, so that, for example, they recognize the requirements of different types of device addressing them and respond accordingly.
- By building extra intelligence into the *network*, in the form of directories, conversion routines and control features, so that it performs a similar role for any devices conducting a dialogue across the network.
- By building this intelligence into the devices operated by network users – *workstations and local systems*.

Each of these places the operating responsibility (although not necessarily responsibility for provision) on to a different person – the provider of the shared services, often the data processing department; the network manager; and the network user, respectively for each of the three options listed above. Leaving aside equipment cost issues, each of them also has particular advantages and disadvantages, which are summarized in Figure 8.7.

Intelligence built into ...	Advantages	Disadvantages
Shared services	Single point of control (or few) makes it easier to provide a consistent high-level interface to all users of the service/application.	Central maintenance overhead for directories, software, etc. can create a bottleneck if requirements are volatile. Inconvenient for peer-to-peer or local traffic that normally need not come near the shared systems.
Corporate network	Makes it easier to provide a consistent session-level interface for users of a range of different services, and to establish company-wide access security schemes and directories.	Increased dependence on network intelligence makes it more difficult to use public network services for fallback when failures occur.
Workstations and/or local systems	Increases local autonomy and flexibility, since local systems can be programmed to reflect precise local needs.	Likely to create problems of version control and software maintenance; network upgrades may make local solutions obsolete.

Figure 8.7 Where should the interconnection intelligence be located?

Generic strategies point to the right approach

Looking at the corporate networks which were being implemented by a range of different, leading-edge organizations in the US and Europe, I recognized five main structural variants. Four of these variants correspond to the four generic strategies described in Chapter 2. Each of them provides a high level of support for non-voice communication, including traffic generated by end-user systems. But the structure of the communications network that handles the non-voice traffic varies, and can be differentiated in two ways:

- By whether it is principally hierarchical, or whether it has a mesh structure intended to support complex patterns of lateral, as well as hierarchical, communication.
- By whether the network couples its users tightly or loosely to shared services and to one another – tight coupling imposes a strict discipline on users' means of access and interworking, in other words takes support higher up the levels of the OSI model, while loose coupling provides services more on a take-it-or-leave-it basis, leaving the onus on the network user to decide how to access and use services.

Hierarchical networks normally have centralized switching, sometimes distributed across two or more major sites interconnected by high-speed lines, to protect against disasters or major failures. Work groups on different sites may have their equipment attached to local switching systems such as local area networks or directly to multiplexers, and traffic from these work groups is channelled to the centralized switching nodes. Mesh networks, by contrast, use distributed switching, with switching nodes on all major sites, interconnected either by switched public networks or by private lines, depending on traffic levels and prevailing tariffs. In terms of the generic strategies, hierarchical networks are preferred by low-autonomy companies; mesh networks by high-autonomy. The choice of tight or loose coupling correlates, as you would expect, with the coupling variable of the generic strategies.

These four corporate network structures are shaped principally by the organization's requirements for internal communication, although they will of course be linked to public networks for telephony, telex and data to provide access to the world outside the organization as well. For some organizations, that external network is affected by the growth of trading networks – electronic data interchange and data acquisition at source. Here there are strong pressures from the carriers to adopt international standards for transport of information, and from industry associations to adopt industry standards for the formatting of documents and transactions. Normally, these same standards will not be adopted universally within the internal network, partly because they are too unwieldy for the purpose, partly because the internal systems already use different protocols. Hence, it is worth thinking in terms of installing a gateway to link internal and external networks, rather than, for example, building an interface directly into the computer(s) running the operational systems. This provides flexibility for the future.

The fifth variant provides only limited support for data communications, by allocating bandwidth as and when needed. The prime purpose of a network such is this is to achieve economies of scale by sharing bandwidth between large sites. I call this the *transport utility*. Networks such as this are commonly installed and operated (in those countries where telecommunications regulation permits) at corporate level by large groups of disparate companies. Effectively, it is a highest-common-factor default option, reflecting how difficult it is to reconcile the different needs of diverse businesses and provide a shared network which gives them all the required level of service. Consequently, such a network is only worthwhile if it can achieve cost savings, whilst remaining transparent to business units' communication applications. The role of the network operator, in effect, is to operate as an enlightened telecommunications carrier within the organization, rather than to provide a service which fully reflects the needs of the businesses in the group. This means that the economics of the *transport utility*, and hence its value to the organization, are highly vulnerable to tariff changes by the carriers.

Deciding the operating philosophy

The new pressures generated by the growth of end-user systems also influence the way the network is operated and managed. Central management is proving increasingly difficult to sustain as rates of change at local level increase. All but relatively small organizations on a single site will need to think about decentralizing at least some aspects of network management.

Central network management is difficult to sustain

The advantage of centralized network management is that it concentrates scarce engineering skills and sophisticated monitoring equipment at one or a few locations. The cost advantages of doing so are well recognized by telecommunications authorities, who reckon to reduce their requirements for engineering staff to maintain public telephone networks by an order of magnitude, by installing equipment that enables exchanges to be monitored and controlled from a few maintenance centres.

That said, it must also be recognized that managing a corporate telephone network day-to-day is very different from managing a non-voice network carrying data, text and similar traffic. To manage a voice network is principally a matter of isolating and repairing faults in the switching and transmission equipment, and occasionally replacing a faulty telephone. Faults arise from a relatively narrow range of causes which, given the right equipment and the right training, are fairly easy to diagnose.

With a non-voice network, by contrast, faults are far more difficult to run to earth. As well as from faults in the network equipment, problems also arise because a personal computer user does something silly; because a new software package or a new version of an operating system has been installed which is not quite compatible with the network or with other devices with which it exchanges information; and for a host of other reasons which have more to do with the people and the applications that are using the network than with the network itself. The manager of one of the UK's largest private non-voice networks told me that most of the faults on his network were down to the carrier (at a time, it should be added, when new digital telecommunications services were going through severe teething problems), and the vast majority of those that were under his direct control were software problems. As far as network users are concerned 'it doesn't work!' and they expect him, as network operator, to put things right. It requires a heavy expenditure on people and monitoring equipment to cope. If provided centrally, these people constitute a highly visible overhead. What is more, they often find it difficult to operate effectively because they are too remote from the people using the network and from their problems. Network management in the end-user systems era is more akin to end-user support than to engineering.

The high rate of change in the end-user systems era introduces further difficulties. DEC (UK), for example, growing consistently at over 25 per cent per annum, found that managing their corporate network centrally severely restricted the flexibility they needed to sustain that growth. Rolls-Royce, operating on ten sites across the UK, adopted a centralized network management approach, both for cost reasons and because security was very important for their work in the defence field. But they soon found the more volatile traffic patterns and the 'churn' – frequent changes in device location – generated by personal computers very difficult to handle. In practical terms, they were able to cope with about 200 device changes a year, and this was no longer enough.

In summary, then, important new features of the information systems scene create powerful pressures to decentralize at least some aspects of network management to local staff who can respond quickly and appropriately to local needs.

The network should be partitioned

I mentioned above that Digital Equipment Company have been experiencing sustained growth in excess of 25 per cent per annum, and they are also an organization with a very wide geographical distribution. In 1987, their internal network connected over 15,000 computers, located on 340 sites in 26 countries. This makes them an extreme example of the pressures to decentralize which I have just outlined, and the methods they have adopted to manage their corporate network can be taken as a

model, to be scaled down for organizations suffering lesser pressures.[3]
They have partitioned their network horizontally into three levels:

- At the lowest level, there is an access network on each building or site, typically a local area network and/or some other site switching system, linking computers and workstations on the site to one another and to the outside world, including the next higher level of the corporate network.
- At the next level, the network is divided into geographical areas reflecting the organizational structure.
- At the highest level, an organization-wide 'backbone' network carries traffic between the areas.

Each building and each area has a manager who is responsible for planning for growth and for operating his/her part of the network, including the interface to the level above. The manager is answerable to his customers for the cost and quality of the service provided. For the building manager, that means the network users themselves; and for the area manager, it means the building managers. The backbone network is run by a central group, which also issues rules or guidelines to area and building managers. These are designed to meet corporate concerns, such as for security, and to ensure that the network operates as a coherent whole and as 'seamlessly' as possible. In other words, the aim is that the internal stucture of the network and its division into three levels should be invisible to network users.

In organizations smaller or less widespread geographically than DEC no more than two levels are needed – an *access network* in every building or site, and a *transport network* linking those access networks to one another and to shared services. In the rest of this chapter, I use those two terms and distinguish only between the two levels.

Linking transport and access networks

Both cost ratios and regulatory constraints are different in the transport and access networks, and for this reason they have to be considered separately. Yet, as is obvious, there is also a close relationship between them. There are essentially two ways of building the links between them:

- A *bridge* extends an access network on one site to that on another site, without switching traffic and without altering it in any way. Its job is to make efficient use of the relatively expensive bandwidth between the sites, and also to detect and correct errors introduced on the private lines or public networks used between the sites, which will normally be less reliable than lines on the site. Thus, a bridge effectively extends the access network across more than one site.
- A *gateway* enables devices on an access network to communicate

across other networks, such as public packet-switching services, or with other systems, such as the corporate data centre, that may not use the same procedures as are used on the access network. Like the bridge, it concerns itself with the efficiency and the reliability of transmission, but it may also take care of access security and collect accounting data. A gateway serving a large site may be a special-purpose dedicated device; on a smaller site or for a single work group, it may be one of the tasks handled by a work-group system, or by a personal computer acting as communications server on a local area network.

For a given information community, or combination of information communities, the choice between bridge and gateway will obviously depend to a large extent on the nature of the traffic crossing the boundary between the local access and transport networks. Bridges, which are inherently simpler, are usually cheaper than gateways. However, the extra intelligence of the gateway can deliver important benefits, both tangible and intangible. The US House of Representatives, for example, reckoned to save $950,000 on external telecommunications charges because the gateway installed there automatically chose least-cost routes for traffic. A protocol conversion feature, centralized in the gateway, can also displace costs. If, for example, IBM 3270 emulation is included in one personal computer acting as gateway, all the other personal computers on the local access network can use simple and low-cost methods to get through to the company mainframe.

Cost of local support against value of local control

Both the organizations I mentioned above that experienced the draw-backs of centralized network management – DEC and Rolls-Royce – are, in the terminology of my four generic strategies, *high autonomy* busi-nesses, since they both manufacture highly complex products with a high service content. As you would expect, this feature of their business operations is reflected in a high rate of change at local level in their infor-mation systems. This, in turn, creates the pressures that make centralized network management impractical. Both, also, operate on a number of major sites – DEC internationally, Rolls-Royce in the UK.

If we compare their experience with a *low autonomy* organization also operating with many sites, we see the same pressures operating in favour of decentralization. But the costs and the compensating benefits of local management are different, and this may result in a different answer. Chemical Bank, for example, decided to install distributed systems in all of its 260 branches, to make it easier to create new branch applications whenever the need arises. Workstations in the branches are attached to local area networks, which are linked via a gateway to the mainframe computers that run the main business applications such as credit card and cheque account maintenance. The same argument that led to distributed systems could be advanced in favour of decentralizing network management, but the bank decided against it, and manages the network centrally all the way through to the workstations. The vice-president responsible for the development explains the decision like this: 'Many things can go wrong between the workstation and the mainframe, so we're very sensitive to being able to centrally control, manage, and even diagnose right down to the workstation. We can't expect to have a technical officer in each of our 260 locations ready to manage the system. They want to be in the banking business, not the DP business'.[4]

Thus, the cost of providing support at site level must be set against the value attributed to having local control. This value will be higher in *high autonomy* businesses, where control over information systems applications is likely to be seen as a vehicle for achieving business objectives, rather than as a distraction.

Assessing the integration options

Finally, I review some of the equipment options, but I do not try to provide a complete guide to the procurement of network equipment. There are far too many equipment options and far too many variations in the nature and tariffing of telecommunications services for that. Instead I concentrate on the integration options, and the key decisions associated with integration. I concentrate on integration for two reasons. First, because a corporate network, stretching perhaps across a number of sites and across the public as well as the private domain, must nonetheless function as a single network. And, second, because the technology and supplier pressures in favour of integration of different forms of traffic are so powerful.

Integration brings mixed blessings

Within the corporate network, integration can be applied at three main levels:

- *In the transport network* – by channeling the traffic from a number of sources on to high-capacity long distance lines, you reduce the overall cost of transmission.
- *In the access network* – by integrating the switching and routing of traffic across company sites, you rationalize site wiring and maintenance, and give users greater freedom to interconnect their systems as and when they wish.
- *At the workstation* – by extending integration all the way out to the

workstation, you can replace telephone, data terminal, personal computer, and whatever, with a single multi–purpose device.

To some extent, the options at these three levels are interdependent, but not entirely so. It is not unusual, for example, for organizations to switch data and voice traffic separately in the access network on the site, but link the separate traffic streams into an integrated inter-site transport network. Conversely, an advanced switching system, such as a digital private telephone exchange, could direct data traffic on to a network optimized for data, such as a packet–switching network, and voice traffic on to a separate (circuit–switched) network optimized for telephony. It is necessary, therefore, to look at the pros and cons at each level separately.

Before I do so, I want to take a closer look at the cost savings that can be achieved through integration. Economies can be achieved in three main ways:

1. Economies of *scale* in transmission and, to a lesser extent, in switching and multiplexing equipment: high-bandwidth telecommunications lines such as MegaStream in the UK or T1 carriers in the US provide bandwidth at something like a fifth of the price of slower lines, so that substantial sums can be saved by using them to carry all the traffic between large sites.
2. Economies of *sharing*: where traffic of different types follows common routes, further economies can be gained by interpolating other traffic into the gaps beween continuous channel traffic such as voice. However, little can be gained where the peaks coincide. The spread of end-user systems is incorporating information processing more and more into routine work patterns, which naturally means that peaks increasingly coincide.
3. Economies of *operation* by combining the staff who run and maintain the network – one network should be cheaper to run than two. As has already been pointed out, however, management of voice and non-voice networks are very different games, and the increasing volatility of network users' requirements militates against management totally from the centre.

The brief outline of the integration options, given above, suggested that integration can lead not only to cost savings, but also to operational gains. Most notably, it promises to rationalize both management and equipment of corporate networks, and to open up the path toward the universal multi-purpose workstation.

But these potential gains are counter-balanced by potential penalties, which include:

•   The problem of achieving security for non-voice applications running in the much more open environment characteristic of telephony.

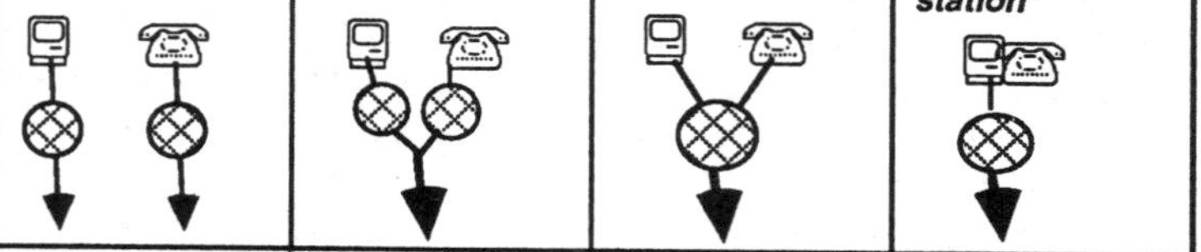

	Separate	Integrated transmission	Integrated switching	Integration at the work-station
Main advantages	Straightforward Separate systems can be developed independently	Saves money on transmission costs	Rationalization of on-site wiring and of site management	The 'multi-function workstation'
Main dis-advantages	Extra wiring Terminals cannot easily interwork	Vulnerability ('all eggs in one basket')		
			Increased risk if growth exceeds expectations	
				Access security may be a problem
Conditions to be met if advantages are to be realized	None	Traffic flows must match – must follow the same routes and ideally peaks should not coincide		
		Enough traffic to give economies of scale on inter-site lines	Signalling schemes – methods used to set up and clear down calls etc – must be compatible	

Figure 8.8 Integration options, pros and cons

- Difficulty in reconciling the very different methods used to control and manage voice and data networks.
- Increased vulnerability, resulting from combining two or more separate systems into one integrated system.
- For the same reason, reduced flexibility and greater exposure – for example, unexpectedly rapid growth in non-voice traffic might degrade service levels for telephone users, or necessitate an expensive upgrade.

These disadvantages do not apply equally at the three levels at which integration can be applied. Figure 8.8 shows the three levels, plus the default option of keeping voice and non-voice traffic separate, and summarizes their pros and cons. It also shows, in the bottom row, the conditions to be met if this option is to be workable. For each of those levels in turn I now look in more detail at the conditions for success and the main options.

The transport network – keep it simple

Suppliers face a central difficulty in reconciling the worlds of voice and

data. It concerns the signalling procedures used to send control information between terminals – telephones and workstations – and switching
equipment, for example to set up and clear down calls. Since many of
these calls will not originate and. terminate on the site, these signalling
procedures must be compatible with those used on external networks,
and particularly on the emerging digital services which will enable the
advantages of integrated switching to be exploited to the full. The
problem is therefore inextricably linked with the international standards–
making process discussed briefly earlier in the book.

At the time of writing, official standards have not been agreed. In the
interim, major equipment suppliers are devising their own standards or
adopting those developed nationally. They will subsequently re-engineer
their equipment to conform with the standards that are agreed. While
this may not cause serious problems, it does represent an added risk.

Furthermore, it appears that a large proportion of the value of
integrating voice and non-voice traffic can be achieved by applying
conventional multiplexing techniques to the non-voice traffic alone. If
this is the case, there is no need to share circuits between voice and non-
voice traffic. Non-voice traffic can occupy part of a high-bandwidth
channel alongside voice. In the absence of compatible signalling standards, channels allocated to voice cannot automatically be switched to
non-voice or *vice versa* when traffic loads vary. In the meantime, this can
be achieved through manual switching.

In a sentence – keep the transport network as clean and as simple as
possible, consistent with reasonably efficient use of transmission
capacity, because the risks involved in integration are considerable.

The access network – two (or more) worlds collide

The natural pattern of business communication is for most of the traffic to
occur locally, within the work group and on the site. The pattern of
electronic communication has been distorted by large centralized transaction processing systems. But, as end-user systems spread, the natural
pattern starts to re-establish itself, and hence the access network grows in
importance. New technologies, including local area networks and voice
plus data telephone exchanges, have come forward to meet the requirement. Unfortunately, excitement about these new technologies has
sometimes drawn attention away from users' real needs and problems.
While there may be money and trouble to save by rationalizing site
wiring, for example, it is unlikely to make long term sense unless at the
same time the end-user at the workstation gains advantage from the
change.

Most telecommunications managers will be uncomfortably aware of
the wiring problem in today's office. For a new office, up to four separate

networks may be required, each using a different wiring scheme – see Figure 8.9. The competing interests of telecommunications and data processing suppliers have, so far, exacerbated rather than resolved this wiring problem.

To integrate switching of voice and non-voice traffic on the site, suppliers need to solve the technical problems in such a way that the cost of their integrated solution compares with that of separate networks. This task is not made easier by continuing cost reductions in the better established technologies of separate switching.

The suppliers' main problem is to develop a cost-effective switching technology capable of coping with the considerable functional differences between voice and non-voice traffic which I referred to earlier in this chapter. Their particular goal is to produce what is referred to as a *nonblocking* switch, which prevents bursty non-voice traffic from interfering with continuous voice calls, and *vice versa*. Although US suppliers have made some progress, the cost-effectiveness of the technology remains uncertain.

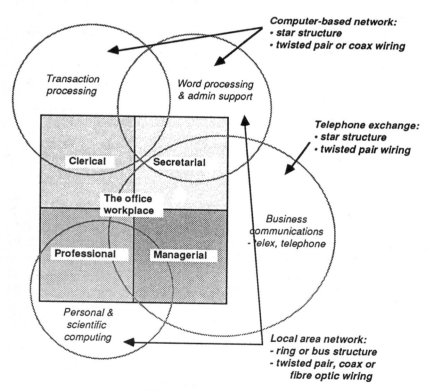

Figure 8.9 The wiring problem

The fact is that the main candidate technologies – local area networks and digital private telephone exchanges (PABXs) – in many respects complement one another rather than compete. The former are optimized for bursty traffic and designed to fit into the communications control philosophy adopted by today's computer systems, while the latter are optimized for telephony and designed to work across public telephone networks. As I have explained, a map of your information communities will show you where there is scope for integration. Here is some guidance on how you should assess the opportunities.

On very large sites, such as the Dublin airport site mentioned earlier or a university campus, the integration opportunity offering the greatest cost saving will usually consist of exploiting telephone wiring and the telephone exchange to carry non-voice traffic. Where there is a business case such as this for voice/data integration, you should not take for granted that it is technically feasible, even at this stage. Pause and ask yourself these questions before going ahead. To be safe, you should either be able to answer them all affirmatively, or have cast-iron guarantees from the potential switch supplier that the underlying problem has been overcome:

- Can the workstations be connected by means of normal telephone wiring, rather than, for example, by coaxial cable?
- Will transparent connection of workstations via the switching system – in other words, a pipeline to carry traffic that does nothing to ensure compatibility or control traffic flow – be adequate?
- Is there no serious risk that the non-voice traffic will overload the switching system or provoke expensive upgrades?
- Will switched access to the inter-site transmission system, rather than via a multiplexer or concentrator that economizes bandwidth, be efficient enough?[5]

Where there are multiple overlapping non-voice information communities, and particularly if one of these uses video, there may be an opportunity to reduce costs significantly by integrating these to operate over a broadband local area network, with telephone traffic switched separately. Cost effectiveness will depend on a sufficient number of devices sharing the local area network to justify the installation and the cost of interfacing devices – interfacing costs are particularly high for these broadband systems. Lower cost local area networks come into their own where there is a high density of non-voice devices, particularly powerful ones generating very bursty traffic.[6]

In summary, the best choice will depend mainly on the cost of wiring and the traffic mix. Additionally, separate networks for voice and non-voice services have advantages where you expect rapid growth in traffic, or where the rate of growth is very uncertain. This is because separate networks reduce the risk of interference between services or of very expensive upgrades. I summarize the alternatives in Figure 8.10, together with the main features of requirements which would point to one of those as the most likely choice.

The workstation – don't chase the technology

Perhaps because they embody technology that is new enough and tangible enough to be exciting, and that is still evolving rapidly, workstations, including personal computers, have tended to be sold more on the delights of their technology than on the value that they can deliver.

The voice plus data workstation, for example, has been promoted strongly by a number of powerful suppliers. As yet, however, it has made little headway in the market. Some staff, such as commercial

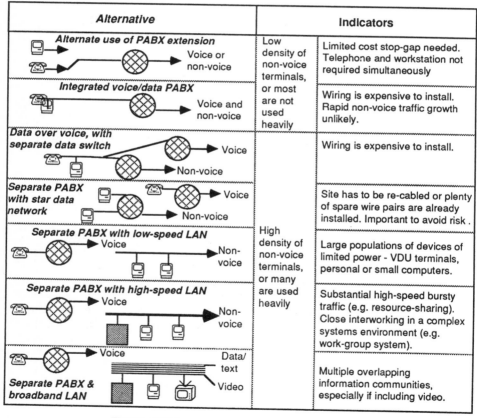

Figure 8.10 Access network alternatives and Indicators of the best choice

managers with geographically dispersed staff, foreign exchange dealers, or buyers of volatile goods, certainly are heavily dependent on rapid access both to their information systems and to their telephones, and may indeed derive considerable value from a good voice plus data workstation, but they are in a minority. No amount of promotion by suppliers can conceal the fact that, in my opinion, integrating voice and data in the workstation gives most staff a second-rate workstation in return for marginal convenience gains.

What many office staff *do* need is integration of a rather different kind – integration of data drawn from different sources, or integration of image and data, for example. In other words, integration driven by their application needs, not integration driven by the technology of integrated switching, which is largely the case with voice/data integration.

The moral, of course, is that you should beware of being distracted by technological possibilities for which there is no real business need. This is hardly a new insight, but always worth stressing. It is perhaps a good note on which to end a chapter that has necessarily dealt with some complex technical issues.

Notes and references

1 Telecommunications people tend to be more enthusiastic about ISDN than computer people. For two contrasting views, see H-E Martin, 'ISDNs: the network solution of the future', *Telecommunications*, 20, 9, Sept 1986, pp. 69-72, 82; and J. McQuillan, 'What's wrong with ISDN?', *Business Communications Review*, Jan/Feb 1987, pp. 37-39.

2 Leon Harding, Worldwide Networks Manager for ICL plc, quoted in *Communicate*, Feb 1986.

3 For a fuller description, see Malcolm Wicks, *The world's largest computer network* (DEC UK, 1987).

4 See 'Grand Net Plan', *Computer Decisions*, March 23 1987, pp. 45-49.

5 See also M. F. Finneran, 'Integrating voice and data in the PBX', *Business Communications Review*, Nov/Dec 1984, pp. 9-14.

6 For a comprehensive description of local area network technologies and their application, see D. Flint, *The data ring main*(Heyden-Wiley, 1983); for a succinct overview, see J. McQuillan, 'Local area networks: yesterday, today, and tomorrow', *Business Communications Review*, Nov/Dec 1984, pp. 38-39.

SUMMARY OF PART TWO:
DEVELOPING THE INFRASTRUCTURE

Here is a summary of the argument and of the main conclusions that have been drawn in Part Two. It is again intended both as a reminder for those who have just finished reading, and for quick and easy reference later.

◊ ◊ ◊ ◊

Part Two explains how to build on the requirements and design principles for the infrastructure identified in Part One, in order to develop a practical and effective solution. It addresses the following questions:

- How should you work towards coherence for the end-user at the workstation?
- How should you distribute processing and storage components, and what steps should you take to maintain overall control?
- How should you manage the interconnection problem?
- How should you plan the corporate network?

I now deal with each of these in turn.

Information power – the workstation

End-users' view of information provided through the workstation is incoherent, and this can be improved by better integrating the various elements which make up that view. As explained in Part One, end-users' integration needs have three dimensions that can be expressed in the form of a *knowledge work support architecture* ...

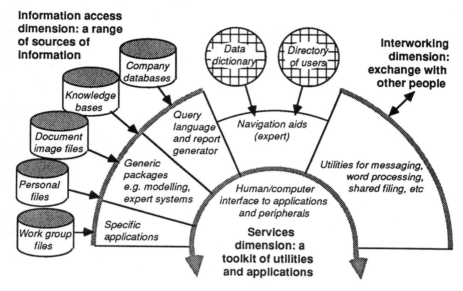

The information access dimension

In the *information access* dimension, the main problem to be overcome is that operational files are usually unsuitable for direct access by end-users, and too narrow in scope to cover their full requirements. The workstation (working in co-operation with other equipment installed locally) contributes to solving these problems by:

- Providing tools for accessing and manipulating data that most end-users can master.
- Providing the means to merge in information from various sources.
- Decoupling end-user activity from the operational systems, thus increasing flexibility and limiting the impact on their performance.

From the common starting point of operational files poorly structured to meet end-users' requirements and end-users equipped with personal computers, here are the main steps to be taken ...

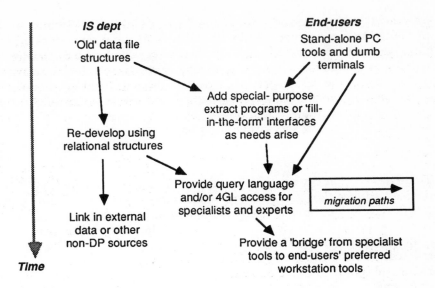

The services dimension

The central aim in the *services* dimension is to make the equipment and its applications easy for end-users to learn and to use. Apple's Macintosh personal computer is a model of what is required. Apart from the striking WIMPs (windows, icon, mouse, pull-down menus) interface, it has presentation management features built into its operating system and reinforced by design guidelines, so that:

- All applications are responsive and operate in a consistent manner.
- The user can switch easily and quickly between applications, carrying information across from one to the next.

Today's personal computers are essentially single-user, single-task machines. So that they can interwork and participate reliably in work group systems, the limitations of their operating software must be overcome. The requirements can be summarized as follows ...

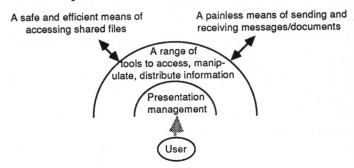

The most likely solution is a personal computer with Macintosh-like presentation management, and with network attachment integrated into the operating software. This would be linked to a shared controller – a work-group system or a centralized mainframe – to handle shared files.

Because of the variety of office workers' needs and the rapid evolution of workstation technology, you should not think in terms of a single, universal prescription, but should provide a framework within which you can match sets of services with different types of user.

The interworking dimension

There has been heavy emphasis on the *interconnection* of computer-based devices, so that they can exchange information in electronic rather than physical form. But the real need is for *interworking* – interconnection is the equivalent of a telephone call, and interworking is the equivalent of the dialogue that ensues. Interconnection only gets us part of the way towards interworking, and is not a prerequisite – paper still has a major role to play. To understand how information technology can support interworking, we must look at business communication as a whole ...

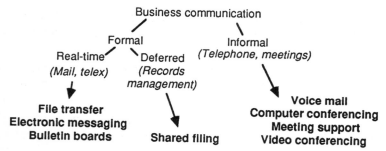

The technologies supporting informal communication are still relatively poorly developed, so the emphasis so far has been on supporting formal communication. Electronic messaging is the key to that support ...

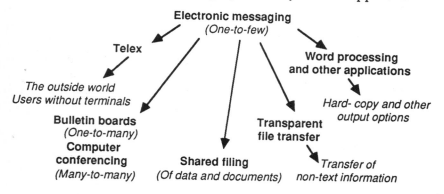

The success of electronic messaging depends on achieving a critical mass of regular users. For this reason you should target initial services at identified groups with characteristics like these ...

	Characteristic of group	Weight
Nature of their work patterns	Complex relationships	Important
	High competitive/external pressures	Important
	Widespread geographically or mobile	Important
	High and regular intercommunication	Important
Nature of the information they exchange	Need to match information or time-sensitive information or volatile information	At least one of these is crucial
	High administration costs	Important
Nature of the environment	Suitable terminals already in place	Influential
	Easy to extend beyond initial service	Influential

Setting priorities

Building the *knowledge work support architecture* as outlined above is a protracted task. Here is some guidance if you are not clear where to start or which step to take next:

- Target highly motivated work groups with real business problems – these are most likely to make the sustained effort necessary to discover the potential of the new systems.
- Concentrate on making progress along one of the dimensions at a time – the interworking dimension is especially important for high-linkage companies, and the services dimension for information-intensive companies.
- Beware the Swiss army knife principle – go for the simplest solution that integrates 80 per cent or so of the needs.

Distributing processing power and information

The starting point for deciding how processing power should be distributed is the logical architecture developed in Chapter 3 (shown over-leaf). As explained in Part One, partitioning is the key principle. To think about the options, it is helpful to see information systems as a hierarchy of three levels:

- *Information* – the resource to be exploited.
- *Services* – the means of manipulating and distributing that resource.

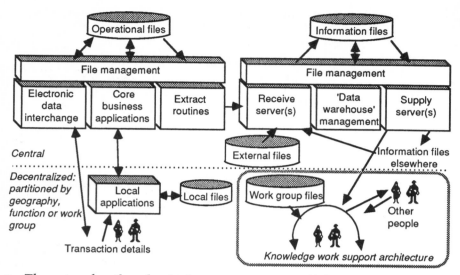

- *The network* – the physical transport system, linking users with the various services they use, and linking services to one another (this is covered later).

Partitioning operational information

Information on the operational files can be partitioned vertically, by business function or by geography, so that operational data files can be held and updated close to where transactions originate. There are basically three ways of decentralizing operational files in this way (illustrated upper right). *Dispersed* processing suits organizations whose work flow is *independent*. *Distributed* processing is more demanding technically, and suits organizations whose work flow is *sequential*. In both cases, performance depends on reasonably high locality of data. *Replicated* processing depends on near 100 per cent locality of data, and suits organizations whose work flow is *facsimile* and those with time-critical centralized functions.

Building the data warehouse

Data warehouse is the term I use to describe the secondary files used to store information for management and planning purposes. Data may be selected from the operational files for inclusion in the data warehouse as shown in the lower figure on the right.

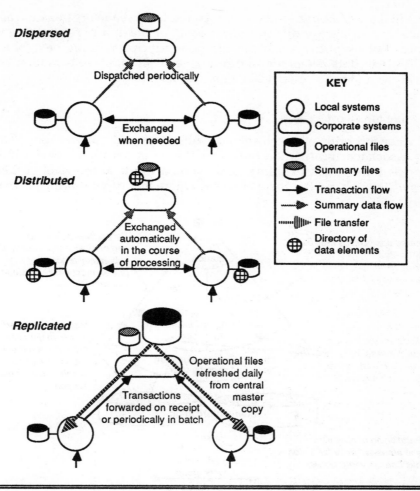

Dispersed

Dispatched periodically

Exchanged when needed

KEY

○ Local systems

⬭ Corporate systems

⬛ Operational files

▨ Summary files

→ Transaction flow

⇢ Summary data flow

⊪ File transfer

⊕ Directory of data elements

Distributed

Exchanged automatically in the course of processing

Replicated

Operational files refreshed daily from central master copy

Transactions forwarded on receipt or periodically in batch

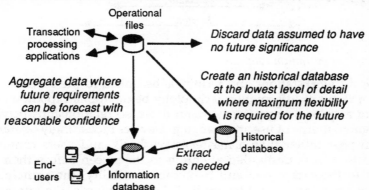

Operational files

Transaction processing applications

Discard data assumed to have no future significance

Aggregate data where future requirements can be forecast with reasonable confidence

Create an historical database at the lowest level of detail where maximum flexibility is required for the future

Historical database

End-users

Extract as needed

Information database

Data in the warehouse should be structured to serve the organization as a whole, rather than individual functions. For maximum flexibility and conceptual simplicity, relational database principles should be applied. Individual data elements should have a simple, well-understood structure, and use a single validation criterion.

Locating the shared services

As a general principle, both shared utilities (general-purpose tools) *plus* the associated information files, and shared applications (performing specific information handling tasks) should reside at the level of their *administrative span*. But there are cases where that general principle may be modified ...

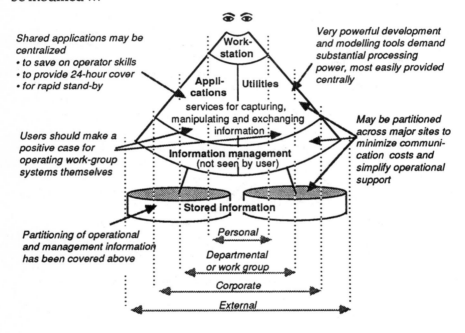

The principle of minimum coupling

How should workstations and terminals be linked to the services they use? As a result of information technology being applied to knowledge work and as processing power decentralizes, so relationships between devices and patterns of use are changing. Devices increasingly operate on a peer-to-peer rather than a master/slave basis, and users cannot be assumed to devote undivided attention to the screen before them. To respond to these changes, and maximize flexibility, the principle of minimum coupling should be applied. In other words, the interaction between the user and the service they are addressing should be kept as loose as possible, consistent with the nature of their exchange. The principle is embodied in two key design concepts that should be applied wherever appropriate within the infrastructure:

- The *agent* assumes responsibility for progressing an information handling activity until it can pass responsibility to another agent, to the service, or back to the user.
- The *server* performs a defined task for its 'clients' on the same network, and is used to share expensive resources, such as laser printers, or to manage common resources, such as work group files.

Managing the interconnection problem

There are three ways you can work towards a solution for the 'interconnection problem':

1. *Divide and link*: a low risk, pragmatic approach. Well-established protocols are chosen that are optimum to support the needs of different categories of user within the organization. Links between these categories are established progressively, via common access points.
2. *Proprietary architecture*: relying on the so-called network architectures developed by major computer suppliers, which are both more mature and more comprehensive at present than products conforming to open interconnection standards. This suits organizations with a heavy commitment to one major supplier. It brings with it the risk of high transition costs to open standards later.
3. *OSI intercept*: a commitment to adopting open standards as soon as practical, accepting the short term risk and cost this entails. A chosen subset of open standards is introduced within selected user communities. Open standards are gradually extended to other communities as conforming products emerge.

Whichever strategy is adopted, certain key products or standards should be chosen to form the backbone of procurement policy. In each of the five dimensions of integration identified earlier, one or two key elements can be identified. These are the 'glue' that holds the infrastructure together ...

- In the *information access* dimension, you should choose the server routines, normally associated with a database management system, that bring data into the data warehouse and distribute extracts. You may also be able to specify the preferred workstation tools to be used by end-users to manipulate information.
- In the *services* dimension, you should choose operating environments for the workstation and for the controller that handles shared

applications, beginning with the more important of those two.

- In the *interworking* dimension, you should choose a standard for electronic messaging and for the associated directory, complemented by word processing routines to be used to access the service.
- In the *development* dimension, organizations that place a high priority on end-user development should choose system building tools, and limit procurement (within defined limits) to the range of equipment with which those tools can be used.
- The key function in the *management* dimension is the security system that prevents unauthorized access. Security products must be chosen and welded together into an effective organization-wide system.

Three measures to help keep the strategy on course ...

- *Chinese walls* can be built around new technologies until the technology stabilizes and reliable standards emerge.
- A set of minimum standards applied to all information technology equipment provide a *safety net* – a guarantee of interconnection at a low level if all else fails.
- *Conformance levels* – different levels of service from the infrastructure, associated with different degrees of restriction on procurement – enable users to balance the relative advantages of the former against those of alternative solutions available to them.

The corporate network

How should you plan and configure the corporate network to support the information systems of the 1990s, while also taking advantage of new digital telecommunications technologies?

Information communities – uncovering the requirements

First, you should take a fresh look at requirements, by picturing these in terms of *information communities*. Information communities are groups of network users who share a need to communicate or exchange information, and who generate a particular type of traffic (see figure top right).

Mapping the information communities within an organization reveals two things:

- Opportunities for integrating network services arise where information communities overlap. Seeing these opportunities in terms of information communities with a given set of characteristics helps to focus on the differences between types of traffic which an integrated network must reconcile effectively. As well as looking at the potential

| Type of Traffic | | Telecommunications Characteristics | | | | |
| | | Burst-iness | Connectivity | | | Band-width |
Name	Description	Typical peak/aver-age ratio	Inter-connect flexibility	Access security	Links to outside world	Typical require-ment (bit/s)
Video	For conferencing or instruction	1:1	Predefined, limited	Not important	None	2M
Telephony	Switched telephone service	1:1	High	Usually un-important	Essential	64K
Image	Bit-mapped facsimiles of documents	10:1	Usually modest	Usually un-important	Often	64K
Convers-ational	Eg text messaging, information retrieval	10:1	Modest	Important or critical	Essential	2.4K
Transaction processing	Eg order processing, credit clearing	100:1	Predefined, limited	Usually important	Usually none	9.6K
Bulk transfer	Of data files or documents	2:1	Can be high Ad hoc	Usually un-important	Sometimes	48K
Resource-sharing	Eg CAD work groups, PCs with shared files	1000:1	Predefined	Important	Sometimes	200K

cost savings arising from integration, you must also take on board the performance implications – How will an integrated network cope with the characteristics of the information communities? How will service to users be affected?

• Organizational and geographical boundaries, and particularly the boundary between the private on-site domain and the public off-site domain, are significant break points, where the degree of control that the network operator can exercise over costs or over procedures changes, sometimes radically. For this reason, it is important to focus on these boundaries, and the methods that are to be used to carry traffic across them. Those methods determine how much control is retained by the network operator.

Deciding network structure

The role of the corporate network has changed. It is no longer mainly a means of limiting telecommunications costs, as it so often was in the past. Now, its main *raison d'être* is to facilitate the exchange of information, and increasingly that means non-voice as well as voice, by the organizational units and the individuals within the organization. Those responsible for planning the network, therefore, must be wary of an excessive concern with traffic volumes and with the cost of transporting bits, important though those are. In terms of its role – what it seeks to do for its users –

and its overall structure, the corporate network today is shaped more by the strategy you adopt to distribute information and processing power than it is by traffic volumes. The generic strategies introduced in Chapter 2 are a valuable guide to the best approach:

- *Low-autonomy* organizations favour straightforward hierarchical networks with centralized switching, while *high-autonomy* companies adopt mesh structures with distributed switching, intended to support complex patterns of lateral as well as hierarchical communication.
- *Tightly* and *loosely-coupled* organizations build that coupling into the design of the network also – tight coupling imposes a strict discipline on users' means of access and interworking, while loose coupling provides services more on a take-it-or-leave-it or utility basis, and leaves more of the onus on the network user to decide how to access and use services.

Deciding the operating philosophy

Central network management is proving increasingly difficult to sustain as rates of change at local level increase. The network should be partitioned into *access* networks on every building and site, linked together by a *transport* network. Large international organizations may need to partition the transport network again by geographical area, and construct a 'backbone' network to link those together.

Cost ratios and regulatory constraints are different in transport and access networks, so they must be considered separately. Intelligent *gateways* should be used to link transport and access networks wherever benefits – tangible or intangible – can be gained. Elsewhere, cheaper *bridges* may be used.

Should the access networks be managed locally or from the centre? *High autonomy* organizations place a higher value on local control and, as a result, are more likely to find the cost of local support justified.

Assessing the integration options

Within the corporate network, integration can be applied at three main levels:

- *In the transport network* – by channeling the traffic from a number of sources on to high-capacity long distance lines, you reduce the overall cost of transmission.
- *In the access network* – by integrating the switching and routing of traffic across company sites, you rationalize site wiring and maintenance, and give users greater freedom to interconnect their systems.

- *At the workstation* – by extending integration all the way to the workstation, you can replace telephone, data terminal, personal computer, and whatever, with a single multi–purpose device.

Integration can save money and rationalize equipment and management of the network, but it also brings potential penalties ...

	Separate	Integrated transmission	Integrated switching	Integration at the work-station
Main advantages	Straightforward Separate systems can be developed independently	Saves money on transmission costs	Rationalization of on-site wiring and of site management	The 'multi-function workstation'
Main disadvantages	Extra wiring Terminals cannot easily interwork	Vulnerability ('all eggs in one basket')		
			Increased risk if growth exceeds expectations	
				Access security may be a problem
Conditions to be met if advantages are to be realized	None	Traffic flows must match – must follow the same routes and ideally peaks should not coincide		
		Enough traffic to give economies of scale on inter-site lines	Signalling schemes – methods used to set up and clear down calls etc – must be compatible	

Here are some guidelines to help you to assess the integration options.

THE TRANSPORT NETWORK
As public telecommunications systems go digital, the risks involved in integration of the transport network remain considerable. The golden rule is to keep the transport network as clean and simple as possible, consistent with reasonably efficient use of transmission capacity.

THE ACCESS NETWORK
The main candidate technologies for the access network – local area networks and digital PABXs – in many respects complement one another rather than compete, so often separate networks make the most sense. The best choice will depend mainly on the cost of wiring and the traffic mix (see overleaf).

THE WORKSTATION

Workstation technology is still evolving rapidly, and that makes it exciting. Remember that the much-vaunted voice plus data workstation has had little commercial success, a classic case of a technological solution chasing a problem that is not widespread. Moral, often said but easily forgotten: don't chase the technology, focus on the business needs.

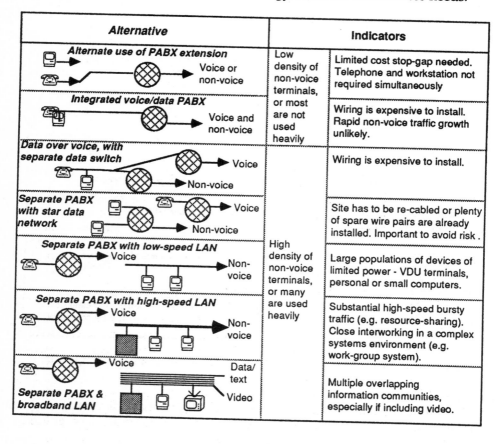

Alternative		Indicators
Alternate use of PABX extension — Voice or non-voice	Low density of non-voice terminals, or most are not used heavily	Limited cost stop-gap needed. Telephone and workstation not required simultaneously
Integrated voice/data PABX — Voice and non-voice		Wiring is expensive to install. Rapid non-voice traffic growth unlikely.
Data over voice, with separate data switch — Voice / Non-voice		Wiring is expensive to install.
Separate PABX with star data network — Voice / Non-voice	High density of non-voice terminals, or many are used heavily	Site has to be re-cabled or plenty of spare wire pairs are already installed. Important to avoid risk .
Separate PABX with low-speed LAN — Voice / Non-voice		Large populations of devices of limited power - VDU terminals, personal or small computers.
Separate PABX with high-speed LAN — Voice / Non-voice		Substantial high-speed bursty traffic (e.g. resource-sharing). Close interworking in a complex systems environment (e.g. work-group system).
Separate PABX & broadband LAN — Voice / Data/text / Video		Multiple overlapping information communities, especially if including video.

CONCLUSION

In the Introduction to this book, I made the point that national governments do not, by and large, attempt to justify expenditure on the transport infrastructure. They just know that, to hold their own in a competitive world, they need to have the best the country can afford. For similar reasons, business organizations, whether engaged in a competitive battle or in a battle to provide the best possible service at the lowest possible cost, need to build the best infrastructure they can afford for the information systems they will depend on in the 1990s and beyond.

We can draw a further lesson from this analogy between the national transport infrastructure and the corporate infrastructure for information systems that I have described in this book. Whatever anyone feels about the relative merits of road, rail and air transport, few will deny that each has its place. And however much anyone relies on the private car for personal transport, few will deny that mass transport of people and bulk carriage of freight also play an essential part. The trick that transport planners try (and sometimes fail) to pull off is to define the right mix, so that all users of the transport infrastructure feel they get a reasonable deal *and* the economy benefits as well. That, in a nutshell, is the trick that those planning the information systems infrastructure must pull off too.

But as with all analogies, we must not stretch this one two far. There is also an important difference. The transport infrastructure takes us and our goods from A to B and that is enough. But, for the information systems infrastructure, transport alone of information is *not* enough. People, and particularly knowledge workers, add value to information by processing it, and the infrastructure must provide for this additional dimension also. Better transport facilities for information without better means of processing that information will merely add to the *too much data, too little information* syndrome that already afflicts many users of today's information systems.

For an organization to succeed in the information era we are now entering, it must have an infrastructure for information systems that enables all its staff to exploit the best tools available to help them to do their jobs. In the last few years, the quality and the range of the tools knowledge workers can use to process information has improved out of all recognition. And believe me, we ain't seen nuthin' yet.

INDEX